LITERATURE FOR ADVENTURES

In the Human Spirit

VOLUME I

edited by

Philip E. Bishop
Valencia Community College

PRENTICE HALL, Upper Saddle River, NJ 07458

Library of Congress Cataloging-in-Publication Data

Literature for Adventures in the human spirit/edited by Philip E.
  Bishop
       p.   cm.
    ISBN 0-13-141251-5 (v. I)
    I. Bishop, Philip E.   II. Bishop, Philip E.   Adventures in the
  human spirit.
  CB245.B57L58   1995
  909'.0981'2—dc20   94-28737
                                                         CIP

Editorial/production supervision
   and interior design: Jordan Ochs and Patricia V. Amoroso
Acquisitions editor: Bud Therien
Editorial assistant: Lee Mamunes
Manufacturing buyer: Robert Anderson
Cover design: John Judy

*Credits and copyright acknowledgments appear on pages ix–x,
which constitute an extension of the copyright page.*

© 1995 by Prentice-Hall, Inc.
A Pearson Education Company
Upper Saddle River, NJ 07458

Printed in the United States of America

10   9   8   7   6   5   4   3   2   1

0-13-141251-5

Prentice-Hall International (UK) Limited,London
Prentice-Hall of Australia Pty. Limited, Sydney
Prentice-Hall Canada Inc., Toronto
Prentice-Hall Hispanoamericana, S.A., Mexico
Prentice-Hall of India Private Limited, New Delhi
Prentice-Hall of Japan, Inc., Tokyo
Pearson Education Asia Pte. Ltd., Singapore
Editora Prentice-Hall do Brasil, Ltda., Rio de Janeiro

Contents

Preface

Literature for Adventures in the Human Spirit is a two-volume companion to my survey of the humanities, *Adventures in the Human Spirit* (Prentice Hall, 1994), offered to instructors and students who wish to enrich the basic text with primary readings. The two volumes are divided to accommodate the most common organization of multisemester humanities courses: Volume I covers the ancient world, classical Greece and Rome, and the Middle Ages; Volume II extends from the Renaissance to the present.

My selections in *Literature for Adventures* have been guided by simple principles. I have tried to represent fairly and concisely the literary and philosophical traditions of Western civilization; to explore the central concepts of Western thought by judicious choice of excerpts; and, most of all, to provoke students to examine and discuss these traditions in light of contemporary experience. Our determination to offer students a convenient and affordable format has limited the scope of these volumes. Still, we have managed to include some representative texts from non-Western traditions and to include a fair sampling of women and minority authors.

In Volume I, "The Ancient World" draws on myths of Egypt and Mesopotamia that offer pointed comparison to the Hebrew Bible stories in Chapter 4. The inclusion of selections by Confucius and Buddha opens possibilities for comparison with classical and Christian religions and ethical teachings.

With ancient Greece and Rome (Chapters 2 and 3), I have included entire chapters of Homer's *Iliad* and *Odyssey* and of Virgil's *Aeneid* in the hopes of rendering some quality of the whole works. We offer the whole text of Sophocles' *Oedipus the King,* that primal drama of the Western imagination, and of Plato's *Apology of Socrates*. Other selections of classical philosophy—from Plato, Aristotle, Lucretius, and Marcus Aurelius—make for fruitful connections to the Asian texts.

Readings from the Christian era include key passages of the Hebrew Bible, New Testament, and Qur'an, emphasizing these religions' common origins. In the Middle Ages, I have sought a balance between the secular and sacred traditions. Both the epic tradition (*Song of Roland,* Dante's *Inferno*) and the lyric mode are repre-sented, while Chaucer's Wife of Bath's Tale epitomizes the medieval romance. With the Wife of Bath and Christine de Pisan, medieval womanhood is heard with a strong and distinctive voice.

Volume II begins with the Renaissance and the humanist writings of Petrarch, Machiavelli, and Pico. Shakespeare's *Hamlet* was chosen for its archetypal Renais-sance hero and Montaigne for his skeptical view of Renaissance humanism. From the baroque and Enlightenment, Cervantes' idealizing hero Don Quixote is set against Voltaire's naive young Candide, while the era's philosophical tensions are revealed by Descartes and Hobbes.

Two of romanticism's great literary heroes, Faust and Frankenstein, open Chapter 3, which includes a generous selection of romantic and symbolist poetry. The nineteenth century closes with the tortured figure of Dostoevsky's Grand In-quisitor, the brilliant portrait of ambivalence. The twentieth century stretches from Eliot's Prufrock to Ellison's invisible man. It includes such pivotal voices of the modern era as Freud, Virginia Woolf, and Sartre. Again, a selection of poetry mirrors the spirit of modernism and the insurgent contemporary voices from groups and cul-tures long denied a voice in the literary and philosophical tradition.

In shaping this collection, I am deeply grateful for the advice of reviewers and colleagues, many of them named below. I have thoughtfully considered their sug-gestions, even where the limitations of space or budget kept me from following them.

ACKNOWLEDGMENTS

For their advice in choosing selections, I am grateful to Andrew Alexander, Don An-drews, Elizabeth Eschbach, Carol Foltz, Rosita Martinez, Diane Maxwell, Lois Mc-Namara, Mary Jo Pecht, Querentia Throm, and others unnamed here. For their un-stinting assistance, I would like to thank Judy Clark, Karin Bonilla, Vicki Pipkin, Mary Beth Elkin, Bunnie Jackson, and the Word Processing staff. Thanks also to my editor Norwell F. Therien, Jr., for his enduring patience and good will. For remind-ing me that there are other things than books, thanks to Shaughna and Aaron, my marvelous children, and to Kira, the perpetual surprise.

For inspiring me always by their courage in the face of difficult truths, I dedi-cate these volumes to my students. With this book, let them make their own truths anew.

Philip E. Bishop

He put forth his hand [to create] the matter he desired
before he let it fall to the ground."
And Atum said:
"That is my daughter, the living female one, Tefnut,
who shall be with her brother Shu.
Life is his name, Order is her name.
[At first] I lived with my two children, my little ones,
the one before me, the other behind me.
Life reposed with my daughter Order,
the one within me, the other without me.
I rose over them, but their arms were around me."

(The text then alludes to Geb, the earth, and Nut, the sky):
"As for Geb, as for my grandson,
after the appearance of my Eye, which I dispatched
while I was still alone in the waters in a state of inertness,
before I had found anywhere to stand or sit,
before Heliopolis had been founded that I might be there,
before a perch had been formed for me to sit on,
before I had created Nut that she might be above my head,
before the first corporation had been born,
before the Primeval Companies of the Gods had come into being.
[In this primordial epoch] Atum said to the Abyss:
I am in a relaxed state, whereof I am very weary,
my humanity are inert,
If earth were alive it would cheer my heart and enliven my bosom.
Let my limbs be assembled for (i.e. to form) him,
and let this great weariness be settled for us.
And the Abyss said to Atum:
Kiss your daughter Order, put her to your nose,
so will your heart live.
Never let her leave you, let Order, who is your daughter,
be with your son Shu, whose name is Life.
You will eat (sic MSS.) with your daughter Order,
while your son Shu will lift you up."
(At this point Shu intervenes to say):
"I am Life, the son of Atum,
he has borne me from his nose.
Let him place me on his neck that he may greet me with
        my sister Order
when he shines every day as he appears from his egg.
The birth of the god is the appearance of daylight,
and he is acclaimed by his scions on the horizon."

MESOPOTAMIAN MYTH

The myths of the ancient world often imagined the world's creation as a violent event, a conflict of titanic forces. Such an image dominates the Babylonian creation myth, the *Enuma Elish* (so called after its opening words, "When on high ..."). In this version, creation begins in the commingling of the fresh waters (Apsu) and salt water (Tiamat), whose union begets additional generations of gods. Disturbed by his raucous offspring, Apsu plots to destroy them all, but instead is killed by Ea. Ea fathers the sixth generation of gods, the great hero-god Marduk, "clothed with the halo of ten gods." Marduk defeats the vengeful Tiamat in a great cosmic combat and carves up her body to create the geography of Mesopotamia. Marduk also creates the first man to be a slave for the gods, fashioning him from the blood of Kingu, instigator of Tiamat's rebellion.

From the *Enuma Elish*

When on high the heaven had not been named,
Firm ground below had not been called by name,
Naught but primordial Apsu, their begetter,
(And) Mummu-Tiamat, she who bore them all,
Their waters commingling as a single body;
No reed hut had been matted, no marsh land had appeared,
When no gods whatever had been brought into being,
Uncalled by name, their destinies undetermined—
Then it was that the gods were formed within them.
Lahmu and Lahamu were brought forth, by name they were called.
For aeons they grew in age and stature.
Anshar and Kishar were formed, surpassing the others.
They prolonged the days, added on the years.
Anu was their son, of his fathers the rival;
Yea, Anshar's first-born, Anu, was his equal.
Anu begot in his image Nudimmud.
This Nudimmud was of his fathers the master;
Of broad wisdom, understanding, mighty in strength,
Mightier by far than his grandfather, Anshar.
He had no rival among the gods, his brothers.
The divine brothers banded together,
They disturbed Tiamat as they surged back and forth,
Yea, they troubled the mood of Tiamat
By their hilarity in the Abode of Heaven.
Apsu could not lessen their clamour
And Tiamat was speechless at their ways.

Their doings were loathsome unto [...].
Unsavoury were their ways; they were overbearing.
Then Apsu, the begetter of the great gods,
Cried out, addressing Mummu, his vizier:
'O Mummu, my vizier, who rejoicest my spirit,
Come hither and let us go to Tiamat!'
They went and sat down before Tiamat,
Exchanging counsel about the gods, their first-born.
Apsu, opening his mouth,
Said unto resplendent Tiamat:
'Their ways are verily loathsome unto me.
By day I find no relief, nor repose by night.
I will destroy, I will wreck their ways,
That quiet may be restored. Let us have rest!'
As soon as Tiamat heard this,
She was wroth and called out to her husband.
She cried out aggrieved, as she raged all alone,
Injecting woe into her mood:
'What? Should we destroy that which we have built?
Their ways are indeed troublesome, but let us attend kindly!'
Then answered Mummu, giving counsel to Apsu;
Ill-wishing and ungracious was Mummu's advice:
'Do destroy, my father, the mutinous ways.
Then shalt thou have relief by day and rest by night!'
When Apsu heard this, his face grew radiant
Because of the evil he planned against the gods, his sons.
As for Mummu, by the neck he embraced him
As (that one) sat down on his knees to kiss him.
(Now) whatever they had plotted between them
Was repeated unto the gods, their first born.
When the gods heard (this), they were astir,
(Then) lapsed into silence and remained speechless.
Surpassing in wisdom, accomplished, resourceful,
Ea, the all-wise, saw through their scheme.
A master design against it he devised and set up,
Made artful his spell against it, surpassing and holy.
He recited it and made it subsist in the deep,
As he poured sleep upon him. Sound asleep he lay.
When Apsu he had made prone, drenched with sleep,
Mummu, the adviser, was impotent to move.
He loosened his band, tore off his tiara,
Removed his halo (and) put it on himself.
Having fettered Apsu, he slew him.

Mummu he bound and left behind lock.
Having thus upon Apsu established his dwelling,
He laid hold on Mummu, holding him by the nose-rope.
After he had vanquished and trodden down his foes,
Ea, his triumph over his enemies secured,
In his sacred chamber in profound peace he rested.
He named it 'Apsu,' for shrines he assigned (it).
In that same place his cult hut he founded.
Ea and Damkina, his wife, dwelled (there) in splendour.
In the chamber of fates, the abode of destinies,
A god was engendered, most potent and wisest of gods.
In the heart of Apsu was Marduk created,
In the heart of holy Apsu was Marduk created.
He who begot him was Ea, his father;
She who conceived him was Damkina, his mother.
The breast of goddesses did she suck.
The nurse that nursed him filled him with awsomeness.
Alluring was his figure, sparkling the lift in his eyes.
Lordly was his gait, commanding from of old.
When Ea saw him, the father who begot him,
He exulted and glowed, his heart filled with gladness.
He rendered him perfect and endowed him with a double godhead.
Greatly exalted was he above them, exceeding throughout.
Perfect were his members beyond comprehension,
Unsuited for understanding, difficult to perceive.
Four were his eyes, four were his ears,
When he moved his lips, fire blazed forth.
Large were all hearing organs,
And the eyes, in like number, scanned all things.
He was the loftiest of the gods, surpassing was his stature;
His members were enormous, he was exceeding tall.
'My little son, my little son!'
My son, the Sun! Sun of the heavens!'
Clothed with the halo of ten gods, he was strong to the utmost,
As their awesome flashes were heaped upon him.

[*The gods incite Tiamat to rebel, and she arms herself with eleven
fearsome monsters. However, Marduk slays Tiamat with his own
cosmic powers, the great winds, and cuts her body in half to make the
firmament and the land. Finally, he creates the first man to free the
gods from labor.*]

When Marduk hears the words of the gods,
His heart prompts (him) to fashion artful works.

Opening his mouth, he addresses Ea
To impart the plan he addresses Ea
To impart the plan he had conceived in his heart:
'Blood I will mass and cause bones to be.
I will establish a savage, "man" shall be his name.
Verily, savage–man I will create.
He shall be charged with the service of the gods
    That they might be at ease!
The ways of the gods I will artfully alter.
Though alike revered, into two (groups) they shall be divided.'
Ea answered him, speaking a word to him,
To relate to him a scheme for the relief of the gods:
'Let but one of their brothers be handed over;
He alone shall perish that mankind may be fashioned.
Let the great gods be here in Assembly,
Let the guilty be handed over that they may endure.'
Marduk summoned the great gods to Assembly;
Presiding graciously, he issued instructions.
To his utterance the gods pay heed.
The king addresses a word to the Anunnaki:
'If your former statement was true,
Do (now) the truth on oath by me declare!
Who was it that contrived the uprising,
And made Tiamat rebel, and joined battle?
Let him be handed over who contrived the uprising.
His guilt I will make him bear that you may dwell in peace!'
The Igigi, the great gods, replied to him,
To Lugaldimmerankia, counsellor of the gods, their lord:
'It was Kingu who contrived the uprising,
And made Tiamat rebel, and joined battle.'
They bound him, holding him before Ea.
They imposed on him his guilt and severed his blood (vessels).
Out of his blood they fashioned mankind.
He imposed the service and let free the gods.

CONFUCIUS

The Chinese philosopher Confucius (a latinization of Kong Fuzi, "Master Kong"; 551–479 B.C.) was the most influential thinker in Chinese history, a figure even more imposing in the Chinese tradition than Socrates in Western philosophy. With good reason, Confucius is often compared to Socrates in his dedication to teaching, his refusal of material gain, and his emphasis on living the examined life. Confucius's interest in social duty and enlightened service to the state also makes a fruitful connection to Roman stoicism, which provided moral guidance to ancient Rome's ruling class.

By his teachings, Confucius successfully altered the Chinese model of human character from an aristocratic ideal of exalted birth and feudal right to an ethical principle of public responsibility and gentle humanity. In his lifetime, Confucius pursued a career in government service, eventually aspiring to influence the conduct of China's rulers. Unsuccessfully, he pushed the rulers of China's feudal states to adopt a personal ethic of wisdom and humanity, and therefore to rule by example and moral persuasion rather than by force.

Confucius stressed the importance of individual virtue, which he termed *jen*, or "human-heartedness." *Jen* meant the cultivation of individual benevolence and humanity, expressed through a life of right action. Thus the attitude of *jen* led to a respect for custom and propriety (*li*, pronounced "lee"), including obedience to one's parents and rulers of the state. *Li* was demonstrated also in the arts, which helped to foster a respect for tradition.

For analysis and interpretation:

1. Summarize Confucius's instructions on the "rectification of the mind."

2. Evaluate Confucius's assertion that "the government of the state depends on the regulation of the family." What evidence from your own experience confirm or contradict this assertion?

3. According to Confucius, how does the conduct of government reflect the inner character of those who govern and those who are governed?

The Great Learning

The way of the great learning consists of clearly exemplifying illustrious virtue, in loving the people, and in resting in the highest good.

Only when one knows where one is to rest can one have a fixed purpose. Only with a fixed purpose can one achieve calmness of mind. Only with calmness of mind can one achieve serene repose. Only in serene repose can one carry on careful deliberation. Only through careful deliberation can one have achievement. Things have their roots and branches; affairs have their beginning and end. He who knows what comes first and what comes last comes himself near the Way.

The ancients who wished clearly to exemplify illustrious virtue throughout the world would first set up good government in their states. Wishing to govern well their states, they would first regulate their families. Wishing to regulate their families, they would first cultivate their persons. Wishing to cultivate their persons, they would first rectify their minds. Wishing to rectify their minds, they would first seek sincerity in their thoughts. Wishing for sincerity in their thoughts, they would first extend their knowledge. The extension of knowledge lay in the investigation of things. For only when things are investigated is knowledge extended; only when knowledge is extended are thoughts sincere; only when thoughts are sincere are minds rectified; only when minds are rectified are our persons cultivated; only when our persons are cultivated are our families regulated; only when families are regulated are states well governed; and only when states are well governed is there peace in the world.

From the emperor down to the common people, all, without exception, must consider cultivation of the individual character as the root. If the root is in disorder, it is impossible for the branches to be in order. To treat the important as unimportant and to treat the unimportant as important—this should never be. This is called knowing the root; this is called the perfection of knowledge. . . .

What is meant by saying that "the cultivation of the person depends on the rectification of the mind" is this: When one is under the influence of anger, one's mind will not be correct; when one is under the influence of anxiety, it will not be correct. When the mind is not there, we gaze at things but do not see; we listen but do not hear; we eat but do not know the flavors. This is what is meant by saying that the cultivation of the person depends on the rectification of the mind. . . .

What is meant by saying that "the government of the state depends on the regulation of the family" is this: One can never teach outsiders if one cannot teach one's own family. Therefore the prince perfects the proper teaching for the whole country without going outside his family; the filial piety wherewith one serves his sovereign, the brotherly respect wherewith one treats his elders, the kindness wherewith one deals with the multitude. There is the saying in the "Announcement to K'ang" [in the *Book of History*]: "Act as if you were rearing an infant." If you set yourself to a task with heart and soul you will not go far wrong even if you do not hit the mark. No girl has ever learned to suckle an infant before she got married.

If one family exemplifies humanity, humanity will abound in the whole country. If one family exemplifies courtesy, courtesy will abound in the whole country. On the other hand, if one man exemplifies greed and wickedness, rebellious disorder will arise in the whole country. Therein lies the secret. Hence the proverb: One word ruins an enterprise; one man determines the fate of an empire. Yao and Shun ruled the empire with humanity, and the people followed them. Chieh and Chou ruled the empire with cruelty, and the people only submitted to them. Since these last commanded actions that they themselves would not like to take, the people refused to follow them. Thus it is that what [virtues] a prince finds in himself he may expect in others, and what [vices] he himself is free from he may condemn in others. It is impossible that a man devoid of every virtue which he might wish to have in others could be able effectively to instruct them.

Thus we see why it is that "the government of the state depends on the regulation of the family." . . .

What is meant by saying that "the establishment of peace in the world is dependent on the government of the state" is this: When superiors accord to the aged their due, then the common people will be inspired to practice filial piety; when superiors accord to elders their due, then the common people will be inspired to practice brotherly respect; when superiors show compassion to the orphaned, then the common people do not do otherwise. Thus a gentleman has a principle with which, as with a measuring square, he may regulate his conduct.

What a man dislikes in his superiors let him not display in his treatment of his inferiors; what he dislikes in his inferiors let him not display in his service to his superiors; what he dislikes in those before him let him not set before those who are behind him; what he dislikes in those behind him let him not therewith follow those who are before him; what he dislikes in those on his right let him not bestow upon those on his left; what he dislikes in those on his left let him not bestow upon those on his right. This is called the regulating principle of the measuring square.

BUDDHA

The life of Siddhartha Gautama (563–483 B.C.), known as the Buddha, or enlightened one, can be compared to many spiritual leaders, including Jesus of Nazareth and St. Francis from the Hebrew and Christian traditions. Buddha was born to a royal family in Nepal, but, at about age twenty-nine, he left his luxurious existence to seek a solution to human suffering (*dukkha*). Seeing his fellow humans caught in an existence of inevitable pain and death, Buddha sought the advice of sages, fasted, and performed other ascetic exercises. Finally, while sitting under a tree (the *bo* tree), Buddha attained enlightenment (*bodhi*). He entered upon a life of preaching, beginning with his sermon at the Deer Park at Sarnath (528 B.C.).

Buddha's doctrine (*dharma*) is summarized in the Four Noble Truths, a prescription for escaping the cycle of *dukkha*. The necessary steps toward this goal are enumerated in the Noble Eightfold Path in a set of instructions that lead the follower from right attitude to right action to the regimen of meditation that will bring enlightenment. Following this strict regimen, the dedicated believer can cease all striving and maintain a mindful detachment from existence. Cultivating this state of being would lead to liberation from suffering, or *nirvana*.

Buddha was deified by his followers, and a great body of sacred legend grew around his life and deeds. As with Christianity in the Roman world, Buddhism spread successfully beyond its native India, even while believers disputed doctrines and divided into sects, or "branches," of different faiths.

For analysis and interpretation:

1. Summarize the four noble truths as Buddha presents them in his teaching.

2. How might the noble truths of Buddhism encourage a monastic life of poverty and solitude?

3. Buddha attributes suffering to desire or attachment. What alternate explanations might be given for the cause of suffering in the world?

4. Evaluate the practicality of living by Buddhist teachings in the modern world. By comparison, how practical are the teachings of Jesus in the Sermon on the Mount (see Chapter 4)?

The Four Noble Truths

17. 'Again, monks, a monk abides contemplating mind-objects as mind-objects in respect of the Four Noble Truths. How does he do so? Here, a monk knows as it really is: "This is suffering"; he knows as it really is: "This is the origin of suffering"; he knows as it really is: "This is the cessation of suffering"; he knows as it really is: "This is the way of practice leading to the cessation of suffering."

18. 'And what, monks, is the Noble Truth of Suffering? Birth is suffering, aging is suffering, death is suffering, sorrow, lamentation, pain, sadness and distress are suffering. Being attached to the unloved is suffering, being separated from the loved is suffering, not getting what one wants is suffering. In short, the five aggregates of grasping are suffering....

'And how, monks, in short, are the five aggregates of grasping suffering? They are as follows: the aggregate of grasping that is form, the aggregate of grasping that is feeling, the aggregate of grasping that is perception, the aggregate of grasping that is the mental formations, the aggregate of grasping that is consciousness. These are, in short, the five aggregates of grasping that are suffering. And that, monks, is called the Noble Truth of Suffering.

19. 'And what, monks, is the Noble Truth of the Origin of Suffering? It is that craving which gives rise to rebirth, bound up with pleasure and lust, finding fresh delight now here, now there: that is to say sensual craving, craving for existence, and craving for non–existence.

'And where does this craving arise and establish itself? Wherever in the world there is anything agreeable and pleasurable, there this craving arises and establishes itself.

'And what is there in the world that is agreeable and pleasurable? The eye in the world is agreeable and pleasurable, the ear..., the nose..., the tongue..., the body..., the mind in the world is agreeable and pleasurable, and there this craving arises and establishes itself. Sights, sounds, smells, tastes, tangibles, mind-objects in the world are agreeable and pleasurable, and there this craving arises and establishes itself.

'The craving for sights, sounds, smells, tastes, tangibles, mind-objects in the world is agreeable and pleasurable, and there this craving arises and establishes itself.

'Thinking of sights, sounds, smells, tastes, tangibles, mind-objects in the world is agreeable and pleasurable, and there this craving arises and establishes itself.

'Pondering on sights, sounds, smells, tastes, tangibles and mind-objects in the world is agreeable and pleasurable, and there this craving arises and establishes itself. And that, monks is called the Noble Truth of the Origin of Suffering.

20. 'And what, monks, is the Noble Truth of the Cessation of Suffering? It is the complete fading-away and extinction of this craving, its forsaking and abandonment, liberation from it, detachment from it. And how does this craving come to be abandoned, how does its cessation come about?...

21. 'And what, monks, is the Noble Truth of the Way of Practice Leading to the Cessation of Suffering? It is just this Noble Eightfold Path, namely:—Right View, Right Thought; Right Speech, Right Action, Right Livelihood; Right Effort, Right Mindfulness, Right Concentration.

'And what, monks, is Right View? It is, monks, the knowledge of suffering, the knowledge of the origin of suffering, the knowledge of the cessation of suffering, and the knowledge of the way of practice leading to the cessation of suffering. This is called Right View.

'And what, monks, is Right Thought? The thought of renunciation, the thought of non-ill-will, the thought of harmlessness. This, monks, is called Right Thought.

'And what, monks, is Right Speech? Refraining from lying, refraining from slander, refraining from harsh speech, refraining from frivolous speech. This is called Right Speech.

'And what, monks, is Right Action? Refraining from taking life, refraining from taking what is not given, refraining from sexual misconduct. This is called Right Action.

'And what, monks, is Right Livelihood? Here, monks, the Ariyan disciple, having given up wrong livelihood, keeps himself by right livelihood.

'And what, monks, is Right Effort? Here, monks, a monk rouses his will, makes an effort, stirs up energy, exerts his mind and strives to prevent the arising of unarisen evil unwholesome mental states. He rouses his will...and strives to overcome evil unwholesome mental states that have arisen. He rouses his will...and strives to produce unarisen wholesome mental states. He rouses his will, makes an effort, stirs up energy, exerts his mind and strives to maintain wholesome mental states that have arisen, not to let them fade away, to bring them to greater growth, to the full perfection of development. This is called Right Effort.

'And what, monks, is Right Mindfulness? Here, monks, a monk abides contemplating body as body, ardent, clearly aware and mindful, having put aside hankering and fretting for the world; he abides contemplating feelings as feelings...; he abides contemplating mind as mind...; he abides contemplating mind-objects as mind-objects, ardent, clearly aware and mindful, having put aside hankering and fretting for the world. This is called Right Mindfulness.

'And what, monks, is Right Concentration? Here, a monk, detached from sense-desires, detached from unwholesome mental states, enters and remains in the first jhāna, which is with thinking and pondering, born of detachment, filled with delight and joy. And with the subsiding of thinking and pondering, by gaining inner tranquillity and oneness of mind, he enters and remains in the second jhāna, which is without thinking and pondering, born of concentration, filled with delight and joy. And with the fading away of delight, remaining imperturbable, mindful and clearly aware, he experiences in himself the joy of which the Noble Ones say: "Happy is he who dwells with equanimity and mindfulness," he enters the third jhāna. And, having given up pleasure and pain, and with the disappearance of former gladness and sadness, he enters and remains in the fourth jhāna, which is beyond pleasure and pain, and purified by equanimity and mindfulness. This is called Right Concentration. And that, monks, is called the way of practice leading to the cessation of suffering.'

2

The Greeks

The Greek literature and philosophy of the period 800 to 300 B.C. is the cornerstone of Western thought, its breadth represented by its variety of forms: the epic poem, the lyric, tragic drama, the Platonic dialogue, the philosophical treatises of Aristotle. The genius of such works lies in their engagement with questions that fascinated and sometimes puzzled the ancient Greeks.

One of these questions is the place of humans among the contending forces of nature and fate. The characters of Homer's epics, for example, understand that their lives and deaths are controlled by forces beyond their power. In the *Iliad*, as Achilles and Priam share their grief, Achilles knows he is fated to die in his youth, while Priam realizes the divinely inspired seduction of Helen has now brought ruin to his proud city. The apparently arbitrary workings of fate cast all humans into the same noble struggle to assert their will and identity, as Odysseus does in his great journey.

The Greeks' reflection on this question of fate reached a new intensity in tragic drama. The tragedy of Oedipus, however, this story of a great man who discovers he is a despicable criminal, is not just a protest against the gods. It is also a praise of human capacity to understand and prevail against their fate. Oedipus has faced the most horrible truth of human vanity and error, and survived to learn.

To his student Plato, the humble philosopher Socrates possessed the qualities of the great heroes of Greek legend. With Greek philosophy comes a shift to rational inquiry as the means for resolving fundamental questions. Socrates's noble search for truth is comparable to Odysseus's determined voyage or Oedipus's insistent pursuit of his identity. In the hands of Plato, Greek philosophy undertook another Greek enterprise, the search for unchanging patterns beneath the capricious and changing events of experience. Finally, the Greeks' concern with living in the world reaches a climax in Aristotle's *Ethics*, which seeks once again to find the right balance in the pursuit of virtue.

THE *ILIAD*

The *Iliad* often strikes modern readers as a particularly brutal and bloody tale of ethnic war. Its heroes are chiefly interested in living and dying by their warrior's code of honor and virtue. Yet Homer's warriors are inspired to acts of great nobility and devotion, and the entire poem is subtly woven together by an author who understood love's tenderness and the pangs of grief.

The story tells of the Achaeans' (Greeks') siege of the city of Troy, ostensibly to recover Helen, wife of an Achaean king, who has eloped with a Trojan prince. However, the Greek hero Achilles has withdrawn from the battle in anger at his humiliation by the chieftain Agamemnon. Despite apologies and gifts from Agamemnon, Achilles refuses to rejoin the combat, although he does permit his dearest friend, Patroclus, to fight in his place. When Patroclus is killed by the Trojan hero Hector, Achilles wrathfully challenges and kills Hector, defiling his body. In the epic's climactic episode, Hector's father, King Priam, steals into the camp of the Greeks and appeals to Achilles to return his son's body. The two enemies share their grief over loved ones fallen in war and reflect on human fate.

This final episode in the poem restores a moral balance that has been disturbed by Achilles' self-indulgent anger and murderous grief. In a tragic pattern repeated often in Greek poetry, the proud hero's error has caused a suffering and loss in which the characters find renewed understanding of the human condition.

For analysis and interpretation:

1. What role do the gods play in the poem's action , and what are the human characters' attitude toward that role?

2. Analyze Achilles' metaphor of Zeus's urn of blessings and evils. How does it reveal the Greeks' understanding of human fate?

The *Iliad*, Book XXIV:

Achilles and Priam

And the games broke up, and the people scattered to go away, each man
to his fast-running ship, and the rest of them took thought of their dinner
and of sweet sleep and its enjoyment; only Achilleus
wept still as he remembered his beloved companion, nor did sleep
who subdues all come over him, but he tossed from one side to the other
in longing for Patroklos, for his manhood and his great strength
and all the actions he had seen to the end with him, and the hardships
he had suffered; the wars of men; hard crossing of the big waters.
Remembering all these things he let fall the swelling tears, lying
sometimes along his side, sometimes on his back, and now again   10
prone on his face; then he would stand upright, and pace turning
in distraction along the beach of the sea, nor did dawn rising

escape him as she brightened across the sea and the beaches.
Then, when he had yoked running horses under the chariot
he would fasten Hektor behind the chariot, so as to drag him,
and draw him three times around the tomb of Menoitios' fallen
son, then rest again in his shelter, and throw down the dead man
and leave him to lie sprawled on his face in the dust. But Apollo
had pity on him, though he was only a dead man, and guarded
the body from all ugliness, and hid all of it under the golden   20
aegis, so that it might not be torn when Achilleus dragged it.
      So Achilleus in his standing fury outraged great Hektor.
The blessed gods as they looked upon him were filled with compassion
and kept urging clear-sighted Argeïphontes to steal the body.
There this was pleasing to all the others, but never to Hera
nor Poseidon, nor the girl of the grey eyes, who kept still
their hatred for sacred Ilion as in the beginning,
and for Priam and his people, because of the delusion of Paris
who insulted the goddesses when they came to him in his courtyard
and favoured her who supplied the lust that led to disaster.   30
But now, as it was the twelfth dawn after the death of Hektor,
Phoibos Apollo spoke his word among the immortals:
'You are hard, you gods, and destructive. Now did not Hektor
burn thigh pieces of oxen and unblemished goats in your honour?
Now you cannot bring yourselves to save him, though he is only
a corpse, for his wife to look upon, his child and his mother
and Priam his father, and his people, who presently thereafter
would burn his body in the fire and give him his rites of burial.
No, you gods; your desire is to help this cursed Achilleus
within whose breast there are no feelings of justice, nor can   40
his mind be bent, but his purposes are fierce, like a lion
who when he has given way to his own great strength and his haughty
spirit, goes among the flocks of men, to devour them.
So Achilleus has destroyed pity, and there is not in him
any shame; which does much harm to men but profits them also.
For a man must some day lose one who was even closer
than this; a brother from the same womb, or a son. And yet
he weeps for him, and sorrows for him, and then it is over,
for the Destinies put in mortal men the heart of endurance.
But this man, now he has torn the heart of life from great Hektor,   50
ties him to his horses and drags him around his beloved companion's
tomb; and nothing is gained thereby for his good, or his honour.
Great as he is, let him take care not make us angry;
for see, he does dishonour to the dumb earth in his fury.'
      Then bitterly Hera of the white arms answered him, saying:
'What you have said could be true, lord of the silver bow, only

if you give Hektor such pride of place as you give to Achilleus.
But Hektor was mortal, and suckled at the breast of a woman,
while Achilleus is the child of a goddess, one whom I myself
nourished and brought up and gave her as bride to her husband   60
Peleus, one dear to the hearts of the immortals, for you all
went, you gods, to the wedding; and you too feasted among them
and held your lyre, o friend of the evil, faithless forever.'
In turn Zeus who gathers the clouds spoke to her in answer:
'Hera, be not utterly angry with the gods, for there shall not
be the same pride of place given both. Yet Hektor also
was loved by the gods, best of all the mortals in Ilion.
I loved him too. He never failed of gifts to my liking.
Never yet has my altar gone without fair sacrifice,
the smoke and the savour of it, since that is our portion of honour.   70
The stealing of him we will dismiss, for it is not possible
to take bold Hektor secretly from Achilleus, since always
his mother is near him night and day; but it would be better
if one of the gods would summon Thetis here to my presence
so that I can say a close word to her, and see that Achilleus
is given gifts by Priam and gives back the body of Hektor.'
        He spoke, and Iris storm-footed sprang away with the message,
and at a point between Samos and Imbros of the high cliffs
plunged in the dark water, and the sea crashed moaning about her.
She plummeted to the sea floor like a lead weight which, mounted   80
along the horn of an ox who ranges the fields, goes downward
and takes death with it to the raw-ravening fish. She found Thetis
inside the hollow of her cave, and gathered about her
sat the rest of the sea goddesses, and she in their midst
was mourning the death of her blameless son, who so soon was destined
to die in Troy of the rich soil, far from the land of his fathers.
Iris the swift-footed came close beside her and spoke to her:
'Rise, Thetis. Zeus whose purposes are infinite calls you.'
        In turn Thetis the goddess, the silver-footed, answered her:
'What does he, the great god, want with me? I feel shamefast   90
to mingle with the immortals, and my heart is confused with sorrows.
But I will go. No word shall be in vain, if he says it.'
        So she spoke, and shining among the divinities took up
her black veil, and there is no darker garment. She went
on her way, and in front of her rapid wind-footed Iris
guided her, and the wave of the water opened about them.
They stepped out on the dry land and swept to the sky. There they found
the son of Kronos of the wide brows, and gathered about him
sat all the rest of the gods, the blessed, who live forever.

She sat down beside Zeus father, and Athene made a place for her.   100
Hera put into her hand a beautiful golden goblet
and spoke to her to comfort her, and Thetis accepting drank from it.
The father of gods and men began the discourse among them:
'You have come to Olympos, divine Thetis, for all your sorrow,
with an unforgotten grief in your heart. I myself know this.
But even so I will tell you why I summoned you hither.
For nine days there has risen a quarrel among the immortals
over the body of Hektor, and Achilleus, stormer of cities.
They keep urging clear-sighted Argeïphontes to steal the body,
but I still put upon Achilleus the honour that he has, guarding   110
your reverence and your love for me into time afterwards. Go then
in all speed to the encampment and give to your son this message:
tell him that the gods frown upon him, that beyond all other
immortals I myself am angered that in his heart's madness
he holds Hektor beside the curved ships and did not give him
back. Perhaps in fear of me he will give back Hektor.
Then I will send Iris to Priam of the great heart, with an order
to ransom his dear son, going down to the ship of the Achaians
and bringing gifts to Achilleus which might soften his anger.'
        He spoke and the goddess silver-foot Thetis did not disobey him   120
but descended in a flash of speed from the peaks of Olympos
and made her way to the shelter of her son, and there found him
in close lamentation, and his beloved companions about him
were busy at their work and made ready the morning meal, and there
stood a great fleecy sheep being sacrificed in the shelter.
His honoured mother came close to him and sat down beside him,
and stroked him with her hand and called him by name and spoke to him:
'My child, how long will you go on eating your heart out in sorrow
and lamentation, and remember neither your food nor going
to bed? It is a good thing even to lie with a woman   130
in love. For you will not be with me long, but already
death and powerful destiny stand closely above you.
But listen hard to me, for I come from Zeus with a message.
He says that the gods frown upon you, that beyond all other
immortals he himself is angered that in your heart's madness
you hold Hektor beside the curved ships and did not redeem him.
Come, then, give him up and accept ransom for the body.'
        Then in turn Achilleus of the swift feet answered her:
'So be it. He can bring the ransom and take off the body,
if the Olympian himself so urgently bids it.'   140
        So, where the ships were drawn together, the son and his mother
conversed at long length in winged words. But the son of Kronos

stirred Iris to go down to sacred Ilion, saying:
'Go forth, Iris the swift, leaving your place on Olympos,
and go to Priam of the great heart within Ilion, tell him
to ransom his dear son, going down to the ships of the Achaians
and bringing gifts to Achilleus which might soften his anger:
alone, let no other man of the Trojans go with him, but only
let one elder herald attend him, one who can manage
the mules and the easily running wagon, so he can carry   150
the dead man, whom great Achilleus slew, back to the city.
Let death not be a thought in his heart, let him have no fear;
such an escort shall I send to guide him, Argeïphontes
who shall lead him until he brings him to Achilleus. And after
he has brought him inside the shelter of Achilleus, neither
will the man himself kill him, but will hold back all the others,
for he is no witless man nor unwatchful, nor is he wicked,
but will in all kindness spare one who comes to him as a suppliant.'
        He spoke, and storm-footed Iris swept away with the message
and came to the house of Priam. There she found outcry and mourning.   160
The sons sitting around their father inside the courtyard
made their clothes sodden with their tears, and among them the old man
sat veiled, beaten into his mantle. Dung lay thick
on the head and neck of the aged man, for he had been rolling
in it, he had gathered and smeared it on with his hands. And his daughters
all up and down the house and the wives of his sons were mourning
as they remembered all those men in their numbers and valour
who lay dead, their lives perished at the hands of the Argives.
The messenger of Zeus stood beside Priam and spoke to him
in a small voice, and yet the shivers took hold of his body: 170
'Take heart, Priam, son of Dardanos, do not be frightened.
I come to you not eyeing you with evil intention
but with the purpose of good toward you. I am a messenger
of Zeus, who far away cares much for you and is pitiful.
The Olympian orders you to ransom Hektor the brilliant,
to bring gifts to Achilleus which may soften his anger:
alone, let no other man of the Trojans go with you, but only
let one elder herald attend you, one who can manage
the mules and the easily running wagon, so he can carry
the dead man, whom great Achilleus slew, back to the city.   180
Let death not be a thought in your heart, you need have no fear,
such an escort shall go with you to guide you, Argeïphontes
who will lead you till he brings you to Achilleus. And after
he has brought you inside the shelter of Achilleus, neither
will the man himself kill you but will hold back all the others;

for he is no witless man nor unwatchful, nor is he wicked
but will in all kindness spare one who comes to him as a suppliant.'
　　So Iris the swift-footed spoke and went away from him.
Thereupon he ordered his sons to make ready the easily rolling
mule wagon, and to fasten upon it the carrying basket.　　　　　　　190
He himself went into the storeroom, which was fragrant
and of cedar, and high-ceilinged, with many bright treasures inside it.
He called out to Hekabe his wife, and said to her:
'Dear wife, a messenger came to me from Zeus on Olympos,
that I must go to the ships of the Achaians and ransom my dear son,
bringing gifts to Achilleus which may soften his anger.
Come then, tell me. What does it seem best to your own mind
for me to do? My heart, my strength are terribly urgent
that I go there to the ships within the wide army of the Achaians.'
　　So he spoke, and his wife cried out aloud, and answered him:　　200
'Ah me, where has that wisdom gone for which you were famous
in time before, among outlanders and those you rule over?
How can you wish to go alone to the ships of the Achaians
before the eyes of a man who has slaughtered in such numbers
such brave sons of yours? The heart in you is iron. For if
he has you within his grasp and lays eyes upon you, that man
who is savage and not to be trusted will not take pity upon you
nor have respect for your rights. Let us sit apart in our palace
now, and weep for Hektor, and the way at the first strong Destiny
spun with his life line when he was born, when I gave birth to him,　　210
that the dogs with their shifting feet should feed on him, far from his parents,
gone down before a stronger man; I wish I could set teeth
in the middle of his liver and eat it. That would be vengeance
for what he did to my son; for he slew him when he was no coward
but standing before the men of Troy and the deep-girdled women
of Troy, with no thoughts in his mind of flight or withdrawal.'
　　In turn the aged Priam, the godlike, answered her saying
'Do not hold me back when I would be going, neither yourself be
a bird of bad omen in my palace. You will not persuade me.
If it had been some other who ordered me, one of the mortals,　　220
one of those who are soothsayers, or priests, or diviners,
I might have called it a lie and we might rather have rejected it.
But now, for I myself heard the god and looked straight upon her,
I am going, and this word shall not be in vain. If it is my destiny
to die there by the ships of the bronze-armoured Achaians,
then I wish that. Achilleus can slay me at once, with my own son
caught in my arms, once I have my fill of mourning above him.'
　　He spoke, and lifted back the fair covering of his clothes-chest

and from inside took out twelve robes surpassingly lovely
and twelve mantles to be worn single, as many blankets,   230
as many great white cloaks, also the same number of tunics.
He weighed and carried out ten full talents of gold, and brought forth
two shining tripods, and four cauldrons, and brought out a goblet
of surpassing loveliness that the men of Thrace had given him
when he went to them with a message, but now the old man spared not
even this in his halls, so much was it his heart's desire
to ransom back his beloved son. But he drove off the Trojans
all from his cloister walks, scolding them with words of revilement:
'Get out, you failures, you disgraces. Have you not also
mourning of your own at home that you come to me with your sorrows?   240
It is not enough that Zeus, son of Kronos, has given me sorrow
in losing the best of my sons? You also shall be aware of this
since you will be all the easier for the Achaians to slaughter
now he is dead. But, for myself, before my eyes look
upon this city as it is destroyed and its people are slaughtered,
my wish is to go sooner down to the house of the death god.'
      He spoke, and went after the men with a stick, and they fled outside
before the fury of the old man. He was scolding his children
and cursing Helenos, and Paris, Agathon the brilliant,
Pammon and Antiphonos, Polites of the great war cry,   250
Deïphobos and Hippothoös and proud Dios. There were nine
sons to whom now the old man gave orders and spoke to them roughly:
'Make haste, wicked children, my disgraces. I wish all of you
had been killed beside the running ships in the place of Hektor.
Ah me, for my evil destiny. I have had the noblest
of sons in Troy, but I say not one of them is left to me,
Mestor like a god and Troilos whose delight was in horses,
and Hektor, who was a god among men, for he did not seem like
one who was child of a mortal man, but of a god. All these
Ares has killed, and all that are left me are the disgraces,   260
the liars and the dancers, champions of the chorus, the plunderers
of their own people in their land of lambs and kids. Well then,
will you not get my wagon ready and be quick about it,
and put all these things on it, so we can get on with our journey?'
      So he spoke, and they in terror at the old man's scolding
hauled out the easily running wagon for mules, a fine thing
new-fabricated, and fastened the carrying basket upon it.
They took away from its peg the mule yoke made of boxwood
with its massive knob, well fitted with guiding rings, and brought forth
the yoke lashing (together with the yoke itself) of nine cubits   270
and snugged it well into place upon the smooth-polished wagon-pole

at the foot of the beam, then slipped the ring over the peg, and lashed it
with three turns on either side to the knob, and afterwards
fastened it all in order and secured it under a hooked guard.
Then they carried out and piled into the smooth-polished mule wagon
all the unnumbered spoils to be given for the head of Hektor,
then yoked the powerful-footed mules who pulled in the harness
and whom the Mysians gave once as glorious presents to Priam;
but for Priam they led under the yoke those horses the old man
himself had kept, and cared for them at his polished manger.   280
    Now in the high house the yoking was done for the herald
and Priam, men both with close counsels in their minds. And now came
Hekabe with sorrowful heart and stood close beside them
carrying in her right hand the kind, sweet wine in a golden
goblet, so that before they went they might pour a drink-offering.
She stood in front of the horses, called Priam by name and spoke to him:
'Here, pour a libation to Zeus father, and pray you may come back
home again from those who hate you, since it seems the spirit
within you drives you upon the ships, though I would not have it.
Make your prayer then to the dark-misted, the son of Kronos   290
on Ida, who looks out on all the Troad, and ask him
for a bird of omen, a rapid messenger, which to his own mind
is dearest of all birds and his strength is the biggest, one seen
on the right, so that once your eyes have rested upon him
you can trust in him and go to the ships of the fast-mounted Danaans.
But if Zeus of the wide brows will not grant you his own messenger,
then I, for one, would never urge you on nor advise you
to go the Argive ships, for all your passion to do it.'
    Then in answer to her again spoke Priam the godlike:
'My lady, I will not disregard this wherein you urge me.   300
It is well to lift hands to Zeus and ask if he will have mercy.'
    The old man spoke, and told the housekeeper who attended them
to pour unstained water over his hands. She standing beside them
and serving them held the washing-bowl in her hands, and a pitcher.
He washed his hands and took the cup from his wife. He stood up
in the middle of the enclosure, and prayed, and poured the wine out
looking up into the sky, and gave utterance and spoke, saying:
'Father Zeus, watching over us from Ida, most high, most honoured:
grant that I come to Achilleus for love and pity; but send me
a bird of omen, a rapid messenger which to your own mind   310
is dearest of all birds and his strength is biggest, one seen
on the right, so that once my eyes have rested upon him
I may trust in him and go to the ships of the fast-mounted Danaans.'
    So he spoke in prayer, and Zeus of the counsels heard him.

Straightway he sent down the most lordly of birds, an eagle,
the dark one, the marauder, called as well the black eagle.
And as big as is the build of the door to a towering chamber
in the house of a rich man, strongly fitted with bars, of such size
was the spread of his wings on either side. He swept through the city
appearing on the right hand, and the people looking upon him   320
were uplifted and the hearts made glad in the breasts of all of them.
        Now in urgent haste the old man mounted into his chariot
and drove out through the forecourt and the thundering close. Before him
the mules hauled the wagon on its four wheels, Idaios
the sober-minded driving them, and behind him the horses
came on as the old man laid the lash upon them and urged them
rapidly through the town, and all his kinsmen were following
much lamenting, as if he went to his death. When the two men
had gone down through the city, and out, and come to the flat land,
the rest of them turned back to go to Ilion, the sons   330
and the sons-in-law. And Zeus of the wide brows failed not to notice
the two as they showed in the plain. He saw the old man and took pity
upon him, and spoke directly to his beloved son, Hermes:
'Hermes, for to you beyond all other gods it is dearest
to be man's companion, and you listen to whom you will, go now
on your way, and so guide Priam inside the hollow ships
of the Achaians, that no man shall see him, none be aware of him,
of the other Danaans, till he has come to the son of Peleus.'
        He spoke, nor disobeyed him the courier, Argeïphontes.
Immediately he bound upon his feet the fair sandals   340
golden and immortal, that carried him over the water
as over the dry land of the main abreast of the wind's blast.
He caught up the staff, with which he mazes the eyes of those mortals
whose eyes he would maze, or wakes again the sleepers. Holding
this in his hands, strong Argeïphontes winged his way onward
until he came suddenly to Troy and the Hellespont, and there
walked on, and there took the likeness of a young man, a noble,
with beard new grown, which is the most graceful time of young manhood.
        Now when the two had driven past the great tomb of Ilos
they stayed their mules and horses to water them in the river,   350
for by this time darkness had descended on the land; and the herald
made out Hermes, who was coming toward them at a short distance.
He lifted his voice and spoke aloud to Priam: 'Take thought,
son of Dardanos. Here is work for a mind that is careful.
I see a man; I think he will presently tear us to pieces.
Come then, let us run away with our horses, or if not, then
clasp his knees and entreat him to have mercy upon us.'

So he spoke, and the old man's mind was confused, he was badly
frightened, and the hairs stood up all over his gnarled body
and he stood staring, but the kindly god himself coming closer   360
took the old man's hand, and spoke to him and asked him a question.
'Where, my father, are you thus guiding your mules and horses
through the immortal night while other mortals are sleeping?
Have you no fear of the Achaians whose wind is fury,
who hate you, who are your enemies, and are near? For if one
of these were to see you, how you are conveying so many
treasures through the swift black night, what then could you think of?
You are not young yourself, and he who attends you is aged
for beating off any man who might pick a quarrel with you.
But I will do you no harm myself, I will even keep off   370
another who would. You seem to me like a beloved father.'
    In answer to him again spoke aged Priam the godlike;
'Yes, in truth, dear child, all this is much as you tell me;
yet still there is some god who has held his hand above me,
who sent such a wayfarer as you to meet me, an omen
of good, for such you are by your form, your admired beauty
and the wisdom in your mind. Your parents are fortunate in you.'
    Then in turn answered him the courier Argeïphontes:
'Yes, old sir, all this that you said is fair and orderly.
But come, tell me this thing and recite it to me accurately.   380
Can it be you convey these treasures in all their numbers and beauty
to outland men, so that they can be still kept safe for you?
Or are all of you by now abandoning sacred Ilion
in fear, such a one was he who died, the best man among you,
your son; who was never wanting when you fought against the Achaians.'
    In answer to him again spoke aged Priam the godlike:
'But who are you, o best of men, and who are your parents?
Since you spoke of my ill-starred son's death, and with honour.'
    Then in turn answered him the courier Argeïphontes:
'You try me out, aged sir. You ask me of glorious Hektor   390
whom many a time my eyes have seen in the fighting where men win
glory, as also on that time when he drove back the Argives
on their ships and kept killing them with the stroke of the sharp bronze,
and we stood by and wondered at him; for then Achilleus
would not let us fight by reason of his anger at Agamemnon.
For I am Achilleus' henchman, and the same strong-wrought vessel
brought us here; and I am a Myrmidon, and my father is
Polyktor; a man of substance, but aged, as you are.
He has six sons beside, and I am the seventh, and I shook
lots with the others, and it was my lot to come on this venture.   400

But now I have come to the plain away from the ships, for at daybreak
the glancing-eyed Achaians will do battle around the city.
They chafe from sitting here too long, nor have the Achaians'
kings the strength to hold them back as they break for the fighting.'
    In answer to him again spoke aged Priam the godlike:
'If then you are henchman to Peleïd Achilleus,
come, tell me the entire truth, and whether my son lies
still beside the ships, or whether by now he has been hewn
limb from limb and thrown before the dogs by Achilleus.'
    Then in turn answered the courier Argeïphontes: 410
'Aged sir, neither have any dogs eaten him, nor have
the birds, but he lies yet beside the ship of Achilleus
at the shelters, and as he was; now here is the twelfth dawn
he has lain there, nor does his flesh decay, nor do worms feed
on him, they who devour men who have fallen in battle.
It is true, Achilleus drags him at random around his beloved
companion's tomb, as dawn on dawn appears, yet he cannot
mutilate him; you yourself can see when you go there
how fresh with dew he lies, and the blood is all washed from him,
nor is there any corruption, and all the wounds have been closed up   420
where he was struck, since many drove the bronze in his body.
So it is that the blessed immortals care for your son, though
he is nothing but a dead man; because in their hearts they loved him.'
    He spoke, and the old man was made joyful and answered him, saying:
'My child, surely it is good to give the immortals
their due gifts; because my own son, if ever I had one,
never forgot in his halls the gods who live on Olympos.
Therefore they remembered him even in death's stage. Come, then,
accept at my hands this beautiful drinking-cup, and give me
protection for my body, and with the gods' grace be my escort   430
until I make my way to the shelter of the son of Peleus.'
    In turn answered him the courier Argeïphontes:
'You try me out, aged sir, for I am young, but you will not
persuade me, telling me to accept your gifts when Achilleus
does not know. I fear him at heart and have too much reverence
to rob him. Such a thing might be to my sorrow hereafter.
But I would be your escort and take good care of you, even
till I came to glorious Argos in a fast ship or following
on foot, and none would fight you because he despised your escort.'
    The kind god spoke, and sprang up behind the horses and into   440
the chariot, and rapidly caught in his hands the lash and the guide reins,
and breathed great strength into the mules and horses. Now after
they had got to the fortifications about the ships, and the ditch, there

were sentries, who had just begun to make ready their dinner,
but about these the courier Argeïphontes drifted
sleep, on all, and quickly opened the gate, and shoved back
the door-bars, and brought in Priam and the glorious gifts on the wagon.
But when they had got to the shelter of Peleus' son: a towering
shelter the Myrmidons had built for their king, hewing
the timbers of pine, and they made a roof of thatch above it   450
shaggy with grass that they had gathered out of the meadows;
and around it made a great courtyard for their king, with hedgepoles
set close together; the gate was secured by a single door-piece
of pine, and three Achaians could ram it home in its socket
and three could pull back and open the huge door-bar; three other
Achaians, that is, but Achilleus all by himself could close it.
At this time Hermes, the kind god, opened the gate for the old man
and brought in the glorious gifts for Peleus' son, the swift-footed,
and dismounted to the ground from behind the horses, and spoke forth:
'Aged sir, I who came to you am a god immortal,   460
Hermes. My father sent me down to guide and go with you.
But now I am going back again, and I will not go in
before the eyes of Achilleus, for it would make others angry
for an immortal god so to face mortal men with favour.
But go you in yourself and clasp the knees of Peleion
and entreat him in the name of his father, the name of his mother
of the lovely hair, and his child, and so move the spirit within him.'
      So Hermes spoke, and went away to the height of Olympos,
but Priam vaulted down to the ground from behind the horses
and left Idaios where he was, for he stayed behind, holding   470
in hand the horses and mules. The old man made straight for the dwelling
where Achilleus the beloved of Zeus was sitting. He found him
inside, and his companions were sitting apart, as two only,
Automedon the hero and Alkimos, scion of Ares,
were busy beside him. He had just now got through with his dinner,
with eating and drinking, and the table still stood by. Tall Priam
came in unseen by the other men and stood close beside him
and caught the knees of Achilleus in his arms, and kissed the hands
that were dangerous and manslaughtering and had killed so many
of his sons. As when dense disaster closes on one who has murdered   480
a man in his own land, and he comes to the country of others,
to a man of substance, and wonder seizes on those who behold him,
so Achilleus wondered as he looked on Priam, a godlike
man, and the rest of them wondered also, and looked at each other.
But now Priam spoke to him in the words of a suppliant:
'Achilleus like the gods, remember your father, one who

is of years like mine, and on the door-sill of sorrowful old age.
And they who dwell nearby encompass him and afflict him,
nor is there any to defend him against the wrath, the destruction.
Yet surely he, when he hears of you and that you are still living,   490
is gladdened within his heart and all his days he is hopeful
that he will see his beloved son come home from the Troad.
But for me, my destiny was evil. I have had the noblest
of sons in Troy, but I say not one of them is left to me.
Fifty were my sons, when the sons of the Achaians came here.
Nineteen were born to me from the womb of a single mother,
and other women bore the rest in my palace; and of these
violent Ares broke the strength in the knees of most of them,
but one was left me who guarded my city and people, that one
you killed a few days since as he fought in defence of his country,   500
Hektor; for whose sake I come now to the ships of the Achaians
to win him back from you, and I bring you gifts beyond number.
Honour then the gods, Achilleus, and take pity upon me
remembering your father, yet I am still more pitiful;
I have gone through what no other mortal on earth has gone through;
I put my lips to the hands of the man who has killed my children.'
        So he spoke, and stirred in the other a passion of grieving
for his own father. He took the old man's hand and pushed him
gently away, and the two remembered, as Priam sat huddled
at the feet of Achilleus and wept close for manslaughtering Hektor   510
and Achilleus wept now for his own father, now again
for Patroklos. The sound of their mourning moved in the house. Then
when great Achilleus had taken full satisfaction in sorrow
and the passion for it had gone from his mind and body, thereafter
he rose from his chair, and took the old man by the hand, and set him
on his feet again, in pity for the grey head and the grey beard,
and spoke to him and addressed him in winged words: 'Ah, unlucky,
surely you have had much evil to endure in your spirit.
How could you dare to come alone to the ships of the Achaians
and before my eyes, when I am one who have killed in such numbers   520
such brave sons of yours? The heart in you is iron. Come, then,
and sit down upon this chair, and you and I will even let
our sorrows lie still in the heart for all our grieving. There is not
any advantage to be won from grim lamentation.
Such is the way the gods spun life for unfortunate mortals,
that we live in unhappiness, but the gods themselves have no sorrows.
There are two urns that stand on the door-sill of Zeus. They are unlike
for the gifts they bestow: an urn of evils, an urn of blessings.
If Zeus who delights in thunder mingles these and bestows them

on man, he shifts, and moves now in evil, again in good fortune.   530
But when Zeus bestows from the urn of sorrows, he makes a failure
of man, and the evil hunger drives him over the shining
earth, and he wanders respected neither of gods nor mortals.
Such were the shining gifts given by the gods to Peleus
from his birth, who outshone all men beside for his riches
and pride of possession, and was lord over the Myrmidons. Thereto
the gods bestowed an immortal wife on him, who was mortal.
But even on him the god piled evil also. There was not
any generation of strong sons born to him in his great house
but a single all-untimely child he had, and I give him   540
no care as he grows old, since far from the land of my fathers
I sit here in Troy, and bring nothing but sorrow to you and your children.
And you, old sir, we are told you prospered once; for as much
as Lesbos, Makar's hold, confines to the north above it
and Phrygia rom the north confines, and enormous Hellespont,
of these, old sir, you were lord once in your wealth and your children.
But now the Uranian gods brought us, an affliction upon you,
forever there is fighting about your city, and men killed.
But bear up, nor mourn endlessly in your heart, for there is not
anything to be gained from grief for your son; you will never   550
bring him back; sooner you must go through yet another sorrow.'
    In answer to him again spoke aged Priam the godlike:
'Do not, beloved of Zeus, make me sit on a chair while Hektor
lies yet forlorn among the shelters; rather with all speed
give him back, so my eyes may behold him, and accept the ransom
we bring you, which is great. You may have joy of it, and go back
to the land of your own fathers, since once you have permitted me
to go on living myself and continue to look on the sunlight.'
    Then looking darkly at him spoke swift-footed Achilleus:
'No longer stir me up, old sir. I myself am minded   560
to give Hektor back to you. A messenger came to me from Zeus,
my mother, she who bore me, the daughter of the sea's ancient.
I know you, Priam, in my heart, and it does not escape me
that some god led you to the running ships of the Achaians.
For no mortal would dare come to our encampment, not even
one strong in youth. He could not get by the pickets, he could not
lightly unbar the bolt that secures our gateway. Therefore
you must not further make my spirit move in my sorrows,
for fear, old sir, I might not let you alone in my shelter,
suppliant as you are; and be guilty before the god's orders.'   570
    He spoke, and the old man was frightened and did as he told him.
The son of Peleus bounded to the door of the house like a lion,

nor went alone, but the two henchmen followed attending,
the hero Automedon and Alkimos, those whom Achilleus
honoured beyond all companions after Patroklos dead. These two
now set free from under the yoke the mules and the horses,
and led inside the herald, the old king's crier, and gave him
a chair to sit in, then from the smooth-polished mule wagon
lifted out the innumerable spoils for the head of Hektor,
but left inside it two great cloaks and a finespun tunic   580
to shroud the corpse in when they carried him home. Then Achilleus
called out to his serving-maids to wash the body and anoint it
all over; but take it first aside, since otherwise Priam
might see his son and in the heart's sorrow not hold in his anger
at the sight, and the deep heart in Achilleus be shaken to anger;
that he might not kill Priam and be guilty before the god's orders.
Then when the serving-maids had washed the corpse and anointed it
with olive oil, they threw a fair great cloak and a tunic
about him, and Achilleus himself lifted him and laid him
on a litter, and his friends helped him lift it to the smooth-polished   590
mule wagon. He groaned then, and called by name on his beloved companion:
'Be not angry with me, Patroklos, if you discover,
though you be in the house of Hades, that I gave back great Hektor
to his loved father, for the ransom he gave me was not unworthy.
I will give you your share of the spoils, as much as is fitting.'
     So spoke great Achilleus and went back into the shelter
and sat down on the elaborate couch from which he had risen,
against the inward wall, and now spoke his word to Priam:
'Your son is given back to you, aged sir, as you asked it.
He lies on a bier. When dawn shows you yourself shall see him   600
as you take him away. Now you and I must remember our supper.
For even Niobe, she of the lovely tresses, remembered
to eat, whose twelve children were destroyed in her palace,
six daughters, and six sons in the pride of their youth, whom Apollo
killed with arrows from his silver bow, being angered
with Niobe, and shaft-showering Artemis killed the daughters;
because Niobe likened herself to Leto of the fair colouring
and said Leto had borne only two, she herself had borne many;
but the two, though they were only two, destroyed all those others.
Nine days long they lay in their blood, nor was there anyone   610
to bury them, for the son of Kronos made stones out of
the people; but on the tenth day the Uranian gods buried them.
But she remembered to eat when she was worn out with weeping.
And now somewhere among the rocks, in the lonely mountains,
in Sipylos, where they say is the resting place of the goddesses

who are nymphs, and dance beside the waters of Acheloios,
there, stone still, she broods on the sorrows that the gods gave her.
Come then, we also, aged magnificent sir, must remember
to eat, and afterwards you may take your beloved son back
to Ilion, and mourn for him; and he will be much lamented.'   620
        So spoke fleet Achilleus and sprang to his feet and slaughtered
a gleaming sheep, and his friends skinned it and butchered it fairly,
and cut up the meat expertly into small pieces, and spitted them,
and roasted all carefully and took off the pieces.
Automedon took the bread and set it out on the table
in fair baskets, while Achilleus served the meats. And thereon
they put their hands to the good things that lay ready before them.
But when they had put aside their desire for eating and drinking,
Priam, son of Dardanos, gazed upon Achilleus, wondering
at his size and beauty, for he seemed like an outright vision   630
of gods. Achilleus in turn gazed on Dardanian Priam
and wondered, as he saw his brave looks and listened to him talking.
But when they had taken their fill of gazing one on the other,
first of the two to speak was the aged man, Priam the godlike:
'Give me, beloved of Zeus, a place to sleep presently, so that
we may even go to bed and take the pleasure of sweet sleep.
For my eyes have not closed underneath my lids since that time
when my son lost life beneath your hands, but always
I have been grieving and brooding over my numberless sorrows
and wallowed in the muck about my courtyard's enclosure.   640
Now I have tasted food again and have let the gleaming
wine go down my throat. Before, I had tasted nothing.'
        He spoke, and Achilleus ordered his serving-maids and companions
to make a bed in the porch's shelter and to lay upon it
fine underbedding of purple, and spread blankets above it
and fleecy robes to be an over-all covering. The maid-servants
went forth from the main house, and in their hands held torches,
and set to work, and presently had two beds made. Achilleus
of the swift feet now looked at Priam and said, sarcastic:
'Sleep outside, aged sir and good friend, for fear some Achaian   650
might come in here on a matter of counsel, since they keep coming
and sitting by me and making plans; as they are supposed to.
But if one of these come through the fleeting black night should notice you,
he would go straight and tell Agamemnon, shepherd of the people,
and there would be delay in the ransoming of the body.
But come, tell me this and count off for me exactly
how many days you intend for the burial of great Hektor.
Tell me, so I myself shall stay still and hold back the people.'

In answer to him again spoke aged Priam the godlike:
'If you are willing that we accomplish a complete funeral   660
for great Hektor, this, Achilleus, is what you could do and give
me pleasure. For you know surely how we are penned in our city,
and wood is far to bring in from the hills, and the Trojans are frightened
badly. Nine days we would keep him in our palace and mourn him,
and bury him on the tenth day, and the people feast by him,
and on the eleventh day we would make the grave-barrow for him,
and on the twelfth day fight again; if so we must do.'
      Then in turn swift-footed brilliant Achilleus answered him:
'Then all this, aged Priam, shall be done as you ask it.
I will hold off our attack for as much time as you bid me.'   670
      So he spoke, and tood the aged king by the right hand
at the wrist, so that his heart might have no fear. Then these two,
Priam and the herald who were both men of close counsel,
slept in the place outside the house, in the porch's shelter;
but Achilleus slept in the inward corner of the strong-built shelter,
and at his side lay Briseis of the fair colouring.
      Now the rest of the gods and men who were lords of chariots
slept nightlong, with the easy bondage of slumber upon them,
only sleep had not caught Hermes the kind god, who pondered
now in his heart the problem of how to escort King Priam   680
from the ships and not be seen by the devoted gate-wardens.
He stood above his head and spoke a word to him, saying:
'Aged sir, you can have no thought of evil from the way
you sleep still among your enemies now Achilleus has left you
unharmed. You have ransomed now your dear son and given much for him.
But the sons you left behind would give three times as much ransom
for you, who are alive, were Atreus' son Agamemnon
to recognize you, and all the other Achaians learn of you.'
      He spoke, and the old man was afraid, and wakened his herald,
and lightly Hermes harnessed for them the mules and the horses   690
and himself drove them through the encampment. And no man knew of them.
      But when they came to the crossing-place of the fair-running river,
of whirling Xanthos, a stream whose father was Zeus the immortal,
there Hermes left them and went away to the height of Olympos,
and dawn, she of the yellow robe, scattered over all earth,
and they drove their horses on to the city with lamentation
and clamour, while the mules drew the body. Nor was any other
aware of them at the first, no man, no fair-girdled woman,
only Kassandra, a girl like Aphrodite the golden,
who had gone up the height of the Pergamos. She saw   700
her dear father standing in the chariot, his herald and crier

with him. She saw Hektor drawn by the mules on a litter.
She cried out then in sorrow and spoke to the entire city:
'Come, men of Troy and Trojan women; look upon Hektor
if ever before you were joyful when you saw him come back living
from battle; for he was a great joy to his city, and all his people.'
     She spoke, and there was no man left there in all the city
nor woman, but all were held in sorrow passing endurance.
They met Priam beside the gates as he brought the dead in.
First among them were Hektor's wife and his honoured mother   710
who tore their hair, and ran up beside the smooth-rolling wagon,
and touched his head. And the multitude, wailing, stood there about them.
And now and there in front of the gates they would have lamented
all day till the sun went down and let fall their tears for Hektor,
except that the old man spoke from the chariot to his people:
'Give me way to get through with my mules; then afterwards
you may sate yourselves with mourning, when I have him inside the palace.'
     So he spoke, and they stood apart and made way for the wagon.
And when they had brought him inside the renowned house, they laid him
then on a carved bed, and seated beside him the singers   720
who were to lead the melody in the dirge, and the singers
chanted the song of sorrow, and the women were mourning beside them.
Andromache of the white arms led the lamentation
of the women, and held in her arms the head of manslaughtering Hektor:
'My husband, you were lost young from life, and have left me
a widow in your house, and the boy is only a baby
who was born to you and me, the unhappy. I think he will never
come of age, for before then head to heel this city
will be sacked, for you, its defender, are gone, you who guarded
the city, and the grave wives, and the innocent children,   730
wives who before long must go away in the hollow ships,
and among them I shall also go, and you, my child, follow
where I go, and there do much hard work that is unworthy
of you, drudgery for a hard master; or else some Achaian
will take you by hand and hurl you from the tower into horrible
death, in anger because Hektor once killed his brother,
or his father, or his son; there were so many Achaians
whose teeth bit the vast earth, beaten down by the hands of Hektor.
Your father was no merciful man in the horror of battle.
Therefore your people are grieving for you all through their city,   740
Hektor, and you left for your parents mourning and sorrow
beyond words, but for me passing all others is left the bitterness
and the pain, for you did not die in bed, and stretch your arms to me,
nor tell me some last intimate word that I could remember

always, all the nights and days of my weeping for you.'
So she spoke in tears, and the women were mourning about her.
Now Hekabe led out the thronging chant of their sorrow:
'Hektor, of all my sons the dearest by far to my spirit;
while you still lived for me you were dear to the gods, and even
in the stage of death they cared about you still. There were others   750
of my sons whom at times swift-footed Achilleus captured,
and he would sell them as slaves far across the unresting salt water
into Samos, and Imbros, and Lemnos in the gloom of the mists. You,
when he had taken your life with the thin edge of the bronze sword,
he dragged again and again around his beloved companion's
tomb, Patroklos', whom you killed, but even so did not
bring him back to life. Now you lie in the palace, handsome
and fresh with dew, in the likeness of one whom he of the silver
bow, Apollo, has attacked and killed with his gentle arrows.'
So she spoke, in tears, and wakened the endless mourning.   760
Third and last Helen led the song of sorrow among them:
'Hektor, of all my lord's brothers dearest by far to my spirit:
my husband is Alexandros, like an immortal, who brought me
here to Troy; and I should have died before I came with him;
and here now is the twentieth year upon me since I came
from the place where I was, forsaking the land of my fathers. In this time
I have never heard a harsh saying from you, not an insult.
No, but when another, one of my lord's brothers or sisters, a fair-robed
wife of some brother, would say a harsh word to me in the palace,
or my lord's mother—but his father was gentle always, a father   770
indeed—then you would speak and put them off and restrain them
by your own gentleness of heart and your gentle words. Therefore
I mourn for you in sorrow of heart and mourn myself also
and my ill luck. There was no other in all the wide Troad
who was kind to me, and my friend; all others shrank when they saw me.'
So she spoke in tears, and the vast populace grieved with her.
Now Priam the aged king spoke forth his word to his people:
'Now, men of Troy, bring timber into the city, and let not
your hearts fear a close ambush of the Argives. Achilleus
promised me, as he sent me on my way from the black ships,   780
that none should do us injury until the twelfth dawn comes.'
He spoke, and they harnessed to the wagons their mules and their oxen
and presently were gathered in front of the city. Nine days
they spent bringing in an endless supply of timber. But when
the tenth dawn had shone forth with her light upon mortals,
they carried out bold Hektor, weeping, and set the body
aloft a towering pyre for burning. And set fire to it.

But when the young dawn showed again with her rosy fingers,
then people gathered around the pyre of illustrious Hektor.
But when all were gathered to one place and assembled together,   790
first with gleaming wine they put out the pyre that was burning,
all where the fury of the fire still was in force, and thereafter
the brothers and companions of Hektor gathered the white bones
up, mourning, as the tears swelled and ran down their cheeks. Then
they laid what they had gathered up in a golden casket
and wrapped this about with soft robes of purple, and presently
put it away in the hollow of the grave, and over it
piled huge stones laid close together. Lightly and quickly
they piled up the grave-barrow, and on all sides were set watchmen
for fear the strong-greaved Achaians might too soon set upon them.   800
They piled up the grave-barrow and went away, and thereafter
assembled in a fair gathering and held a glorious
feast within the house of Priam, king under God's hand.
Such was their burial of Hektor, breaker of horses.

—Translated by Richmond Lattimore

THE *ODYSSEY*

In the *Odyssey*, the hero's aim is not winning great prizes on the field of battle, but returning home from Troy to his homeland and faithful wife. Odysseus's challenge, then, is to endure the trials and temptations that might prevent him from completing the circuit of his voyage.

The tale consists of parallel dramas. In the ten years since the fall of Troy, Odysseus's wife Penelope has delayed the suitors who would replace Odysseus, while the hero has had to prove himself in many difficult adventures, including a journey into the underworld where he must escape the spell of the sorceress Circe. With each adventure, Odysseus proves his bravery and cunning while deepening his understanding of the world.

We learn of most of Odysseus's adventures through his own tale recounted at great length to the Phaeacians, who have rescued him from the sea. At the story's end, Odysseus returns to Ithaca disguised as a beggar, secretly enters his own household, slays the suitors, and is reunited with Penelope.

In the episode provided here, Odysseus describes his encounter with the Cyclops (Kyklopes), a race of giant one-eyed shepherds. Odysseus's curiosity (and his desire for plunder) draw him into a test of his guile and eloquence. Odysseus' encounter with Polyphemus is, in a sense, a struggle with a more primitive human self. Odysseus is able to deny his own famous name to escape Polyphemus, but cannot resist a gloating boast from his ship, a boast that calls down the revenge of the sea-god Poseidon, Polyphemus's father.

For analysis and interpretation:
    1. Describe Odysseus's most admirable qualities, based on his own account of his adventures. How well would such a hero be suited for the challenge of life today?
    2. Analyze the symbolism in Odysseus's trickery of Polyphemus. What analogy can be made to other stories of humans' encounters with primitives?

The *Odyssey*, Book IX:
The Kyklops

Now this was the reply Odysseus made:

"Alkínoös, king and admiration of men,
how beautiful this is, to hear a minstrel
gifted as yours: a god he might be, singing!
There is no boon in life more sweet, I say,
than when a summer joy holds all the realm,
and banqueters sit listening to a harper
in a great hall, by rows of tables heaped
with bread and roast meat, while a steward goes
to dip up wine and brim your cups again.
Here is the flower of life, it seems to me!
But now you wish to know my cause for sorrow—
and thereby give me cause for more.
                      What shall I
say first? What shall I keep until the end?
The gods have tried me in a thousand ways.
But first my name: let that be known to you,
and if I pull away from pitiless death,
friendship will bind us, though my land lies far.

I am Laërtês' son, Odysseus.
                      Men hold me
formidable for guile in peace and war:
this fame has gone abroad to the sky's rim.
My home is on the peaked sea-mark of Ithaka
under Mount Neion's wind-blown robe of leaves,
in sight of other islands—Doulíkhion,
Samê, wooded Zakynthos—Ithaka
being most lofty in that coastal sea,
and northwest, while the rest lie east and south.
A rocky isle, but good for a boy's training;
I shall not see on earth a place more dear,

though I have been detained long by Kalypso,
loveliest among goddesses, who held me
in her smooth caves, to be her heart's delight,
as Kirkê of Aiaia, the enchantress,
desired me, and detained me in her hall.
But in my heart I never gave consent.
Where shall a man find sweetness to surpass
his own home and his parents? In far lands
he shall not, though he find a house of gold.

What of my sailing, then, from Troy?
                                   What of those years
of rough adventure weathered under Zeus?
The wind that carried west from Ilion
brought me to Ismaros, on the far shore,
a strongpoint on the coast of Kikonês.
I stormed that place and killed the men who fought.
Plunder we took, and we enslaved the women,
to make division, equal shares to all—
but on the spot I told them: 'Back, and quickly!
Out to sea again!' My men were mutinous,
fools, on stores of wine. Sheep after sheep
they butchered by the surf, and shambling cattle,
feasting,—while fugitives went inland, running
to call to arms the main force of Kikonês.
This was an army, trained to fight on horseback
or, where the ground required, on foot. They came
with dawn over that terrain like the leaves
and blades of spring. So doom appeared to us,
dark word of Zeus for us, our evil days.
My men stood up and made a fight of it—
backed on the ships, with lances kept in play,
from bright morning through the blaze of noon
holding our beach, although so far outnumbered;
but when the sun passed toward unyoking time,
then the Akhaians, one by one, gave way.
Six benches were left empty in every ship
that evening when we pulled away from death.
And this new grief we bore with us to sea:
our precious lives we had, but not our friends.
No ship made sail next day until some shipmate
had raised a cry, three times, for each poor ghost
unfleshed by the Kikonês on that field.

Now Zeus the lord of cloud roused in the north
a storm against the ships, and driving veils
of squall moved down like night on land and sea.
The bows went plunging at the gust; sails
cracked and lashed out strips in the big wind.
We saw death in that fury, dropped the yards,
unshipped the oars, and pulled for the nearest lee:
then two long days and nights we lay offshore
worn out and sick at heart, tasting our grief,
until a third Dawn came with ringlets shining.
Then we put up our masts, hauled sail, and rested,
letting the steersman and the breeze take over.

I might have made it safely home, that time,
but as I came round Malea the current
took me out to sea, and from the north
a fresh gale drove me on, past Kythera.
Nine days I drifted on the teeming sea
before dangerous high winds. Upon the tenth
we came to the coastline of the Lotos Eaters,
who live upon that flower. We landed there
to take on water. All ships' companies
mustered alongside for the mid-day meal.
Then I sent out two picked men and a runner
to learn what race of men that land sustained.
They fell in, soon enough, with Lotos Eaters,
who showed no will to do us harm, only
offering the sweet Lotos to our friends—
but those who ate this honeyed plant, the Lotos,
never cared to report, nor to return:
they longed to stay forever, browsing on
that native bloom, forgetful of their homeland.
I drove them, all three wailing, to the ships,
tied them down under their rowing benches,
and called the rest: 'All hands aboard:
come, clear the beach and no one taste
the Lotos, or you lose your hope of home.'
Filing in to their places by the rowlocks
my oarsmen dipped their long oars in the surf,
and we moved out again on our sea faring.

In the next land we found were Kyklopês,
giants, louts, without a law to bless them.
In ignorance leaving the fruitage of the earth in mystery

to the immortal gods, they neither plow
nor sow by hand, nor till the ground, though grain—
wild wheat and barley—grows untended, and
wine-grapes, in clusters, ripen in heaven's rain.
Kyklopês have no muster and no meeting,
no consultation or old tribal ways,
but each one dwells in his own mountain cave
dealing out rough justice to wife and child,
indifferent to what the others do.
                        Well, then:
across the wide bay from the mainland
there lies a desert island, not far out,
but still not close inshore. Wild goats in hundreds
breed there; and no human being comes
upon the isle to startle them—no hunter
of all who ever tracked with hounds through forests
or had rough going over mountain trails.
The isle, unplanted and untilled, a wilderness,
pastures goats alone. And this is why:
good ships like ours with cheekpaint at the bows
are far beyond the Kyklopês. No shipwright
toils among them, shaping and building up
symmetrical trim hulls to cross the sea
and visit all the seaboard towns, as men do
who go and come in commerce over water.
This isle—seagoing folk would have annexed it
and built their homesteads on it: all good land,
fertile for every crop in season: lush
well-watered meads along the shore, vines in profusion,
prairie, clear for the plow, where grain would grow
chin high by harvest time, and rich sub-soil.
The island cove is landlocked, so you need
no hawsers out astern, bow-stones or mooring:
run in and ride there till the day your crews
chafe to be under sail, and a fair wind blows.
You'll find good water flowing from a cavern
through dusky poplars into the upper bay.
Here we made harbor. Some god guided us
that night, for we could barely see our bows
in the dense fog around us, and no moonlight
filtered through the overcast. No look-out,
nobody saw the island dead ahead,
nor even the great landward rolling billow

that took us in: we found ourselves in shallows,
keels grazing shore: so furled our sails
and disembarked when the low ripples broke.
There on the beach we lay, and slept till morning.

When Dawn spread out her finger tips of rose
we turned out marveling, to tour the isle,
while Zeus's shy nymph daughters flushed wild goats
down from the heights—a breakfast for my men.
We ran to fetch our hunting bows and long-shanked
lances from the ships, and in three companies
we took our shots. Heaven gave us game a-plenty:
for every one of twelve ships in my squadron
nine goats fell to be shared; my lot was ten.
So there all day, until the sun went down,
we made our feast on meat galore, and wine—
wine from the ship, for our supply held out,
so many jars were filled at Ismaros
from stores of the Kikonês that we plundered.
We gazed, too, at Kyklopês Land, so near,
we saw their smoke, heard bleating from their flocks.
But after sundown, in the gathering dusk,
we slept again above the wash of ripples.

When the young Dawn with finger tips of rose
came in the east, I called my men together
and made a speech to them:
                              'Old shipmates, friends,
the rest of you stand by; I'll make the crossing
in my own ship, with my own company,
and find out what the mainland natives are—
for they may be wild savages, and lawless,
or hospitable and god fearing men.'

At this I went aboard, and gave the word
to cast off by the stern. My oarsmen followed,
filing in to their benches by the rowlocks,
and all in line dipped oars in the grey sea.

As we rowed on, and nearer to the mainland,
at one end of the bay, we saw a cavern
yawning above the water, screened with laurel,
and many rams and goats about the place
inside a sheepfold—made from slabs of stone
earthfast between tall trunks of pine and rugged

towering oak trees.
                    A prodigious man
slept in this cave alone, and took his flocks
to graze afield—remote from all companions,
knowing none but savage ways, a brute
so huge, he seemed no man at all of those
who eat good wheaten bread; but he seemed rather
a shaggy mountain reared in solitude.
We beached there, and I told the crew
to stand by and keep watch over the ship;
as for myself I took my twelve best fighters
and went ahead. I had a goatskin full
of that sweet liquor that Euanthês' son,
Maron, had given me. He kept Apollo's
holy grove at Ismaros; for kindness
we showed him there, and showed his wife and child,
he gave me seven shining golden talents
perfectly formed, a solid silver winebowl,
and then this liquor—twelve two-handled jars
of brandy, pure and fiery. Not a slave
in Maron's household knew this drink; only
he, his wife and the storeroom mistress knew;
and they would put one cupful—ruby-colored,
honey-smooth—in twenty more of water,
but still the sweet scent hovered like a fume
over the winebowl. No man turned away
when cups of this came round.
                                A wineskin full
I brought along, and victuals in a bag,
for in my bones I knew some towering brute
would be upon us soon—all outward power,
a wild man, ignorant of civility.

We climbed, then, briskly to the cave. But Kyklops
had gone afield, to pasture his fat sheep,
so we looked round at everything inside:
a drying rack that sagged with cheeses, pens
crowded with lambs and kids, each in its class:
firstlings apart from middlings, and the "dewdrops,"
or newborn lambkins, penned apart from both.
And vessels full of whey were brimming there—
bowls of earthenware and pails for milking.
My men came pressing round me, pleading:
                                        'Why not

take these cheeses, get them stowed, come back,
throw open all the pens, and make a run for it?
We'll drive the kids and lambs aboard. We say
put out again on good salt water!'
how sound that was! Yet I refused. I wished
to see the caveman, what he had to offer—
no pretty sight, it turned out, for my friends.

We lit a fire, burnt an offering,
and took some cheese to eat; then sat in silence
around the embers, waiting. When he came
he had a load of dry boughs on his shoulder
to stoke his fire at suppertime. He dumped it
with a great crash into that hollow cave,
and we all scattered fast to the far wall.
Then over the broad cavern floor he ushered
the ewes he meant to milk. He left his rams
and he-goats in the yard outside, and swung
high overhead a slab of solid rock
to close the cave. Two dozen four-wheeled wagons,
with heaving wagon teams, could not have stirred
the tonnage of that rock from where he wedged it
over the doorsill. Next he took his seat
and milked his bleating ewes. A practiced job
he made of it, giving each ewe her suckling;
thickened his milk, then, into curds and whey,
sieved out the curds to drip in withy baskets,
and poured the whey to stand in bowls
cooling until he drank it for his supper.
When all these chores were done, he poked the fire,
heaping on brushwood. In the glare he saw us.

'Strangers,' he said, 'who are you? And where from?
What brings you here by sea ways—a fair traffic?
Or are you wandering rogues, who cast your lives
like dice, and ravage other folk by sea?'

We felt a pressure on our hearts, in dread
of that deep rumble and that mighty man.
But all the same I spoke up in reply:

'We are from Troy, Akhaians, blown off course
by shifting gales on the Great South Sea;
homeward bound, but taking routes and ways
uncommon; so the will of Zeus would have it.

We served under Agamémnon, son of Atreus—
the whole world knows what city
he laid waste, what armies he destroyed.
It was our luck to come here; here we stand,
beholden for your help, or any gifts
you give—as custom is to honor strangers.
We would entreat you, great Sir, have a care
for the god's courtesy; Zeus will avenge
the unoffending guest.'

                He answered this
from his brute chest, unmoved:
                        'You are a ninny,
or else you come from the other end of nowhere,
telling me, mind the gods! We Kyklopês
care not a whistle for your thundering Zeus
or all the gods in bliss; we have more force by far.
I would not let you go for fear of Zeus—
you or your friends—unless I had a whim to.
Tell me, where was it, now, you left your ship—
around the point, or down the shore, I wonder?'

He thought he'd find out, but I saw through this,
and answered with a ready lie:

                  'My ship?
Poseidon Lord, who sets the earth a-tremble,
broke it up on the rocks at your land's end.
A wind from seaward served him, drove us there.
We are survivors, these good men and I.'

Neither reply nor pity came from him,
but in one stride he clutched at my companions
and caught two in his hands like squirming puppies
to beat their brains out, spattering the floor.
Then he dismembered them and made his meal,
gaping and crunching like a mountain lion—
everything: innards, flesh, and marrow bones.
We cried aloud, lifting our hands to Zeus,
powerless, looking on at this, appalled;
but Kyklops went on filling up his belly
with manflesh and great gulps of whey,
then lay down like a mast among his sheep.
My heart beat high now at the chance of action,
and drawing the sharp sword from my hip I went

along his flank to stab him where the midriff
holds the liver. I had touched the spot
when sudden fear stayed me: if I killed him
we perished there as well, for we could never
move his ponderous doorway slab aside.
So we were left to groan and wait for morning.

When the young Dawn with finger tips of rose
lit up the world, the Kyklops built a fire
and milked his handsome ewes, all in due order,
putting the sucklings to the mothers. Then,
his chores being all dispatched, he caught
another brace of men to make his breakfast,
and whisked away his great door slab
to let his sheep go through—but he, behind,
reset the stone as one would cap a quiver.
There was a din of whistling as the Kyklops
rounded his flock to higher ground, then stillness.
And now I pondered how to hurt him worst,
if but Athena granted what I prayed for.
Here are the means I thought would serve my turn:

a club, or staff, lay there along the fold—
an olive tree, felled green and left to season
for Kyklops' hand. And it was like a mast
a lugger of twenty oars, broad in the beam—
a deep-sea-going craft—might carry:
so long, so big around, it seemed. Now I
chopped out a six foot section of this pole
and set it down before my men, who scraped it;
and when they had it smooth, I hewed again
to make a stake with pointed end. I held this
in the fire's heart and turned it, toughening it,
then hid it, well back in the cavern, under
one of the dung piles in profusion there.
Now came the time to toss for it: who ventured
along with me? Whose hand could bear to thrust
and grind that spike in Kyklops' eye, when mild
sleep had mastered him? As luck would have it,
the men I would have chosen won the toss—
four strong men, and I made five as captain.

At evening came the shepherd with his flock,
his woolly flock. The rams as well, this time,

entered the cave: by some sheep-herding whim—
or a god's bidding—none were left outside.
He hefted his great boulder into place
and sat him down to milk the bleating ewes
in proper order, put the lambs to suck,
and swiftly ran through all his evening chores.
Then he caught two more men and feasted on them.
My moment was at hand, and I went forward
holding an ivy bowl of my dark drink,
looking up, saying:

        'Kyklops, try some wine.
Here's liquor to wash down your scraps of men.
Taste it, and see the kind of drink we carried
under our planks. I meant it for an offering
if you would help us home. But you are mad,
unbearable, a bloody monster! After this,
will any other traveler come to see you?'

He seized and drained the bowl, and it went down
so fiery and smooth he called for more:

'Give me another, thank you kindly. Tell me,
how are you called? I'll make a gift will please you.
Even Kyklopês know the wine-grapes grow
out of grassland and loam in heaven's rain,
but here's a bit of nectar and ambrosia!'

Three bowls I brought him, and he poured them down.
I saw the fuddle and flush come over him,
then I sang out in cordial tones:

        'Kyklops,
you ask my honorable name? Remember
the gift you promised me, and I shall tell you.
My name is Nohbdy: mother, father, and friends,
everyone calls me Nohbdy.'

        And he said:
'Nohbdy's my meat, then, after I eat his friends.
Others come first. There's a noble gift, now.'

Even as he spoke, he reeled and tumbled backward,
his great head lolling to one side; and sleep
took him like any creature. Drunk, hiccuping,
he dribbled streams of liquor and bits of men.

Now, by the gods, I drove my big hand spike
deep into the embers, charring it again,
and cheered my men along with battle talk
to keep their courage up: no quitting now.
The pike of olive, green though it had been,
reddened and glowed as if about to catch.
I drew it from the coals and my four fellows
gave me a hand, lugging it near the Kyklops
as more than natural force nerved them; straight
forward they sprinted, lifted it, and rammed it
deep in his crater eye, and I leaned on it
turning it as a shipwright turns a drill
in planking, having men below to swing
the two-handled strap that spins it in the groove.
So with our brand we bored that great eye socket
while blood ran out around the red hot bar.
Eyelid and lash were seared; the pierced ball
hissed broiling, and the roots popped.

                                             In a smithy
one sees a white-hot axehead or an adze
plunged and wrung in a cold tub, screeching steam—
the way they make soft iron hale and hard—:
just so that eyeball hissed around the spike.
The Kyklops bellowed and the rock roared round him,
and we fell back in fear. Clawing his face
he tugged the bloody spike out of his eye,
threw it away, and his wild hands went groping;
then he set up a howl for Kyklopês
who lived in caves on windy peaks nearby.
Some heard him; and they came by divers ways
to clump around outside and call:

                                             'What ails you,
Polyphêmos? Why do you cry so sore
in the starry night? You will not let us sleep.
Sure no man's driving off your flock? No man
has tricked you, ruined you?'
                                             Out of the cave
the mammoth Polyphêmos roared in answer:
'Nohbdy, Nohbdy's tricked me, Nohbdy's ruined me!'

To this rough shout they made a sage reply:

'Ah well, if nobody has played you foul

there in you lonely bed, we are no use in pain
given by great Zeus. Let it be your father,
Poseidon Lord, to whom you pray.'

                             So saying
they trailed away. And I was filled with laughter
to see how like a charm the name deceived them.
Now Kyklops, wheezing as the pain came on him,
fumbled to wrench away the great doorstone
and squatted in the breach with arms thrown wide
for any silly beast of man who bolted—
hoping somehow I might be such a fool.
But I kept thinking how to win the game:
death sat there huge; how could we slip away?
I drew on all my wits, and ran through tactics,
reasoning as a man will for dear life,
until a trick came—and it pleased me well.
The Kyklops' rams were handsome, fat, with heavy
fleeces, a dark violet.
                  Three abreast
I tied them silently together, twining
cords of willow from the ogre's bed;
then slung a man under each middle one
to ride there safely, shielded left and right.
So three sheep could convey each man. I took
the woolliest ram, the choicest of the flock,
and hung myself under his kinky belly,
pulled up tight, with fingers twisted deep
in sheepskin ringlets for an iron grip.
So, breathing hard, we waited until morning.

When Dawn spread out her finger tips of rose
the rams began to stir, moving for pasture,
and peals of bleating echoed round the pens
where dams with udders full called for a milking.
Blinded, and sick with pain from his head wound,
the master stroked each ram, then let it pass,
but my men riding on the pectoral fleece
the giant's blind hands blundering never found.
Last of them all my ram, the leader, came,
weighted by wool and me with my meditations.
The Kyklops patted him, and then said:

'Sweet cousin ram, why lag behind the rest

in the night cave? You never linger so,
but graze before them all, and go afar
to crop sweet grass, and take your stately way
leading along the streams, until at evening
you run to be the first one in the fold.
Why, now, so far behind? Can you be grieving
over your Master's eye? That carrion rogue
and his accurst companions burnt it out
when he had conquered all my wits with wine.
Nohbdy will not get out alive, I swear.
Oh, had you brain and voice to tell
where he may be now, dodging all my fury!
Bashed by this hand and bashed on this rock wall
his brains would strew the floor, and I should have
rest from the outrage Nohbdy worked upon me.'
He sent us into the open, then. Close by,
I dropped and rolled clear of the ram's belly,
going this way and that to untie the men.
With many glances back, we rounded up
his fat, stiff-legged sheep to take aboard,
and drove them down to where the good ship lay.
We saw, as we came near, our fellows' faces
shining; then we saw them turn to grief
tallying those who had not fled from death.
I hushed them, jerking head and eyebrows up,
and in a low voice told them: 'Load this herd;
move fast, and put the ship's head toward the breakers.'
They all pitched in at loading, then embarked
and struck their oars into the sea. Far out,
as far off shore as shouted words would carry,
I sent a few back to the adversary:

'O Kyklops! Would you feast on my companions?
Puny, am I, in a Caveman's hands?
How do you like the beating that we gave you,
you damned cannibal? Eater of guests
under your roof! Zeus and the gods have paid you!'

The blind thing in his doubled fury broke
a hilltop in his hands and heaved it after us.
Ahead of our black prow it struck and sank
whelmed in a spuming geyser, a giant wave
that washed the ship stern foremost back to shore.
I got the longest boathook out and stood

fending us off, with furious nods to all
to put their backs into a racing stroke—
row, row, or perish. So the long oars bent
kicking the foam sternward, making head
until we drew away, and twice as far.
Now when I cupped my hands I heard the crew
in low voices protesting:

                'Godsake, Captain!
Why bait the beast again? Let him alone!'
'That tidal wave he made on the first throw
all but beached us.'

            'All but stove us in!'

'Give him our bearing with your trumpeting,
he'll get the range and lob a boulder.'

                  'Aye
He'll smash our timbers and our heads together!'

I would not heed them in my glorying spirit,
but let my anger flare and yelled:

                'Kyklops,
if ever mortal man inquire
how you were put to shame and blinded, tell him
Odysseus, raider of cities, took your eye:
Laërtês' son, whose home's on Ithaka!'

At this he gave a mighty sob and rumbled:

'Now comes the weird upon me, spoken of old.
A wizard, grand and wondrous, lived here—Télemos,
a son of Eurymos; great length of days
he had in wizardry among the Kyklopês,
and these things he foretold for time to come:
my great eye lost, and Odysseus' hands.
Always I had in mind some giant, armed
in giant force, would come against me here.
But this, but you—small, pitiful and twiggy—
you put me down with wine, you blinded me.
Come back, Odysseus, and I'll treat you well,
praying the god of earthquake to befriend you—
his son I am, for he by his avowal
fathered me, and, if he will, he may

heal me of this black wound—he and no other
of all the happy gods or mortal men.'

Few words I shouted in reply to him:
'If I could take your life I would and take
your time away, and hurl you down to hell!
The god of earthquake could not heal you there!'

At this he stretched his hands out in his darkness
toward the sky of stars, and prayed Poseidon:

'O hear me, lord, blue girdler of the islands,
if I am thine indeed, and thou art father:
grant that Odysseus, raider of cities, never
see his home: Laërtês' son, I mean,
who kept his hall on Ithaka. Should destiny
intend that he shall see his roof again
among his family in his father land,
far be that day, and dark the years between.
Let him lose all companions, and return
under strange sail to bitter days at home.'

In these words he prayed, and the god heard him.
Now he laid hands upon a bigger stone
and wheeled around, titanic for the cast
to let it fly in the black-prowed vessel's track.
But it fell short, just aft the steering oar,
and whelming seas rose giant above the stone
to bear us onward toward the island.
                                                    There
as we ran in we saw the squadron waiting,
the trim ships drawn up side by side, and all
our troubled friends who waited, looking seaward.
We beached her, grinding keel in the soft sand,
and waded in, ourselves, on the sandy beach.
Then we unloaded all the Kyklops' flock
to make division, share and share alike,
only my fighters voted that my ram,
the prize of all, should go to me. I slew him
by the sea side and burnt his long thighbones
to Zeus beyond the stormcloud, Kronos' son,
who rules the world. But Zeus disdained my offering;
destruction for my ships he had in store
and death for those who sailed them, my companions.
Now all day long until the sun went down
we made our feast on mutton and sweet wine,

till after sunset in the gathering dark
we went to sleep above the wash of ripples.

When the young Dawn with finger tips of rose
touched the world, I roused the men, gave orders
to man the ships, cast off the mooring lines;
and filing in to sit beside the rowlocks
oarsmen in line dipped oars in the grey sea.
So we moved out, sad in the vast offing,
having our precious lives, but not our friends.

—Translated by Robert Fitzgerald

SAPPHO

The lyric poet Sappho (born ca. 620 B.C.) was esteemed by ancient commentators as the greatest of Greek lyric poets. She wrote principally short lyrics, such as the invocations of Aphrodite, goddess of love, reprinted here. Nearly all her poetry, which is known mostly in fragments, concerns itself with the intimate circle of family and female friends for whom Sappho clearly felt great passion.

For analysis and interpretation:

1. Describe Sappho's attitude toward the goddess Aphrodite, especially as compared to the attitudes of Homer's characters in the *Iliad* and *Odyssey*.

2. Compare Sappho's poignant regret over the loss of her beloved Anaktoria to Achilles' grief over the death of Patroclus.

Poems to Aphrodite

1

Throned in splendor, deathless, O Aphrodite,
child of Zeus, charm-fashioner, I entreat you
not with griefs and bitternesses to break my
    spirit, O goddess;

standing by me rather, if once before now
far away you heard, when I called upon you,
left your father's dwelling place and descended,
    yoking the golden

chariot to sparrows, who fairly drew you
down in speed aslant the black world, the bright air
trembling at the heart to the pulse of countless
    fluttering wingbeats.

Swiftly then they came, and you, blessed lady,
smiling on me out of immortal beauty,
asked me what affliction was on me, why I
    called thus upon you,

what beyond all else I would have befall my
tortured heart: "Whom then would you have Persuasion
force to serve desire in your heart? Who is it,
    Sappho, that hurt you?

Though she now escape you, she soon will follow;
though she take not gifts from you, she will give them:
though she love not, yet she will surely love you
    even unwilling."

In such guise come even again and set me
free from doubt and sorrow; accomplish all those
things my heart desires to be done; appear and
    stand at my shoulder.

2

Like the very gods in my sight is he who
sits where he can look in your eyes, who listens
close to you, to hear the soft voice, its sweetness
    murmur in love and

laughter, all for him. But it breaks my spirit;
underneath my breast all the heart is shaken.
Let me only glance where you are, the voice dies,
    I can say nothing,

but my lips are stricken to silence, underneath my skin the tenuous flame suffuses;
nothing shows in front of my eyes, my ears are
    muted in thunder.

And the sweat breaks running upon me, fever
shakes my body, paler I turn than grass is;
I can feel that I have been changed, I feel that
    death has come near me.

3

Some there are who say that the fairest thing seen
on the black earth is an array of horsemen;
some, men marching; some would say ships; but I say
    she whom one loves best

is the loveliest. Light were the work to make this
plain to all, since she, who surpassed in beauty
all mortality, Helen, once forsaking
    her lordly husband,

fled away to Troy-land across the water.
Not the thought of child nor beloved parents
was remembered, after the Queen of Cyprus
    won her at first sight.

Since young brides have hearts that can be persuaded
easily, light things, palpitant to passion
as am I, remembering Anaktória
    who has gone from me

and whose lovely walk and the shining pallor
of her face I would rather see before my
eyes than Lydia's chariots in all their glory
    armored for battle.

—Translated by Richmond Lattimore

SOPHOCLES

The poet Sophocles (ca. 496-406 B.C.) developed Greek tragic drama to its highest
point, with his mastery of character and sense of dramatic tension. In his *Poetics*, Aristotle credited Sophocles with several innovations in tragedy, including the expansion
of the chorus and the use of painted scenery. Sophocles was most praised for his tight-
ly constructed plots, in which the tragic action unfolds with a compelling necessity.

    No Greek tragedy was more compelling than Sophocles' saga of Oedipus, king
of Thebes, who has won the throne and the hand of Queen Jocasta by his cunning response to the sphinx. That Oedipus has succeeded by his human intelligence only in-
creases the irony in the play's horrifying turn of events: unknowingly, Oedipus is
guilty of the most unspeakable crimes, patricide and incest. Compelled by events and
his own questing nature to discover his identity, Oedipus uncovers the horrible truth
of his own ignorance and folly.

For analysis and interpretation:

    1. Identify which actions in the play's scenario represent the free choice of the
characters and which are controlled or fated by the gods.

    2. Analyze the conflict in the play between the pious belief in the truth of prophe-
cy and the humanist belief in humans' ability to know and discover for themselves.

    3. If Oedipus were to write out a confession of his crimes, for what reasons
would he hold himself guilty and deserving of punishment? How would you agree or
disagree with his assessment?

Oedipus the King

CHARACTERS

Oedipus, *The King of Thebes*
Priest of Zeus, *Leader of the Suppliants*
Creon, *Oedipus's Brother-in-law*
Chorus, *a group of Theban Elders*
Choragos, *Spokesman of the Chorus*
Tiresias, *a blind Seer or Prophet*
Jocasta, *The Queen of Thebes*
Messenger, *from Corinth, once a Shepherd*
Herdsman, *once a Servant of Laius*
Second Messenger, *a Servant of Oedipus*

MUTES

Suppliants, *Thebans seeking Oedipus's help*
Attendants, *for the Royal Family*
Servants, *to lead Tiresias and Oedipus*
Antigone, *Daughter of Oedipus and Jocasta*
Ismene, *Daughter of Oedipus and Jocasta*

[*The action takes place during the day in front of the royal palace in Thebes. There are two altars (left and right) on the Proscenium and several steps leading down to the Orchestra. As the play opens, Thebans of various ages who have come to beg Oedipus for help are sitting on these steps and in part of the Orchestra. These suppliants are holding branches of laurel or olive which have strips of wool wrapped around them. Oedipus enters from the palace (the central door of the Skene).*]

PROLOGUE

OEDIPUS.   My children, ancient Cadmus, newest care,
   why have you hurried to those seats, your boughs
   wound with the emblems of the suppliant?
   The city is weighed down with fragrant smoke,

Oedipus: The name means "swollen foot." It refers to the mutilation of Oedipus's feet done by his father, Laius, before the infant was sent to Mount Cithaeron to be put to death by exposure. Stage direction *wool*: Branches wrapped with wool are traditional symbols of prayer or supplication. 1 *Cadmus*: Oedipus's great great grandfather (although he does not know this) and the founder of Thebes.

with hymns to the Healer and the cries of mourners.   5
I thought it wrong, my sons, to hear your words
through emissaries, and have come out myself,
I, Oedipus, a name that all men know.
[OEDIPUS *addresses the* PRIEST.]
Old man—for it is fitting that you speak
for all—what is your mood as you entreat me,   10
fear or trust? You may be confident
that I'll do anything. How hard of heart
if an appeal like this did not rouse my pity!

PRIEST. You, Oedipus, who hold the power here,
you see our several ages, we who sit   15
before your altars—some not strong enough
to take long flight, some heavy in old age,
the priests, as I of Zeus, and from our youths
a chosen band. The rest sit with their windings
in the markets, at the twin shrines of Pallas,   20
and the prophetic embers of Ismēnos.
Our city, as you see yourself, is tossed
too much, and can no longer lift its head
above the troughs of billows red with death.
It dies in the fruitful flowers of the soil,   25
it dies in its pastured herds, and in its women's
barren pangs. And the fire-bearing god
has swooped upon the city, hateful plague,
and he has left the house of Cadmus empty.
Black Hades is made rich with moans and weeping.   30
Not judging you an equal of the gods,
do I and the children sit here at your hearth,
but as the first of men, in troubled times
and in encounters with divinities.
You came to Cadmus' city and unbound   35
the tax we had to pay to the harsh singer,

---

5 *Healer:* Apollo, god of prophecy, light, healing, justice, purification, and destruction. 18 *Zeus:* father and king of the gods. 20 *Pallas:* Athena, goddess of wisdom, arts, crafts, and war. 21 *Ismēnos:* a reference to the temple of Apollo near the river Ismēnos in Thebes. Prophecies were made here by "reading" the ashes of the altar fires. 27 *fire-bearing god:* contagious fever viewed as a god. 30 *Black Hades:* refers to both the underworld where the spirits of the dead go and the god of the underworld. 36 *harsh singer:* the Sphinx, a monster with a woman's head, a lion's body, and wings. The "tax" that Oedipus freed Thebes from was the destruction of all the young men who failed to solve the Sphinx's riddle and were subsequently devoured. The sphinx always asked the same riddle: "What goes on four legs in the morning, two legs at noon, and three legs in the evening, and yet is weakest when supported by the largest number of feet?" Oedipus discovered the correct answer—man, who crawls in infancy, walks in his prime, and uses a stick in old age— and that ended the Sphinx's reign of terror. The Sphinx destroyed herself when Oedipus answered the riddle. Oedipus's reward for freeing Thebes of the Sphinx was the throne and the hand of the recently widowed Jocasta.

did it without a helpful word from us,
with no instruction; with a god's assistance
you raised up our life, so we believe.
Again now Oedipus, our greatest power,   40
we plead with you, as suppliants, all of us,
to find us strength, whether from a god's response,
or learned in some way from another man.
I know that the experienced among men
give counsels that will prosper best of all.   45
Noblest of men, lift up our land again!
Think also of yourself; since now the land
calls you its Savior for your zeal of old,
oh let us never look back at your rule
as men helped up only to fall again!   50
Do not stumble! Put our land on firm feet!
The bird of omen was auspicious then,
when you brought that luck; be that same man again!
The power is yours; if you will rule our country,
rule over men, not in an empty land.   55
A towered city or a ship is nothing
if desolate and no man lives within.

OEDIPUS.   Pitiable children, oh I know, I know
the yearnings that have brought you. Yes, I know
that you are sick. And yet, though you are sick,   60
there is not one of you so sick as I.
For your affliction comes to each alone,
for him and no one else, but my soul mourns
for me and for you, too, and for the city.
You do not waken me as from a sleep,   65
for I have wept, bitterly and long,
tried many paths in the wanderings of thought,
and the single cure I found by careful search
I've acted on: I sent Menoeceus' son,
Creon, brother of my wife, to the Pythian   70
halls of Phoebus, so that I might learn
what I must do or say to save this city.
Already, when I think what day this is,
I wonder anxiously what he is doing.
Too long, more than is right, he's been away.   75
But when he comes, then I shall be a traitor
if I do not do all that the god reveals.

70-71 *Pythian. . .Phoebus*: The temple of Phoebus Apollo's oracle or prophet at Delphi.

PRIEST. Welcome words! But look, those men have signaled
    that it is Creon who is now approaching!
OEDIPUS. Lord Apollo! May he bring Savior Luck,   80
    a Luck as brilliant as his eyes are now!
PRIEST. His news is happy, it appears. He comes,
    forehead crowned with thickly berried laurel.
OEDIPUS. We'll know, for he is near enough to hear us.

[*Enter* CREON *along one of the Parados.*]

    Lord, brother in marriage, son of Menoeceus!   85
    What is the god's pronouncement that you bring?
CREON. It's good. For even troubles, if they chance
    to turn out well, I always count as lucky.
OEDIPUS. But what was the response? You seem to say
    I'm not to fear—but not to take heart either.   90
CREON. If you will hear me with these with men present,
    I'm ready to report—or go inside.

[CREON *moves up the steps toward the palace.*]

OEDIPUS. Speak out to all! The grief that burdens me
    concerns these men more that it does my life.
CREON. Then I shall tell you what I heard from the god.   95
    The task Lord Phoebus sets for us is clear:
    drive out pollution sheltered in our land,
    and do not shelter what is incurable.
OEDIPUS. What is our trouble? How shall we cleanse ourselves?
CREON. We must banish or murder to free ourselves   100
    from a murder that blows storms through the city.
OEDIPUS. What man's bad luck does he accuse in this?
CREON. My Lord, a king named Laius ruled our land
    before you came to steer the city straight.
OEDIPUS. I know. So I was told—I never saw him.   105
CREON. Since he was murdered, you must raise your hand
    against the men who killed him with their hands.
OEDIPUS. Where are they now? And how can we ever find
    the track of ancient guilt now hard to read?
CREON. In our own land, he said. What we pursue,   110
    that can be caught; but not what we neglect.
OEDIPUS. Was Laius home, or in the countryside—
    or was he murdered in some foreign land?
CREON. He left to see a sacred rite, he said:

83 *laurel*: Creon is wearing a garland of laurel leaves, sacred to Apollo.

He left, but never came home from his journey.   115
OEDIPUS.   Did none of his party see it and report—
    someone we might profitably question?
CREON.   They were all killed but one, who fled in fear,
    and he could tell us only one clear fact.
OEDIPUS.   What fact? One thing could lead us on to more   120
    if we could get a small start on our hope.
CREON.   He said that bandits chanced on them and killed him—
    with the force of many hands, not one alone.
OEDIPUS.   How could a bandit dare so great an act—
    unless this was a plot paid off from here!   125
CREON.   We thought of that, but when Laius was killed,
    we had no one to help us in our troubles.
OEDIPUS.   It was your very kingship that was killed!
    What kind of trouble blocked you from a search?
CREON.   The subtle-singing Sphinx asked us to turn   130
    from the obscure to what lay at our feet.
OEDIPUS.   Then I shall begin again and make it plain.
    It was quite worthy of Phoebus, and worthy of you,
    to turn our thoughts back to the murdered man,
    and right that you should see me join the battle   135
    for justice to our land and to the god.
    Not on behalf of any distant kinships,
    it's for myself I will dispel this stain.
    Whoever murdered him may also wish
    to punish me—and with the selfsame hand.   140
    In helping him I also serve myself.
    Now quickly, children: up from the altar steps,
    and raise the branches of the suppliant!
    Let someone go and summon Cadmus' people:
    say I'll do anything.

[*Exit an* ATTENDANT *along one of the Parados.*]

Our luck will prosper   145
    if the god is with us, or we have already fallen.
PRIEST.   Rise, my children: that for which we came,
    he has himself proclaimed he will accomplish.
    May Phoebus, who announced this, also come
    as Savior and reliever from the plague.   150

[*Exit* OEDIPUS *and* CREON *into the Palace. The* PRIEST *and the* SUPPLIANTS *exit left
and right along the Parados. After a brief pause, the* CHORUS *(including the*
CHORAGOS) *enters the Orchestra from the Parados.*)

PARADOS
Strophe 1

CHORUS. Voice from Zeus, sweetly spoken, what are you
    that have arrived from golden
    Pytho to our shining
    Thebes? I am on the rack, terror
        shakes my soul.   155
    Delian Healer, summoned by "iē!"
    I await in holy dread what obligation, something new
    or something back once more with the revolving years,
        you'll bring about for me.
    Oh tell me, child of golden Hope,   160
    deathless Response!

Antistrophe 1

I appeal to you first, daughter of Zeus,
    deathless Athena,
    and to your sister who protects this land,
Artemis, whose famous throne is the whole circle   165
    of the marketplace,
and Phoebus, who shoots from afar: iō!
Three-fold defenders against death, appear!
If ever in the past, to stop blind ruin
    sent against the city,   170
you banished utterly the fires of suffering,
    come now again!

Strophe 2

Ah! Ah! Unnumbered are the miseries
I bear. The plague claims all
our comrades. Nor has thought found yet a spear   175
by which a man shall be protected. What our glorious
earth gives birth to does not grow. Without a birth
from cries of labor
    do the women rise.
One person after another   180
    you may see, like flying birds,

151,162 *Strophe, Antistrophe*: probably refer to the direction in which the Chorus danced while reciting
specific stanzas. Strophe may have indicated dance steps to stage left, antistrophe to stage right. 151 *Voice
from Zeus*: a reference to Apollo's prophecy. Zeus taught Apollo how to prophesy. 153 *Pytho*: Delphi. 156
Delian Healer: Apollo. 165 *Artemis*: goddess of virginity, childbirth, and hunting.

faster than indomitable fire, sped
to the shore of the god that is the sunset.

Antistrophe 2

And with their deaths unnumbered dies the city.
Her children lie unpitied on the ground,   185
spreading death, unmourned.
Meanwhile young wives, and gray-haired mothers with them,
on the shores of the altars, from this side and that,
suppliants from mournful trouble,
  cry out their grief.   190
A hymn to the Healer shines,
  the flute a mourner's voice.
Against which, golden goddess, daughter of Zeus,
  send lovely Strength.

Strophe 3

Cause raging Ares—who,   195
  armed now with no shield of bronze,
burns me, coming amid loud cries—
to turn his back and run from my land,
with a fair wind behind to the great
  hall of Amphitritē,   200
or to the anchorage that welcomes no one.
Thrace's troubled sea!
If night lets something get away at last,
  it comes by day.
Fire-bearing god...   205
  you who dispense the might of lightning,
Zeus! Father! Destroy him with your thunderbolt!

[*Enter* OEDIPUS *from the palace.*]

Antistrophe 3

Lycēan Lord! From you looped
  bowstring, twisted gold,
I wish indomitable missiles might be scattered   210

---

183 *god...sunset*: Hades, god of the underworld. 195 *Ares*: god of war and destruction. 200 *Amphitritë*: the Atlantic Ocean. 208 *Lycëan Lord*: Apollo.

and stand forward, our protectors; also fire-bearing
radiance of Artemis, with which
     she darts across the Lycian mountains.
I call the god whose head is bound in gold,
with whom this country shares its name,   215
Bacchus, wine-flushed, summoned by "euoi!,"
     Maenads' comrade
to approach ablaze
     with gleaming...
pine, opposed to that god-hated god.   220

EPISODE 1

OEDIPUS. I hear your prayer. Submit to what I say
    and to the labors that the plague demands
    and you'll get help and a relief from evils.
    I'll make the proclamation, though a stranger
    to the report and to the deed. Alone,   225
    had I no key, I would soon lose the track.
    Since it was only later that I joined you,
    to all the sons of Cadmus I say this:
    whoever has clear knowledge of the man
    who murdered Laius, son of Labdacus,   230
    I command him to reveal it all to me—
    nor fear if, to remove the charge, he must
    accuse himself: his fate will not be cruel—
    he will depart unstumbling into exile.
    But if you know another, or a stranger,   235
    to be the one whose hand is guilty, speak:
    I shall reward you and remember you.
    But if you keep your peace because of fear,
    and shield yourself or kin from my command,
    hear you what I shall do in that event: 240
    I charge all in this land where I have throne
    and power, shut out that man—no matter who—
    both from your shelter and all spoken words,
    nor in your prayers or sacrifices make
    him partner, nor allot him lustral water.   245
    All men shall drive him from their homes: for he
    is the pollution that the god-sent Pythian
    response has only now revealed to me.
    In this way I ally myself in war

216 *Bacchus*: Dionysus, god of fertility and wine. 245 *lustral*: purifying.

with the divinity and the deceased.   250
And this curse, too, against the one who did it,
whether alone in secrecy, or with others:
may he wear out his life unblest and evil!
I pray this, too: if he is at my hearth
and in my home, and I have knowledge of him,   255
may the curse pronounced on others come to me.
All this I lay to you to execute,
for my sake, for the god's, and for this land
now ruined, barren, abandoned by the gods.
Even if no god had driven you to it,   260
you ought not to have left this stain uncleansed,
the murdered man a nobleman, a king!
You should have looked! But now, since, as it happens,
It's I who have the power that he had once,
and have his bed, and a wife who shares our seed,   265
and common bond had we had common children
(had not his hope of offspring had bad luck—
but as it happened, luck lunged at his head);
because of this, as if for my own father,
I'll fight for him, I'll leave no means untried,   270
to catch the one who did it with his hand,
for the son of Labdacus, of Polydōrus,
of Cadmus before him, and of Agēnor.
This prayer against all those who disobey:
the gods send out no harvest from their soil,   275
nor children from their wives. Oh, let them die
victims of this plague, or of something worse.
Yet for the rest of us, people of Cadmus,
we the obedient, may Justice, our ally,
and all the gods, be always on our side!   280
CHORAGOS.   I speak because I feel the grip of your curse:
     the killer is not I. Nor can I point
     to him. The one who set us to this search,
     Phoebus, should also name the guilty man.
OEDIPUS.   Quite right, but to compel unwilling gods—   285
     no man has ever had that kind of power.
CHORAGOS.   May I suggest to you a second way?
OEDIPUS.   A second or third—pass over nothing!
CHORAGOS.   I know of no one who sees more of what
     Lord Phoebus sees than Lord Tiresias.   290
     My lord, one might learn brilliantly from him.

---

250 *the deceased*: Laius. 272-273 *Son...Agēnor*: refers to Laius by citing his genealogy.

OEDIPUS. Nor is this something I have been slow to do.
    At Creon's word I sent an escort—twice now!
    I am astonished that he has not come.
CHORAGOS. The old account is useless. It told us nothing.   295
OEDIPUS. But tell it to me. I'll scrutinize all stories.
CHORAGOS. He is said to have been killed by travelers.
OEDIPUS. I have heard, but the one who did it no one sees.
CHORAGOS. If there is any fear in him at all,
    he won't stay here once he has heard that curse.   300
OEDIPUS. He won't fear words: he had no fear when he did it.

    [*Enter* TIRESIAS *from the right, led by a* SERVANT *and two of Oedipus's*
    ATTENDANTS.]

CHORAGOS. Look there! There is the man who will convict him!
    It's the god's prophet they are leading here,
    one gifted with the truth as no one else.
OEDIPUS. Tiresias, master of all omens—   305
    public and secret, in the sky and on the earth—
    your mind, if not your eyes, sees how the city
    lives with a plague, against which Thebes can find
    no Saviour or protector, Lord, but you.
    For Phoebus, as the attendants surely told you,   310
    returned this answer to us: liberation
    from the disease would never come unless
    we learned without a doubt who murdered Laius—
    put them to death, or sent them into exile.
    Do not begrudge us what you may learn from birds   315
    or any other prophet's path you know!
    Care for yourself, the city, care for me,
    care for the whole pollution of the dead!
    We're in your hands. To do all that he can
    to help another is man's noblest labor.   320
TIRESIAS. How terrible to understand and get
    no profit from the knowledge! I knew this,
    but I forgot, or I had never come.
OEDIPUS. What's this? You've come with very little zeal.
TIRESIAS. Let me go home! If you will listen to me,   325
    You will endure your troubles better—and I mine.
OEDIPUS. A strange request, not very kind to the land
    that cared for you—to hold back this oracle!
TIRESIAS. I see your understanding comes to you
    inopportunely. So that won't happen to me...   330
OEDIPUS. Oh, by the gods, if you understand about this,
    don't turn away! We're on our knees to you.

TIRESIAS.   None of you understands! I'll never bring
    my grief to light—I will not speak of yours.
OEDIPUS.   You know and won't declare it! Is your purpose   335
    to betray us and to destroy this land!
TIRESIAS.   I will grieve neither of us. Stop this futile
    cross-examination. I'll tell you nothing!
OEDIPUS.   Nothing? You vile traitor! You could provoke
    a stone to anger! You still refuse to tell?   340
    Can nothing soften you, nothing convince you?
TIRESIAS.   You blamed anger in me—you haven't seen.
    Can nothing soften you, nothing convince you?
OEDIPUS.   Who wouldn't fill with anger, listening
    to words like yours which now disgrace this city?   345
TIRESIAS.   It will come, even if my silence hides it.
OEDIPUS.   If it will come, then why won't you declare it?
TIRESIAS.   I'd rather say no more. Now if you wish,
    respond to that with all your fiercest anger!
OEDIPUS.   Now I am angry enough to come right out   350
    with this conjecture: you, I think, helped plot
    the deed; you did it—even if your hand
    cannot have struck the blow. If you could see,
    I should have said the deed was yours alone.
TIRESIAS.   Is that right! Then I charge you to abide   355
    by the decree you have announced: from this day
    say no word to either these or me,
    for you are the vile polluter of this land!
OEDIPUS.   Aren't you appalled to let a charge like that
    come bounding forth? How will you get away?   360
TIRESIAS.   You cannot catch me. I have the strength of truth.
OEDIPUS.   Who taught you this? Not your prophetic craft!
TIRESIAS.   You did. You made me say it. I didn't want to.
OEDIPUS.   Say what? Repeat it so I'll understand.
TIRESIAS.   I made no sense? Or are you trying me?   365
OEDIPUS.   No sense I understood. Say it again!
TIRESIAS.   I say you are the murderer you seek.
OEDIPUS.   Again that horror! You'll wish you hadn't said that.
TIRESIAS.   Shall I say more, and raise your anger higher?
OEDIPUS.   Anything you like! Your words are powerless.   370
TIRESIAS.   You live, unknowing, with those nearest to you
    in the greatest shame. You do not see the evil.
OEDIPUS.   You won't go on like that and never pay!
TIRESIAS.   I can if there is any strength in truth.
OEDIPUS.   In truth, but not in you! You have no strength,   375
    blind in your ears, your reason, and your eyes.

TIRESIAS. Unhappy man! Those jeers you hurl at me
    before long all these men will hurl at you.
OEDIPUS. You are the child of endless night; it's not
    for me or anyone who sees to hurt you.   380
TIRESIAS. It's not my fate to be struck down by you.
    Apollo is enough. That's his concern.
OEDIPUS. Are these inventions Creon's or your own?
TIRESIAS. No, your affliction is yourself, not Creon.
OEDIPUS. Oh success!—in wealth, kingship, artistry,   385
    in any life that wins much admiration—
    the envious ill will stored up for you!
    to get at my command, a gift I did not
    seek, which the city put into my hands,
    my loyal Creon, colleague from the start,   390
    longs to sneak up in secret and dethrone me.
    So he's suborned this fortuneteller—schemer!
    deceitful beggar-priest!—who has good eyes
    for gains alone, though in his craft he's blind.
    Where were your prophet's powers ever proved?   395
    Why, when the dog who chanted verse was here,
    did you not speak and liberate this city?
    Her riddle wasn't for a man chancing by
    to interpret; prophetic art was needed,
    but you had none, it seems—learned from birds   400
    or from a god. I came along, yes I,
    Oedipus the ignorant, and stopped her—
    by using thought, not augury from birds.
    And it is I whom you now wish to banish,
    so you'll be close to the Creontian throne.   405
    You—and the plot's concocter—will drive out
    pollution to your grief: you look quite old
    or you would be the victim of that plot!
CHORAGOS. It seems to us that this man's words were said
    in anger, Oedipus, and yours as well.   410
    Insight, not angry words, is what we need,
    the best solution to the god's response.
TIRESIAS. You are the king, and yet I am your equal
    in my right to speak. In that I too am Lord,
    for I belong to Loxias, not you.   415
    I am not Creon's man. He's nothing to me.
    Hear this, since you have thrown my blindness at me:
    Your eyes can't see the evil to which you've come,

396 *dog...verse*: The Sphinx. 415 *Loxias*: Apollo.

nor where you live, nor who is in your house.
Do you know your parents? Not knowing, you are   420
their enemy, in the underworld and here.
A mother's and a father's double-lashing
terrible-footed curse will soon drive you out.
Now you can see, then you will stare into darkness.
What place will not be harbor to your cry,   425
or what Cithaeron not reverberate
when you have heard the bride-song in your palace
to which you sailed? Fair wind to evil harbor!
Nor do you see how many other woes
will level you to yourself and to your children.   430
So, at my message, and at Creon, too,
splatter muck! There will never be a man
ground into wretchedness as you will be.

OEDIPUS.   Am I to listen to such things from him!
May you be damned! Get out of here at once!   435
Go! Leave my palace! Turn around and go!

[*TIRESIAS begins to move away from OEDIPUS.*]

TIRESIAS.   I wouldn't have come had you not sent for me.
OEDIPUS.   I did not know you'd talk stupidity,
    or I wouldn't have rushed to bring you to my house.
TIRESIAS.   Stupid I seem to you, yet to your parents   440
    who gave you natural birth I seemed quite shrewd.
OEDIPUS. Who? Wait! Who is the one who gave me birth?
TIRESIAS. This day will give you birth, and ruin too.
OEDIPUS.   What murky, riddling things you always say!
TIRESIAS.   Don't you surpass us all at finding out?   445
OEDIPUS.   You sneer at what you'll find has brought me greatness.
TIRESIAS.   And that's the very luck that ruined you.
OEDIPUS.   I wouldn't care, just so I saved the city.
TIRESIAS.   In that case I shall go. Boy, lead the way!
OEDIPUS.   Yes, let him lead you off. Here, underfoot,   450
    you irk me. Gone, you'll cause no further pain.
TIRESIAS.   I'll go when I have said what I was sent for.
    Your face won't scare me. You can't ruin me.
    I say to you, the man whom you have looked for
    as you pronounced your curses, your decrees   455
    on the bloody death of Laius—he is here!
    A seeming stranger, he shall be shown to be

---

426 *Cithaeron*: reference to the mountain on which Oedipus was to be exposed as an infant.   443 *give you birth*: that is, identify your parents.

a Theban born, though he'll take no delight
in that solution. Blind, who once could see,
a beggar who was rich, through foreign lands   460
he'll go and point before him with a stick.
To his beloved children, he'll be shown
a father who is also brother; to the one
who bore him, son and husband; to his father,
his seed-fellow and killer. Go in   465
and think this out; and if you find I've lied,
say then I have no prophet's understanding!

[*Exit TIRESIAS, led by a SERVANT. OEDIPUS exits into the palace with his ATTENDANTS.*]

STASIMON 1
Strophe 1

CHORUS. Who is the man of whom the inspired
            rock of Delphi said
he has committed the unspeakable   470
            with blood-stained hands?
Time for him to ply a foot
mightier than those of the horses
            of the storm in his escape;
upon him mounts and plunges the weaponed   475
son of Zeus, with fire and thunderbolts,
and in his train the dreaded goddesses
of Death, who never miss.

Antistrophe 1

The message has just blazed,
            gleaming from the snows   480
of Mount Parnassus: we must track
            everywhere the unseen man.
He wanders, hidden by wild
forests, up through caves
            and rocks, like a bull,   485
anxious, with an anxious foot, forlorn.
He puts away from him the mantic words come from earth's
navel, at its center, yet these live
forever and still hover round him.

---

469 *rock of Delphi*: Apollo's oracle at Delphi. 476 *son of Zeus*: Apollo. 487 *mantic*: prophetic. 487-88
earth's navel: Delphi

Strophe 2

Terribly he troubles me,   490
    the skilled interpreter of birds!
I can't assent, nor speak against him.
    Both paths are closed to me.
I hover on the wings of doubt,
    not seeing what is here nor what's to come.   495
What quarrel started in the house of Labdacus
or in the house of Polybus,
    either ever in the past
    or now, I never
heard, so that . . . with this fact for my touchstone   500
I could attack the public
    fame of Oedipus, by the side of Labdaceans
an ally, against the dark assassination.

Antistrophe 2

No, Zeus and Apollo
    understand and know things   505
mortal; but that another man
    can do more as a prophet than I can—
for that there is no certain test,
    though, skill to skill,
one man might overtake another.   510
No, never, not until
    I see the charges proved,
when someone blames him shall I nod assent.
For once, as we all saw, the winged Maiden came
against him: he was seen then to be skilled,   515
    proved by that touchstone, dear to the people. So,
never will my mind convict him of the evil.

EPISODE 2

[*Enter* CREON *from the right door of the skene and speaks to the* CHORUS.]

CREON. Citizens, I hear that a fearful charge
    is made against me by King Oedipus!
    I had to come. If, in this crisis,   520

---

491 *interpreter of birds*: Tiresias. The Chorus is troubled by his accusations. 496 *house of Labdacus*: the line of Laius. 497 *Polybus*: Oedipus's foster father. 514 *winged maiden*: The Sphinx.

he thinks that he has suffered injury
from anything that I have said or done,
I have no appetite for a long life—
bearing a blame like that! It's no slight blow
the punishment I'd take from what he said: 525
it's the ultimate hurt to be called traitor
by the city, by you, by my own people!
CHORAGOS. The thing that forced that accusation out
could have been anger, not the power of thought.
CREON. But who persuaded him that thoughts of mine   530
had led the prophet into telling lies?
CHORAGOS. I do not know the thought behind his words.
CREON. But did he look straight at you? Was his mind right
when he said that I was guilty of this charge?
CHORAGOS. I have no eyes to see what rulers do.   535
But here he comes himself out of the house.

[*Enter OEDIPUS from the palace.*]

OEDIPUS. What? You here? And can you really have
the face and daring to approach my house
when you're exposed as its master's murderer
and caught, too, as the robber of my kingship?   540
Did you see cowardice in me, by the gods,
or foolishness, when you began this plot?
Did you suppose that I would not detect
your stealthy moves, or that I'd not fight back?
It's your attempt that's folly, isn't it—   545
tracking without followers or connections,
kingship which is caught with wealth and numbers?
CREON. Now wait! Give me as long to answer back!
Judge me for yourself when you have heard me!
OEDIPUS. You're eloquent, but I'd be slow to learn   550
from you, now that I've seen your malice toward me.
CREON. That I deny. Hear what I have to say.
OEDIPUS. Don't you deny it! You are the traitor here!
CREON. If you consider mindless willfulness
a prized possession, you are not thinking sense.   555
OEDIPUS. If you think you can wrong a relative
and get off free, you are not thinking sense.
CREON. Perfectly just, I won't say no. And yet
what is this injury you say I did you?
OEDIPUS. Did you persuade me, yes or no, to send   560
someone to bring that solemn prophet here?
CREON. And I still hold to the advice I gave.

OEDIPUS. How many years ago did your King Laius…
CREON. Laius! Do what? Now I don't understand.
OEDIPUS. Vanish—victim of a murderous violence? 565
CREON. That is a long count back into the past.
OEDIPUS. Well, was this seer then practicing his art?
CREON. Yes, skilled and honored just as he is today.
OEDIPUS. Did he, back then, ever refer to me?
CREON. He did not do so in my presence ever. 570
OEDIPUS. You did inquire into the murder then.
CREON. We had to, surely, though we discovered nothing.
OEDIPUS. But the "skilled" one did not say this then? Why not?
CREON. I never talk when I am ignorant.
OEDIPUS. But you're not ignorant of your own part. 575
CREON. What do you mean? I'll tell you if I know.
OEDIPUS. Just this: if he had not conferred with you
    he'd not have told about my murdering Laius.
CREON. If he said that, you are the one who knows.
    But now it's fair that you should answer me. 580
OEDIPUS. Ask on! You won't convict me as the killer.
CREON. Well then, answer. My sister is your wife?
OEDIPUS. Now there's a statement that I can't deny.
CREON. You two have equal power in this country?
OEDIPUS. She gets from me whatever she desires. 585
CREON. And I'm a third? The three of us are equals?
OEDIPUS. That's where you're treacherous to your kinship!
CREON. But think about this rationally, as I do.
    First look at this: do you think anyone
    prefers the anxieties of being king 590
    to troubled sleep—if he has equal power?
    I'm not the kind of man who falls in love
    with kingship. I am content with a king's power.
    And so would any man who's wise and prudent.
    I get all things from you, with no distress; 595
    as king I would have onerous duties, too.
    How could the kingship bring me more delight
    than this untroubled power and influence?
    I'm not misguided yet to such a point
    that profitable honors aren't enough. 600
    As it is, all wish me well and all salute;
    those begging you for something have me summoned,
    for their success depends on that alone.
    Why should I lose all this to become king?
    A prudent mind is never traitorous. 605
    Treason's a thought I'm not enamored of;

nor could I join a man who acted so.
In proof of this, first go yourself to Pytho
and ask if I brought back the true response.
Then, if you find I plotted with that portent   610
reader, don't have me put to death by your vote
only—I'll vote myself for my conviction.
Don't let an unsupported thought convict me!
It's not right mindlessly to take the bad
for good or to suppose the good are traitors.   615
Rejecting a relation who is loyal
is like rejecting life, our greatest love.
In time you'll know securely without stumbling,
for time alone can prove a just man just,
though you can know a bad man in a day.   620
CHORAGOS. Well said, to one who's anxious not to fall.
      Swift thinkers, Lord, are never safe from stumbling.
OEDIPUS. But when a swift and secret plotter moves
      against me, I must make swift counterplot.
      If I lie quiet and await his move,   625
      he'll have achieved his aims and I'll have missed.
CREON. You surely cannot mean you want me exiled!
OEDIPUS. Not exiled, no. Your death is what I want!
CREON. If you would first define what envy is...
OEDIPUS. Are you still stubborn? Still disobedient?   630
CREON. I see you cannot think!
OEDIPUS.   For me I can.
CREON. You should for me as well!
OEDIPUS.   But you're a traitor!
CREON. What if you're wrong?
OEDIPUS.   Authority must be maintained
CREON. Not if the ruler's evil.
OEDIPUS.   Hear that, Thebes!
CREON. It is my city too, not yours alone!   635
CHORAGOS. Please don't, my Lords! Ah, just in time, I see
      Jocasta there, coming from the palace.
      With her help you must settle your quarrel.

[Enter JOCASTA from the Palace.]

JOCASTA. Wretched men! What has provoked this ill-
      advised dispute? Have you no sense of shame,   640
      with Thebes so sick, to stir up private troubles?
      Now go inside! And Creon, you go home!

608 *Pytho*: Delphi. 610-611 *portent reader*: Apollo's oracle or prophet.

Don't make a general anguish out of nothing!
CREON. My sister, Oedipus your husband here   645
    sees fit to do one of two hideous things:
    to have me banished from the land—or killed!
OEDIPUS. That's right: I caught him, Lady, plotting harm
    against my person—with a malignant science.
CREON. May my life fail, may I die cursed, if I   650
    did any of the things you said I did!
JOCASTA. Believe his words, for the god's sake, Oedipus,
    in deference above all to his oath
    to the gods. Also for me, and for these men!

KOMMOS

Strophe 1

CHORUS. Consent, with will and mind,
    my king, I beg of you!   655
OEDIPUS. What do you wish me to surrender?
CHORUS. Show deference to him who was not feeble in time past
    and is now great in the power of his oath!
OEDIPUS. Do you know what you're asking?
CHORUS.   Yes.
OEDIPUS.   Tell me then.
CHORUS. Never to cast into dishonored guilt, with an unproved   660
    assumption, a kinsman who has bound himself by curse.
OEDIPUS. Now you must understand, when you ask this,
    you ask my death or banishment from the land.

Strophe 2

CHORUS. No, by the god who is the foremost of all gods,
    the Sun! No! Godless,   665
        friendless, whatever death is worst of all,
    let that be my destruction, if this
        thought ever moved me!
    But my ill-fated soul
        this dying land   670
    wears out—the more if to these older troubles
    she adds new troubles from the two of you!
OEDIPUS. Then let him go, though it must mean my death,
    or else disgrace and exile from the land.
    My pity is moved by your words, not by his—   675
    he'll only have my hate, wherever he goes.

---

654 *Kommos*: a dirge or lament sung by the Chorus and one or more of the chief characters.

CREON. You're sullen as you yield; you'll be depressed
    when you've passed through this anger. Natures like yours
    are hardest on themselves. That's as it should be.
OEDIPUS. Then won't you go and let me be?
CREON.   I'll go.   680
    Though you're unreasonable, they know I'm righteous.

[*Exit* CREON.]

Antistrophe 1

CHORUS. Why are you waiting, Lady?
    Conduct him back into the palace!
JOCASTA. I will, when I have heard what chanced.   685
CHORUS. Conjectures—words alone, and nothing based on thought.
    But even an injustice can devour a man.
JOCASTA. Did the words come from both sides?
CHORUS.   Yes.
JOCASTA.   What was said?
CHORUS. To me it seems enough! enough! the land already troubled,   690
    that this should rest where it has stopped.
OEDIPUS. See what you've come to in your honest thought,
    in seeking to relax and blunt my heart?

Antistrophe 2

CHORUS. I have not said this only once, my Lord.
    That I had lost my sanity,   695
        without a path in thinking—
    be sure this would be clear
        if I put you away
    who, when my cherished land
        wandered crazed   700
    with suffering, brought her back on course.
    Now, too, be a lucky helmsman!

JOCASTA. Please, for the god's sake, Lord, explain to me
    the reason why you have conceived this wrath?
OEDIPUS. I honor you, not them, and I'll explain   705
    to you how Creon has conspired against me.
JOCASTA. All right, if that will explain how the quarrel started.
OEDIPUS. He says I am the murderer of Laius!
JOCASTA. Did he claim knowledge or that someone told him?
OEDIPUS. Here's what he did: he sent that vicious seer   710
    so he could keep his own mouth innocent.

705 *them*: the Chorus.

JOCASTA. Ah then, absolve yourself of what he charges!
 Listen to this and you'll agree, no mortal
 is ever given skill in prophecy.
 I'll prove this quickly with one incident.   715
 It was foretold to Laius—I shall not say
 by Phoebus himself, but by his ministers—
 that when his fate arrived he would be killed
 by a son who would be born to him and me.
 And yet, so it is told, foreign robbers   720
 murdered him, at a place where three roads meet.
 As for the child I bore him, not three days passed
 before he yoked the ball-joints of its feet,
 then cast it, by others' hands, on a trackless mountain.
 That time Apollo did not make our child   725
 a patricide, or bring about what Laius
 feared, that he be killed by his own son.
 That's how prophetic words determined things!
 Forget them. The things a god must track
 he will himself painlessly reveal.   730
OEDIPUS. Just now, as I was listening to you, Lady,
 what a profound distraction seized my mind!
JOCASTA. What made you turn around so anxiously?
OEDIPUS. I thought you said that Laius was attacked
 and butchered at a place where three roads meet.   735
JOCASTA. That is the story, and it is told so still.
OEDIPUS. Where is the place where this was done to him?
JOCASTA. The land's called Phocis, where a two-forked road
 comes in from Delphi and from Daulia.
OEDIPUS. And how much time has passed since these events?   740
JOCASTA. Just prior to your presentation here
 as king this news was published to the city.
OEDIPUS. Oh, Zeus, what have you willed to do to me?
JOCASTA. Oedipus, what makes your heart so heavy?
OEDIPUS. No, tell me first of Laius' appearance,   745
 what peak of youthful vigor he had reached.
JOCASTA. A tall man, showing his first growth of white.
 He had a figure not unlike your own.
OEDIPUS. Alas! It seems that in my ignorance
 I laid those fearful curses on myself.   750
JOCASTA. What is it , Lord? I flinch to see your face.
OEDIPUS. I'm dreadfully afraid the prophet sees.
 But I'll know better with one more detail.

---

723 *ball-joints of its feet*: the ankles.

JOCASTA. I'm frightened too. But ask: I'll answer you.
OEDIPUS. Was his retinue small, or did he travel   755
    with a great troop, as would befit a prince?
JOCASTA. There were just five in all, one a herald.
    There was a carriage, too, bearing Laius.
OEDIPUS. Alas! Now I see it! But who was it,
    Lady, who told you what you know about this?   760
JOCASTA. A servant who alone was saved unharmed.
OEDIPUS. By chance, could he be now in the palace?
JOCASTA. No, he is not. When he returned and saw
    you had the power of the murdered Laius,
    he touched my hand and begged me formally   765
    to send him to the fields and to the pastures,
    so he'd be out of sight, far from the city.
    I did. Although a slave, he well deserved
    to win this favor, and indeed far more.
OEDIPUS. Let's have him called back in immediately.   770
JOCASTA. That can be done, but why do you desire it?
OEDIPUS. I fear, Lady, I have already said
    too much. That's why I wish to see him now.
JOCASTA. Then he shall come; but it is right somehow
    that I, too, Lord, should know what troubles you.   775
OEDIPUS. I've gone so deep into the things I feared
    I'll tell you everything. Who has a right
    greater than yours, while I cross through the chance?
    Polybus of Corinth was my father,
    my mother was the Dorian Meropē.   780
    I was first citizen, until this chance
    attacked me—striking enough, to be sure,
    but not worth all the gravity I gave it.
    This: at a feast a man who'd drunk too much
    denied, at the wine, I was my father's son.   785
    I was depressed and all that day I barely
    held it in. Next day I put the question
    to my mother and father. They were enraged
    at the man who'd let this fiction fly at me.
    I was much cheered by them. And yet it kept   790
    grinding into me. His words kept coming back.
    Without my mother's or my father's knowledge
    I went to Pytho. But Phoebus sent me away
    dishonoring my demand. Instead, other
    wretched horrors he flashed forth in speech.   795
    He said that I would be my mother's lover,
    show offspring to mankind they could not look at,

and be his murderer whose seed I am.
When I heard this, and ever since, I gauged
the way to Corinth by the stars alone,   800
running to a place where I would never see
the disgrace in the oracle's words come true.
But I soon came to the exact location
where, as you tell of it, the king was killed.
Lady, here is the truth. As I went on,   805
when I was just approaching those three roads,
a herald and a man like him you spoke of
came on, riding a carriage drawn by colts.
Both the man out front and the old man himself
tried violently to force me off the road.   810
The driver, when he tried to push me off.
I struck in anger. The old man saw this, watched
me approach, then leaned out and lunged down
with twin prongs at the middle of my head!
He got more than he gave. Abruptly—struck   815
once by the staff in this my hand—he tumbled
out, head first, from the middle of the carriage.
And then I killed them all. But if there is
a kinship between Laius and this stranger,
who is more wretched than the man you see?   820
Who was there born more hated by the gods?
For neither citizen nor foreigner
may take me in his home or speak to me.
No, they must drive me off. And it is I
who have pronounced these curses on myself!   825
I stain the dead man's bed with these my hands,
by which he died. Is not my nature vile?
Unclean?—if I am banished and even
in exile I may not see my own parents,
or set foot in my homeland, or else be yoked   830
in marriage to my mother, and kill my father,
Polybus, who raised me and gave me birth?
If someone judged a cruel divinity
did this to me, would he not speak the truth?
You pure and awful gods, may I not ever   835
see that day, may I be swept away
from men before I see so great and so
calamitous a stain fixed on my person!

---

798 *be…am*: that is, murder my father. 809 *old man himself*: Laius. 813-814 *lunged…prongs*: Laius
strikes Oedipus with a two-pronged horse goad or whip.

CHORAGOS. These things seem fearful to us, Lord, and yet
    until you hear it from the witness, keep hope!   840
OEDIPUS. That is the single hope that's left to me,
    to wait for him, that herdsman—until he comes.
JOCASTA. When he appears, what are you eager for?
OEDIPUS. Just this: if his account agrees with yours
    then I shall have escaped this misery.   845
JOCASTA. But what was it that struck you in my story?
OEDIPUS. You said he spoke of robbers as the ones
    who killed him. Now: if he continues still
    to speak of many, then I could not have killed him.
    One man and many men just do not jibe.   850
    But if he says one belted man, the doubt
    is gone. The balance tips toward me. I did it.
JOCASTA. No! He told it as I told you. Be certain.
    He can't reject that and reverse himself.
    The city heard these things, not I alone.   855
    But even if he swerves from what he said,
    he'll never show that Laius' murder, Lord,
    occurred just as predicted. For Loxias
    expressly said my son was doomed to kill him.
    The boy—poor boy—he never had a chance   860
    to cut him down, for he was cut down first.
    Never again, just for some oracle
    will I shoot frightened glances right and left.
OEDIPUS. That's full of sense. Nonetheless, send a man
    to bring that farm hand here. Will you do it?
JOCASTA. I'll send one right away. But let's go in.   865
    Would I do anything against your wishes?

[*Exit OEDIPUS and JOCASTA through the central door into the palace.*]

STASIMON 2
Strophe 1

CHORUS. May there accompany me
    the fate to keep a reverential purity in what I say,
    in all I do, for which the laws have been set forth   870
    and walk on high, born to traverse the brightest,
    highest upper air: Olympus only
    is their father, nor was it
    mortal nature
    that fathered them, and never will   875
    oblivion lull them into sleep;
    the god in them is great and never ages.

872 *Olympus*: Mount Olympus, home of the gods, treated as a god.

Antistrophe 1

The will to violate, seed of the tyrant,
if it has drunk mindlessly of wealth and power,
without a sense of time or true advantage,   880
mounts to a peak, then
plunges to an abrupt...destiny,
where the useful foot
is of no use. But the kind
of struggling that is good for the city   885
I ask the god never to abolish.
The god is my protector: never will I give that up.

Strophe 2

But if a man proceeds disdainfully
    in deeds of hand or word
and has no fear of Justice   890
    or reverence for shrines of the divinities
(may a bad fate catch him
    for his luckless wantonness!),
if he'll not gain what he gains with justice
and deny himself what is unholy,   895
or if he clings, in foolishness, to the untouchable
(what man, finally, in such an action, will have strength
enough to fend off passion's arrows from his soul?),
if, I say, this kind of
    deed is held in honor—   900
why should I join the sacred dance?

Antistrophe 2

No longer shall I visit and revere
    Earth's navel, the untouchable,
nor visit Abae's temple,
    or Olympia,   905
if the prophecies are not matched by events
    for all the world to point to.
No, you who hold the power, if you are rightly called
Zeus the king of all, let this matter not escape you
and your ever-deathless rule,   910

903 *Earth's navel*: Delphi. 904 *Abae*: a town in Phocis where there were was another oracle of Apollo. 905 *Olympia*: site of the oracle of Zeus.

for the prophecies to Laius fade...
and men already disregard them;
nor is Apollo anywhere
    glorified with honors.
Religion slips away. 915

EPISODE 3

[*Enter* JOCASTA *from the palace carrying a branch wound with wool and a jar of incense. She is attended by two women.*]

JOCASTA. Lords of the realm, the thought has come to me
    to visit shrines of the divinities
    with suppliant's branch in hand and fragrant smoke.
    For Oedipus excites his soul too much
    with alarms of all kinds. He will not judge 920
    the present by the past, like a man of sense.
    He's at the mercy of all terror-mongers.

[JOCASTA *approaches the altar on the right and kneels.*]

    Since I can do no good by counseling,
    Apollo the Lycēan!—you are the closest—
    I come a suppliant, with these my vows, 925
    for a cleansing that will not pollute him.
    For when we see him shaken we are all
    afraid, like people looking at their helmsman.

[*Enter a* MESSENGER *along one of the Parados. He sees* JOCASTA *at the altar and then addresses the* CHORUS.]

MESSENGER. I would be pleased if you would help me, stranger.
    Where is the palace of King Oedipus? 930
    Or tell me where he is himself, if you know.
CHORUS. This is his house, stranger. He is within.
    This is his wife and mother of his children.
MESSENGER. May she and her family find prosperity,
    if, as you say, her marriage is fulfilled. 935
JOCASTA. You also, stranger, for you deserve as much
    for your gracious words. But tell me why you've come.
    What do you wish? Or what have you to tell us?
MESSENGER. Good news, my Lady, both for your house and
    husband.
JOCASTA. What is your news? And who has sent you to us? 940
MESSENGER. I come from Corinth. When you have heard my news
    you will rejoice, I'm sure—and grieve perhaps.

JOCASTA. What is it? How can it have this double power?
MESSENGER. They will establish him their king, so say
    the people of the land of Isthmia.   945
JOCASTA. But is old Polybus not still in power?
MESSENGER. He's not, for death has clasped him in the tomb.
JOCASTA. What's this? Has Oedipus' father died?
MESSENGER. If I have lied then I deserve to die.
JOCASTA. Attendant! Go quickly to your master,   950
    and tell him this.

    [*Exit an* ATTENDANT *into the palace.*]

    Oracles of the gods!
    Where are you now? The man whom Oedipus
    fled long ago, for fear that he should kill him—
    he's been destroyed by chance and not by him!

    [*Enter* OEDIPUS *from the palace.*]

OEDIPUS. Darling Jocasta, my beloved wife.   955
    Why have you called me from the palace?
JOCASTA. First hear what this man has to say. Then see
    what the god's grave oracle has come to now!
OEDIPUS. Where is he from? What is this news he brings me?
JOCASTA. From Corinth. He brings news about your father: 960
    that Polybus is no more! that he is dead!
OEDIPUS. What's this, old man? I want to hear you say it.
MESSENGER. If this is what must first be clarified,
    please be assured that he is dead and gone.
OEDIPUS. By treachery or by the touch of sickness?   965
MESSENGER. Light pressures tip aged frames into their sleep.
OEDIPUS. You mean the poor man died of some disease.
MESSENGER. And of the length of years he had tallied.
OEDIPUS. Aha! Then why should we look to Pytho's vapors,
    or to the birds that scream above our heads?   970
    If we could really take those things for guides,
    I would have killed my father. But he's dead!
    He is beneath the earth, and here am I,
    who never touched a spear. Unless he died
    of longing for me and I "killed" him that way!   975
    No, in this case, Polybus, by dying, took
    the worthless oracle to Hades with him.
JOCASTA. And wasn't I telling you that just now?

---

945 *land of Isthmia*: Corinth, which was on an isthmus. 969 *Pytho's vapors*: the prophecies of the oracle at Delphi. 970 *birds...heads*: the prophecies derived from interpreting the flights of birds.

OEDIPUS. You were indeed. I was misled by fear.
JOCASTA. You should not care about this anymore.   980
OEDIPUS. I must care. I must stay clear of my mother's bed.
JOCASTA. What's there for man to fear? The realm of chance
    prevails. True foresight isn't possible.
    His life is best who lives without a plan.
    This marriage with your mother—don't fear it.   985
    How many times have men in dreams, too, slept
    with their own mothers! Those who believe such things
    mean nothing endure their lives most easily.
OEDIPUS. A fine, bold speech, and you are right, perhaps,
    except that my mother is still living,   990
    so I must fear her, however well you argue.
JOCASTA. And yet your father's tomb is a great eye.
OEDIPUS. Illuminating, yes. But I still fear the living.
MESSENGER. Who is the woman who inspires this fear?
OEDIPUS. Meropē, Polybus' wife, old man.   995
MESSENGER. And what is there about her that alarms you?
OEDIPUS. An oracle, god-sent and fearful, stranger.
MESSENGER. Is it permitted that another know?
OEDIPUS. It is. Loxias once said to me
    I must have intercourse with my own mother   1000
    and take my father's blood with these my hands.
    So I have long lived far away from Corinth.
    This has indeed brought much good luck, and yet,
    to see one's parents' eyes is happiest.
MESSENGER. Was it for this that you have lived in exile?   1005
OEDIPUS. So I'd not be my father's killer, sir.
MESSENGER. Had I not better free you from this fear, my
    Lord? That's why I came—to do you service.
OEDIPUS. Indeed, what a reward you'd get for that!
MESSENGER. Indeed, this is the main point of my trip,   1010
    to be rewarded when you get back home.
OEDIPUS. I'll never regain the givers of my seed!
MESSENGER. My son, clearly you don't know what you're doing.
OEDIPUS. But how is that, old man? For the god's sake, tell me!
MESSENGER. If it's because of them you won't go home.   1015
OEDIPUS. I fear that Phoebus will have told the truth.
MESSENGER. Pollution from the ones who gave you seed?
OEDIPUS. That is the thing, old man, I always fear.
MESSENGER. Your fear is groundless. Understand that.

1012 *givers of my seed*: that is, my parents. Oedipus still thinks Meropē and Polybus are his parents.

OEDIPUS.   Groundless? Not if I was born their son.   1020
MESSENGER.   But Polybus is not related to you.
OEDIPUS.   Do you mean Polybus was not my father?
MESSENGER.   No more than I. We're both the same to you.
OEDIPUS.   Same? One who begot me and one who didn't?
MESSENGER.   He didn't beget you any more than I did.   1025
OEDIPUS.   But then, why did he say I was his son?
MESSENGER.   He got you as a gift from my own hands.
OEDIPUS.   He loved me so, though from another's hands?
MESSENGER.   His former childlessness persuaded him.
OEDIPUS.   But had you bought me, or begotten me?   1030
MESSENGER.   Found you. In the forest hallows of Cithaeron.
OEDIPUS.   What were you doing traveling in that region?
MESSENGER.   I was in charge of flocks which grazed those mountains.
OEDIPUS.   A wanderer who worked the flocks for hire?
MESSENGER.   Ah, but that day I was your savior, son.   1035
OEDIPUS.   From what? What was my trouble when you took me?
MESSENGER.   The ball-joints of your feet might testify.
OEDIPUS.   What's that? What makes you name that ancient trouble?
MESSENGER.   Your feet were pierced and I am your rescuer.
OEDIPUS.   A fearful rebuke those tokens left for me!   1040
MESSENGER.   That was the chance that names you who you are.
OEDIPUS.   By the gods, did my mother or my father do this?
MESSENGER.   That I don't know. He might who gave you to me.
OEDIPUS.   From someone else? You didn't chance on me?
MESSENGER.   Another shepherd handed you to me.   1045
OEDIPUS.   Who was he? Do you know? Will you explain!
MESSENGER.   They called him one of the men of—was it Laius?
OEDIPUS.   The one who once was king here long ago?
MESSENGER.   That is the one! The man was shepherd to him.   1050
OEDIPUS.   And is he still alive so I can see him?
MESSENGER.   But you who live here ought to know that best.
OEDIPUS.   Does any one of you now present know
           about the shepherd whom this man has named?
           Have you seen him in town or in the fields? Speak out!
           The time has come for the discovery!   1055
CHORAGOS.   The man he speaks of, I believe, is the same
           as the field hand you have already asked to see.
           But it's Jocasta who would know this best.
OEDIPUS.   Lady, do you remember the man we just
           now sent for—is that the man he speaks of?   1060
JOCASTA.   What? The man he spoke of? Pay no attention!
           His words are not worth thinking about. It's nothing.
OEDIPUS.   With clues like this within my grasp, give up?

Fail to solve the mystery of my birth?
JOCASTA. For the love of the gods, and if you love your life,   1065
    give up this search! My sickness is enough.
OEDIPUS. Come! Though my mothers for three generations
    were in slavery, you'd not be lowborn!
JOCASTA. No, listen to me! Please! Don't do this thing!
OEDIPUS. I will not listen; I will search out the truth.   1070
JOCASTA. My thinking is for you—it would be best.
OEDIPUS. This "best" of yours is starting to annoy me.
JOCASTA. Doomed man! Never find out who you are!
OEDIPUS. Will someone go and bring that shepherd here?
    Leave her to glory in her wealthy birth!   1075
JOCASTA. Man of misery! No other name
    shall I address you by, ever again.

[*Exit JOCASTA into the palace after a long pause.*]

CHORAGOS. Why has your lady left, Oedipus,
    hurled by a savage grief? I am afraid
    disaster will come bursting from this silence.   1080
OEDIPUS. Let it burst forth! However low this seed
    of mine may be, yet I desire to see it.
    She, perhaps—she has a woman's pride—
    is mortified by my base origins.
    But I who count myself the child of Chance,   1085
    the giver of good, shall never know dishonor.
    She is my mother, and the months my brothers
    who first marked out my lowness, then my greatness.
    I shall not prove untrue to such a nature
    by giving up the search for my own birth.   1090

STASIMON 3
Strophe

CHORUS. If I have mantic power
    and excellence in thought,
    by Olympus
       you shall not, Cithaeron, at tomorrow's
    full moon,   1095
    fail to hear us celebrate you as the countryman
    of Oedipus, his nurse and mother,
    or fail to be the subject of our dance,
       since you have given pleasure
    to our king.   1100
    Phoebus, whom we summon by "iē!,"
    may this be pleasing to you!

Antistrophe

Who was your mother, son?
which of the long-lived nymphs
after lying with Pan,   1105
    the mountain roaming...Or was it a bride
of Loxias?
For dear to him are all the upland pastures.
Or was it Mount Cyllēnē's lord,
or the Bacchic god,   1110
    dweller of the mountain peaks,
who received you as a joyous find
from one of the nymphs of Helicon,
the favorite sharers of his sport?

EPISODE 4

OEDIPUS. If someone like myself, who never met him,   1115
    may calculate—elders, I think I see
    the very herdsman we've been waiting for.
    His many years would fit that man's age,
    and those who bring him on, if I am right,
    are my own men. And yet, in real knowledge,   1120
    you can outstrip me, surely: you've seen him.

[*Enter the old* HERDSMAN *escorted by two of Oedipus's* ATTENDANTS. *At first,
the* HERDSMAN *will not look at* OEDIPUS.]

CHORAGOS. I know him, yes, a man of the house of Laius,
    a trusty herdsman if he ever had one.
OEDIPUS. I ask you first, the stranger come from Corinth:
    is this the man you spoke of?
MESSENGER. That's he you see.   1125
OEDIPUS. Then you, old man. First look at me! Now answer:
    did you belong to Laius' household once?
HERDSMAN. I did. Not a purchased slave but raised in the palace.
OEDIPUS. How have you spent your life? What is your work?
HERDSMAN. Most of my life now I have tended sheep.   1130
OEDIPUS. Where is the usual place you stay with them?
HERDSMAN. On Mount Cithaeron. Or in that district.
OEDIPUS. Do you recall observing this man there?
HERDSMAN. Doing what? Which is the man you mean?

1087 *She...mother*: Chance is my mother.1105 *Pan*: god of shepherds and woodlands, half man and half
goat.1107 *Loxias*: Apollo. 1109 *Mount Cyllēnē's lord*: Hermes, *messenger of the gods.* 1110 *Bacchic god*:
Dionysus.

OEDIPUS. This man right here. Have you had dealings with him? 1135
HERDSMAN. I can't say right away. I don't remember.
MESSENGER. No wonder, master. I'll bring clear memory
    to his ignorance. I'm absolutely sure
    he can recall it, the district was Cithaeron,
    he with a double flock, and I, with one, 1140
    lived close to him, for three entire seasons,
    six months long, from spring to Arcturus.
    Then for the winter I'd drive mine to my fold,
    and he'd drive his to Laius' pen again.
    Did any of the things I say take place? 1145
HERDSMAN. You speak the truth, though it's from long ago.
MESSENGER. Do you remember giving me, back then,
    a boy I was to care for as my own?
HERDSMAN. What are you saying? Why do you ask me that?
MESSENGER. There, sir, is the man who was that boy! 1150
HERDSMAN. Damn you! Shut your mouth! Keep your silence!
OEDIPUS. Stop! Don't you rebuke his words.
    Your words ask for rebuke far more than his.
HERDSMAN. But what have I done wrong, most royal master?
OEDIPUS. Not telling of the boy of whom he asked. 1155
HERDSMAN. He's ignorant and blundering toward ruin.
OEDIPUS. Tell it willingly—or under torture.
HERDSMAN. Oh god! Don't—I am old—don't torture me!
OEDIPUS. Here! Someone put his hands behind his back!
HERDSMAN. But why? What else would you find out, poor man? 1160
OEDIPUS. Did you give him the child he asks about?
HERDSMAN. I did. I wish that I had died that day!
OEDIPUS. You'll come to that if you don't speak the truth.
HERDSMAN. It's if I speak that I shall be destroyed.
OEDIPUS. I think this fellow struggles for delay. 1165
HERDSMAN. No, no! I said already that I gave him.
OEDIPUS. From your own home, or got from someone else?
HERDSMAN. Not from my own. I got him from another.
OEDIPUS. Which of these citizens? What sort of house?
HERDSMAN. Don't—by the gods!—don't, master, ask me more! 1170
OEDIPUS. It means your death if I must ask again.
HERDSMAN. One of the children of the house of Laius.
OEDIPUS. A slave—or born into the family?
HERDSMAN. I have come to the dreaded thing, and I shall say it.
OEDIPUS. And I to hearing it, but hear I must. 1175
HERDSMAN. He was reported to have been—his son.
    Your lady in the house could tell you best.

1142 *Arcturus*: a star that is first seen in September in the Grecian sky.

OEDIPUS. Because she gave him to you?
HERDSMAN.   Yes, my lord.
OEDIPUS. What was her purpose?
HERDSMAN.   I was to kill the boy.
OEDIPUS. The child she bore?
HERDSMAN.   She dreaded prophecies.   1180
OEDIPUS. What were they?
HERDSMAN.   The word was that he'd kill his parents.
OEDIPUS. Then why did you give him up to this old man?
HERDSMAN. In pity, master—so he would take him home,
    to another land. But what he did was save him
    for his supreme disaster. If you are the one   1185
    he speaks of—know your evil birth and fate!
OEDIPUS. Ah! All of it was destined to be true!
    Oh light, now may I look my last upon you,
    shown monstrous in my birth, in marriage monstrous,
    a murderer monstrous in those I killed.   1190

[*Exit OEDIPUS, running into the palace.*]

STASIMON 4

Strophe 1

CHORUS. Oh generations of mortal men,
    while you are living, I will
        appraise your lives at zero!
    What man
    comes closer to seizing lasting blessedness   1195
    than merely to seize its semblance,
    and after living in this semblance, to plunge?
    With your example before us,
    with your destiny, yours,
        suffering Oedipus, no mortal   1200
    can I judge fortunate.

Antistrophe 1

For he, outranging everybody,
    shot his arrow and became the lord
        of wide prosperity and blessedness,
    oh Zeus, after destroying   1205
    the virgin with the crooked talons,

1202 *he*: Oedipus. 1203 *shot his arrow*: took his chances; made a guess at the Sphinx's riddle. 1206 *virgin...talons*: the Sphinx.

singer of oracles; and against death,
in my land, he arose a tower of defense.
From which time you were called my king
and granted privileges supreme—in mighty   1210
Thebes the ruling lord.

Strophe 2

But now—whose story is more sorrowful than yours?
Who is more intimate with fierce calamities,
with labors, now that your life is altered?
Alas, my Oedipus, whom all men know: 1215
one great harbor—
one alone sufficed for you,
as son and father,
when you tumbled, plowman of the woman's chamber.
How, how could your paternal   1220
        furrows, wretched man,
endure you silently so long.

Antistrophe 2

Time, all-seeing, surprised you living an unwilled life
and sits from of old in judgment on the marriage, not a marriage,
where the begetter is the begot as well.   1225
Ah, son of Laius…,
would that—oh, would that
I had never seen you!
I wail, my scream climbing beyond itself
from my whole power of voice. To say it straight: 1230
        from you I got new breath—
but I also lulled my eye to sleep.

EXODUS

[*Enter the* SECOND MESSENGER *from the palace.*]

SECOND MESSENGER. You who are first among the citizens,
what deeds you are about to hear and see!
What grief you'll carry, if, true to your birth,   1235
you still respect the house of Labdacus!
Neither the Ister nor the Phasis river

1216 *one great harbor*: metaphorical allusion to Jocasta's body. 1219 *tumbled*: were born and had sex. *plowman*: Plowing is used here as a sexual metaphor. 1232 *I…sleep*: I failed to see the corruption you brought.

could purify this house, such suffering
does it conceal, or soon must bring to light—
willed this time, not unwilled. Griefs hurt worst   1240
which we perceive to be self-chosen ones.
CHORAGOS.   They were sufficient, the things we knew before,
to make us grieve. What can you add to those?
SECOND MESSENGER.   The thing that's quickest said and quickest heard:
our own, our royal one, Jocasta's dead.   1245
CHORAGOS.   Unhappy queen! What was responsible?
SECOND MESSENGER.   Herself. The bitterest of these events
is not for you, you were not there to see,
but yet, exactly as I can recall it,
you'll hear what happened to that wretched lady.   1250
She came in anger through the outer hall,
and then she ran straight to her marriage bed,
tearing her hair with the fingers of both hands.
Then, slamming shut the doors when she was in,
she called to Laius, dead so many years,   1255
remembering the ancient seed which caused
his death, leaving the mother to the son
to breed again an ill-born progeny.
She mourned the bed where she, alas, bred double—
husband by husband, children by her child.   1260
From this point on I don't know how she died,
for Oedipus then burst in with a cry,
and did not let us watch her final evil.
Our eyes were fixed on him. Wildly he ran
to each of us, asking for his spear   1265
and for his wife—no wife: where he might find
the double mother-field, his and his children's.
He raved, and some divinity then showed him—
for none of us did so who stood close by.
With a dreadful shout—as if some guide were leading—   1270
he lunged through the double doors; he bent the hollow
bolts from the sockets, burst into the room,
and there we saw her, hanging from above,
entangled in some twisted hanging strands.
He saw, was stricken, and with a wild roar   1275
ripped down the dangling noose. When she, poor woman,
lay on the ground, there came a fearful sight:
he snatched the pins of worked gold from her dress,
with which her clothes were fastened: these he raised
and struck into the ball-joints of his eyes.   1280

1280 *ball-joints of his eyes*: his eyeballs. Oedipus blinds himself in both eyes at the same time.

He shouted that they would no longer see
the evils he had suffered or had done,
see in the dark those he should not have seen,
and know no more those he once sought to know.
While chanting this, not once but many times   1285
he raised his hand and struck into his eyes.
Blood from his wounded eyes poured down his chin,
not freed in moistening drops, but all at once
a stormy rain of black blood burst like hail.
These evils, coupling them, making them one,   1290
have broken loose upon both man and wife.
The old prosperity that they had once
was true prosperity, and yet today,
mourning, ruin, death, disgrace, and every
evil you could name—not one is absent.   1295
CHORAGOS. Has he allowed himself some peace from all this grief?
SECOND MESSENGER. He shouts that someone slide the bolts and show
to all the Cadmeians the patricide,
his mother's—I can't say it, it's unholy—
so he can cast himself out of the land,   1300
not stay and curse his house by his own curse.
He lacks the strength, though, and he needs a guide,
for his is a sickness that's too great to bear.
Now you yourself will see: the bolts of the doors
are opening. You are about to see   1305
a vision even one who hates must pity.

[*Enter the blinded* OEDIPUS *from the palace, led in by a household*
SERVANT.]

CHORAGOS. This suffering sends terror through men's eyes,
terrible beyond any suffering
my eyes have touched. Oh man of pain,
what madness reached you? Which god from far off,   1310
surpassing in range his longest spring,
struck hard against your god-abandoned fate?
Oh man of pain,
I cannot look upon you—though there's so much
I would ask you, so much to hear,   1315
so much that holds my eyes—
so awesome the convulsions you send through me.
OEDIPUS. Ah! Ah! I am a man of misery.
Where am I carried? Pity me! Where
is my voice scattered abroad on wings?   1320
Divinity, where has your lunge transported me?
CHORAGOS. To something horrible, not to be heard or seen.

KOMMOS

Strophe 1

OEDIPUS. Oh, my cloud
      of darkness, abominable, unspeakable as it attacks me,
      not to be turned away, brought by an evil wind!   1325
      Alas!
      Again alas! Both enter me at once:
      the sting of the prongs, the memory of evils!
CHORUS. I do not marvel that in these afflictions
      you carry double griefs and double evils.

Antistrophe 1   1330

OEDIPUS. Ah, friend,
      so you at least are there, resolute servant!
      Still with a heart to care for me, the blind man.
      Oh! Oh!
      I know that you are there. I recognize,   1335
      even inside my darkness, that voice of yours.
CHORUS. Doer of horror, how did you bear to quench
      your vision? What divinity raised your hand?

Strophe 2

OEDIPUS. It was Apollo there, Apollo, friends,
      who brought my sorrows, vile sorrows to their perfection,   1340
          these evils that were done to me.
      But the one who struck them with his hand,
          that one was none but I, in wretchedness.
      For why was I to see
      when nothing I could see would bring me joy?   1345
CHORUS. Yes, that is how it was.
OEDIPUS. What could I see, indeed,
      or what enjoy—what greeting
      is there I could hear with pleasure, friends?
      Conduct me out of the land   1350
          as quickly as you can!
      Conduct me out, my friends,
          the man utterly ruined,
      supremely cursed,
          the man who is by gods   1355
      the most detested of all men!

1328 *prongs*: refers to both the whip that Laius used and the two gold pins Oedipus used to blind himself.

CHORUS.   Wretched in disaster and in knowledge:
      oh, I could wish you'd never come to know!

Antistrophe 2

OEDIPUS.   May he be destroyed, whoever freed the savage shackles
      from my feet when I'd been sent to the wild pasture,   1360
          whoever rescued me from murder
      and became my savior—
          a bitter gift:
      if I had died then,
      I'd not have been such grief to self and kin.   1365
CHORUS.   I also would have had it so.
OEDIPUS.   I'd not have returned to be my father's
      murderer; I'd not be called by men
      my mother's bridegroom.
      Now I'm without a god,   1370
          child of a polluted parent,
      fellow progenitor with him
          who gave me birth in misery.
      If there's an evil that   1375
          surpasses evils, that
      has fallen to the lot of Oedipus.
CHORAGOS.   How can I say that you have counseled well?
      Better not to be than live a blind man.
OEDIPUS.   That this was not the best thing I could do—
      don't tell me that, or advise me any more!   1380
      Should I descend to Hades and endure
      to see my father with these eyes? Or see
      my poor unhappy mother? For I have done,
      to both of these, things too great for hanging.
      Or is the sight of children to be yearned for,   1385
      to see new shoots that sprouted as these did?
      Never, never with these eyes of mine!
      Nor city, nor tower, nor holy images
      of the divinities! For I, all-wretched,
      most nobly raised—as no one else in Thebes—   1390
      deprived myself of these when I ordained
      that all expel the impious one—god-shown
      to be polluted, and the dead king's son!
      Once I exposed this great stain upon me,

1391-1393 *I...son*: Oedipus refers to his own curse against the murderer as well as his sins of patricide and incest.

could I have looked on these with steady eyes?   1395
No! No! And if there were a way to block
the source of hearing in my ears, I'd gladly
have locked up my pitiable body,
so I'd be blind and deaf. Evils shut out—
that way my mind could live in sweetness.   1400
Alas, Cithaeron, why did you receive me?
Or when you had me, not killed me instantly?
I'd not have had to show my birth to mankind.
Polybus, Corinth, halls—ancestral,
they told me—how beautiful was your ward,   1405
a scar that held back festering disease!
Evil my nature, evil my origin.
You, three roads, and you, secret ravine,
you oak grove, narrow place of those three paths
that drank my blood from these my hands, from him   1410
who fathered me, do you remember still
the things I did to you? When I'd come here,
what I then did once more? Oh marriages! Marriages!
You gave us life and when you'd planted us
you sent the same seed up, and then revealed   1415
fathers, brothers, sons, and kinsman's blood,
and brides, and wives, and mothers, all the most
atrocious things that happen to mankind!
One should not name what never should have been.
Somewhere out there, then, quickly, by the gods,   1420
cover me up, or murder me, or throw me
to the ocean where you will never see me more!

[OEDIPUS *moves toward the* CHORUS *and they back away from him.*]

Come! Don't shrink to touch this wretched man!
Believe me, do not be frightened! I alone
of all mankind can carry these afflictions.   1425

[*Enter* CREON *from the palace with* ATTENDANTS.]

CHORAGOS. Tell Creon what you wish for. Just when we need him
    he's here. He can act, he can advise you.
    He's now the land's sole guardian in your place.
OEDIPUS. Ah! Are there words that I can speak to him?
    What ground for trust can I present? It's proved   1430
    that I was false to him in everything.

1401 *Cithaeron:* the mountain on which the infant Oedipus was supposed to be exposed. 1410 *my blood:* that is, the blood of my father, Laius. 1436 *Hëlius:* the sun.

CREON. I have not come to mock you, Oedipus,
    nor to reproach you for your former falseness.
    You men, if you have no respect for sons
    of mortals, let your awe for the all-feeding   1435
    flames of lordly Hēlius prevent
    your showing unconcealed so great a stain,
    abhorred by earth and sacred rain and light.
    Escort him quickly back into the house!
    If blood kin only see and hear their own   1440
    afflictions, we'll have no impious defilement.
OEDIPUS. By the gods, you've freed me from one terrible fear,
    so nobly meeting my unworthiness:
    grant me something—not for me; for you!
CREON. What do you want that you should beg me so?   1445
OEDIPUS. To drive me from the land at once, to a place
    where there will be no man to speak to me!
CREON. I would have done just that—had I not wished
    to ask first of the god what I should do.
OEDIPUS. His answer was revealed in full—that I,   1450
    the patricide, unholy, be destroyed.
CREON. He said that, but our need is so extreme,
    it's best to have sure knowledge what must be done.
OEDIPUS. You'll ask about a wretched man like me?
CREON. Is it not time you put your trust in the god?   1455
OEDIPUS. But I bid you as well, and shall entreat you.
    Give her who is within what burial
    you will—you'll give your own her proper rites;
    but me—do not condemn my father's land
    to have me dwelling here while I'm alive,   1460
    but let me live on mountains—on Cithaeron
    famed as mine, for my mother and my father,
    while they yet lived, made it my destined tomb,
    and I'll be killed by those who wished my ruin!
    And yet I know: no sickness will destroy me,   1465
    nothing will: I'd never have been saved
    when left to die unless for some dread evil.
    Then let my fate continue where it will!
    As for my children, Creon, take no pains
    for my sons—they're men and they will never lack   1470
    the means to live, wherever they may be—
    but my two wretched, pitiable girls,
    who never ate but at my table, never
    were without me—everything that I
    would touch, they'd always have a share of it—   1475

please care for them! Above all, let me touch
them with my hands and weep aloud my woes!
Please, my Lord!
Please, noble heart! Touching with my hands,
I'd think I held them as when I could see.   1480

[Enter ANTIGONE and ISMENE from the palace with ATTENDANTS.]

What's this?
Oh gods! do I hear, somewhere, my two dear ones
sobbing? Has Creon really pitied me
and sent to me my dearest ones, my children?
Is that it?   1485
CREON.   Yes, I prepared this for you, for I knew
you'd feel this joy, as you have always done.
OEDIPUS.   Good fortune, then, and, for your care, be guarded
far better by divinity than I was!
Where are you, children? Come to me! Come here   1490
to these my hands, hands of your brother, hands
of him who gave you seed, hands that made
these once bright eyes to see now in this fashion.

[OEDIPUS embraces his daughters.]

He, children, seeing nothing, knowing nothing,
he fathered you where his own seed was plowed.   1495
I weep for you as well, though I can't see you,
imagining your bitter life to come,
the life you will be forced by men to live.
What gatherings of townsmen will you join,
what festivals, without returning home   1500
in tears instead of watching holy rites?
And when you've reached the time for marrying,
where, children, is the man who'll run the risk
of taking on himself the infamy
that will wound you as it did my parents?   1505
What evil is not here? Your father killed
his father, plowed the one who gave him birth,
and from the place where he was sown, from there
he got you, from the place he too was born.
These are the wounds: then who will marry you?   1510
No man, my children. No, it's clear that you
must wither in dry barrenness, unmarried.

[OEDIPUS addresses CREON.]

Son of Menoeceus! You are the only father
left to them—we two who gave them seed
are both destroyed: watch that they don't become   1515
poor, wanderers, unmarried—they are your kin.
Let not my ruin be their ruin, too!
No, pity them! You see how young they are,
bereft of everyone, except for you.
Consent, kind heart, and touch me with your hand!   1520

[CREON *grasps* OEDIPUS'S *right hand.*]

You, children, if you had reached an age of sense,
I would have counseled much. Now, pray you may live
always where it's allowed, finding a life
better than his was, who gave you seed.
CREON. Stop this now. Quiet your weeping. Move away, into the house.   1525
OEDIPUS. Bitter words, but I obey them.
CREON.   There's an end to all things.
OEDIPUS. I have first this request.
CREON.   I will hear it.
OEDIPUS. Banish me from my homeland.
CREON.   You must ask that of the god.
OEDIPUS. But I am the gods' most hated man!
CREON.   Then you will soon get what you want.
OEDIPUS. Do you consent?
CREON.   I never promise when, as now, I'm ignorant.   1530
OEDIPUS. Then lead me in.
CREON.   Come. But let your hold fall from your children.
OEDIPUS. Do not take them from me, ever!
CREON.   Do not wish to keep all of the power.
You had power, but that power did not follow you through life.

[OEDIPUS'S *daughters are taken from his hand and led into the palace by*
ATTENDANTS. OEDIPUS *is led into the palace by a* SERVANT. CREON *and the*
other ATTENDANTS *follow. Only the* CHORUS *remains.*]

CHORUS. People of Thebes, my country, see: here is that Oedipus—
he who "knew" the famous riddle, and attained the highest power,   1535
whom all citizens admired, even envying his luck!
See the billows of wild troubles which he has entered now!
Here is the truth of each man's life: we must wait, and see his end,
scrutinize his dying day, and refuse to call him happy
till he has crossed the border of his life without pain.   1540

[*Exit the* CHORUS *along each of the Parados.*]

—Translated by Thomas Gould

PLATO

We know the teachings of the Athenian philosopher Socrates almost exclusively through the writings of Plato, his most able student. Plato's *Apology of Socrates* and several other dialogues recount the events of Socrates' last days, though their accuracy cannot be reliably assessed. In later dialogues, including the *Republic*, the figure of Socrates has become a mouthpiece for Plato's own philosophical ideas. These ideas, illustrated in the famous "Allegory of the Cave," are among the most important and influential in the history of Western philosophy.

In the *Apology*, Socrates defends himself against his accusers by explaining his divinely inspired mission to seek a man wiser than he. When he is convicted, Socrates proposes as his "punishment" the honor of eating at the public banquet table, in recognition of his service to Athens. Faced with the death sentence, he reassures his followers that he is going to a better place, perhaps to commune with the great poets in a life of true justice.

The ideal world that Socrates anticipates is described in Plato's graphic metaphor, the "Allegory of the Cave,", excerpted from the *Republic*.

For analysis and interpretation:

1. Evaluate Socrates as a model teacher, based on his self-described mission to demonstrate his own ignorance.

2. Explain what Socrates means by saying the gods have sent him as a "gadfly" to sting the city of Athens. What people do you know who might be seen as "gadflies" in the same sense?

3. Apply Plato's vision of the human condition in the cave to contemporary circumstances. What people are the equivalent to those chained in front of the cave wall? What noble few have freed themselves to leave the cave and achieve enlightenment?

The Apology of Socrates

I do not know what effect my accusers have had upon you, gentlemen, but for my own part I was almost carried away by them; their arguments were so convincing. On the other hand, scarcely a word of what they said was true. I was especially astonished at one of their many misrepresentations: I mean when they told you that you must be careful not to let me deceive you—the implication being that I am a skillful speaker. I thought that it was peculiarly brazen of them to tell you this without a blush, since they must know that they will soon be effectively confuted, when it becomes obvious that I have not the slightest skill as a speaker—unless, of course, by a skillful speaker they mean one who speaks the truth. If that is what they mean, I would agree that I am an orator, though not after their pattern.

My accusers, then, as I maintain, have said little or nothing that is true, but from me you shall hear the whole truth; not, I can assure you, gentlemen, in flowery language like theirs, decked out with fine words and phrases; no, what you will hear will be a straightforward speech in the first words that occur to me, confident as I am in the justice of my cause; and I do not want any of you to expect anything different. It would hardly be suitable, gentlemen, for a man of my age to address you in the artificial language of a schoolboy orator. One thing, however, I do most earnestly beg and entreat of you: if you hear me defending myself in the same language which it has been my habit to use, both in the open spaces of this city (where many of you have heard me), and elsewhere, do not be surprised, and do not interrupt. Let me remind you of my position. This is my first appearance in a court of law, at the age of seventy; and so I am a complete stranger to the language of this place. Now if I were really from another country, you would naturally excuse me if I spoke in the manner and dialect in which I had been brought up; and so in the present case I make this request of you, which I think is only reasonable: to disregard the manner of my speech—it may be better or it may be worse—and to consider and concentrate your attention upon this one question, whether my claims are fair or not. That is the first duty of the juryman, just as it is the pleader's duty to speak the truth.

The proper course for me, gentlemen of the jury, is to deal first with the earliest charges that have been falsely brought against me, and with my earliest accusers; and then with the later ones. I make this distinction because I have already been accused in your hearing by a great many people for a great many years, though without a word of truth; and I am more afraid of those people than I am of Anytus and his colleagues, although they are formidable enough. But the others are still more formidable; I mean the people who took hold of so many of you when you were children and tried to fill your minds with untrue accusations against me, saying 'There is a clever man called Socrates who has theories about the heavens and has investigated everything below the earth, and can make the weaker argument defeat the stronger.' It is these people, gentlemen, the disseminators of these rumours, who are my dangerous accusers; because those who hear them suppose that anyone who inquires into such matters must be an atheist. Besides, there are a great many of these accusers, and they have been accusing me now for a great many years; and what is more, they approached you at the most impressionable age, when some of you were children or adolescents; and they literally won their case by default, because there was no one to defend me. And the most fantastic thing of all is that it is impossible for me even to know and tell you their names, unless one of them happens to be a playwright. All these people, who have tried to set you against me out of envy and love of slander-and some too merely passing on what they have been told by others—all these are very difficult to deal with. It is impossible to bring them here for cross-examination; one simply has to conduct one's defence and argue one's case against an invisible opponent, because there is no one to answer. So I ask you to accept my statement that my critics fall into two classes: on the one hand my immediate accusers, and on the other those earlier ones whom I have mentioned; and you must suppose that I have first to defend myself against the latter. After all, you heard them abusing me longer ago and much more violently than these more recent accusers.

Very well, then; I must begin my defence, gentlemen, and I must try, in the short time that I have, to rid your minds of a false impression which is the work of many years. I should like this to be the result, gentlemen, assuming it to be for your advantage and my own; and I should like to be successful in my defence; but I think that it will be difficult, and I am quite aware of the nature of my task. However, let that turn out as God wills; I must obey the law and make my defence.

Let us go back to the beginning and consider what the charge is that has made me so unpopular, and has encouraged Meletus to draw up this indictment. Very well; what did my critics say in attacking my character? I must read out their affidavit, so to speak, as though they were my legal accusers. 'Socrates is guilty of criminal meddling, in that he inquires into things below the earth and in the sky, and makes the weaker argument defeat the stronger, and teaches others to follow his example.' It runs something like that. You have seen it for yourselves in the play by Aristophanes, where Socrates goes whirling round, proclaiming that he is walking on air, and uttering a great deal of other nonsense about things of which I know nothing whatsoever. I mean no disrespect for such knowledge, if anyone really is versed in it—I do not want any more lawsuits brought against me by Meletus—but the fact is, gentlemen, that I take no interest in it. What is more, I call upon the greater part of you as witnesses to my statement, and I appeal to all of you who have ever listened to me talking (and there are a great many to whom this applies) to clear your neighbours' minds on this point. Tell one another whether any one of you has ever heard me discuss such questions briefly or at length; and then you will realize that the other popular reports about me are equally unreliable.

The fact is that there is nothing in any of these charges; and if you have heard anyone say that I try to educate people and charge a fee, there is no truth in that either. I wish that there were, because I think that it is a fine thing if a man is qualified to teach, as in the case of Gorgias of Leontin and Prodicus of Ceos and Hippias of Elis. Each one of these is perfectly capable of going into any city and actually persuading the young men to leave the company of their fellow-citizens, with any of whom they can associate for nothing, and attach themselves to him, and pay money for the privilege, and be grateful into the bargain. There is another expert too from Patos who I discovered was here on a visit. I happened to meet a man who has paid more in sophists' fees than all the rest put together-I mean Callias the son of Hipponicus; so I asked him (he has two sons, you see): 'Callias,' I said, 'if your sons had colts or calves, we should have had no difficulty in finding and engaging a trainer to perfect their natural qualities; and this trainer would have been some sort of horse-dealer or agriculturalist. But seeing that they are human beings, whom do you intend to get as their instructor? Who is the expert in perfecting the human and social qualities? I assume from the fact of your having sons that you must have considered the question. Is there such a person or not?' 'Certainly,' said he. 'Who is he, and where does he come from?' said I, 'and what does he charge?' 'Evenus of Paros, Socrates,' said he, 'and his fee is 500 drachmae.' I felt that Evenus was to be congratulated if he really was a master of this art and taught it at such a moderate fee. I should certainly plume myself and give myself airs if I understood these things; but in fact, gentlemen, I do not.

Here perhaps one of you might interrupt me and say 'But what is it that you do, Socrates? How is it that you have been misrepresented like this? Surely all this talk and gossip about you would never have arisen if you had confined yourself to ordinary activities, but only if your behavior was abnormal. Tell us the explanation, if you do not want us to invent it for ourselves.' This seems to me to be a reasonable request, and I will try to explain to you what it is that has given me this false notoriety; so please give me your attention. Perhaps some of you will think that I am not being serious; but I assure you that I am going to tell you the whole truth.

I have gained this reputation, gentlemen, from nothing more or less than a kind of wisdom. What kind of wisdom do I mean? Human wisdom, I suppose. It seems that I really am wise in this limited sense. Presumably the geniuses whom I mentioned just now are wise in a wisdom that is more than human; I do not know how else to account for it. I certainly have no knowledge of such wisdom, and anyone who says that I have is a liar and willful slanderer. Now, gentlemen, please do not interrupt me if I seem to make an extravagant claim; for what I am going to tell you is not my own opinion; I am going to refer you to an unimpeachable authority. I shall call as witness to my wisdom (such as it is) the god at Delphi.

You know Chaerephon, of course. He was a friend of mine from boyhood, and a good democrat who played his part with the rest of you in the recent expulsion and restoration. And you know what he was like; how enthusiastic he was over anything that he had once undertaken. Well, one day he actually went to Delphi and asked this question of the god—as I said before, gentlemen, please do not interrupt—he asked whether there was anyone wiser than myself. The priestess replied that there was no one. As Chaerephon is dead, the evidence for my statement will be supplied by his brother, who is here in court.

Please consider my object in telling you this. I want to explain to you how the attack upon my reputation first started. When I heard about the oracle's answer, I said to myself 'What does the god mean? Why does he not use plain language? I am only too conscious that I have no claim to wisdom, great or small; so what can he mean by asserting that I am the wisest man in the world? He cannot be telling a lie; that would not be right for him.'

After puzzling about it for some time, I set myself at last with considerable reluctance to check the truth of it in the following way. I went to interview a man with a high reputation for wisdom, because I felt that here if anywhere I should succeed in disproving the oracle and pointing out to my divine authority 'You said that I was the wisest of men, but here is a man who is wiser than I am.'

Well, I gave a thorough examination to this person—I need not mention his name, but it was one of our politicians that I was studying when I had this experience—and in conversation with him I formed the impression that although in many people's opinion, and especially in his own, he appeared to be wise, in fact he was not. Then when I began to try to show him that he only thought he was wise and was not really so, my efforts were resented both by him and by many of the other people present. However, I reflected as I walked away: 'Well, I am certainly wiser than this man. It is only too likely that neither of us has any knowledge to boast of; but he thinks that he knows something which he does not know, whereas I am quite conscious of my ignorance. At any rate it seems that I am wiser than he is to this small extent, that I do not think that I know what I do not know.'

After this I went on to interview a man with an even greater reputation for wisdom, and I formed the same impression again; and here too I incurred the resentment of the man himself and a number of others.

From that time on I interviewed one person after another. I realized with distress and alarm that I was making myself unpopular, but I felt compelled to put my religious duty first; since I was trying to find out the meaning of the oracle, I was bound to interview everyone who had a reputation for knowledge. And by Dog, gentlemen! (for I must be frank with you) my honest impression was this: it seemed to me, as I pursued my investigation at the god's command, that the people with the greatest reputations were almost entirely deficient, while others who were supposed to be their inferior were much better qualified in practical intelligence.

I want you to think of my adventures as a sort of pilgrimage undertaken to establish the truth of the oracle once for all. After I had finished with the politicians I turned to the poets, dramatic, lyric, and all the rest, in the belief that here I should expose myself as a comparative ignoramus. I used to pick up what I thought were some of their most perfect works and question them closely about the meaning of what they had written, in the hope of incidentally enlarging my own knowledge. Well, gentlemen, I hesitate to tell you the truth, but it must be told. It is hardly an exaggeration to say that any of the bystanders could have explained those poems better than their actual authors. So I soon made up my mind about the poets too: I decided that it was not wisdom that enabled them to write their poetry, but a kind of instinct or inspiration, such as you find in seers and prophets who deliver all their sublime messages without knowing in the least what they mean. It seemed clear to me that the poets were in much the same case; and I also observed that the very fact that they were poets made them think that they had a perfect understanding of all other subjects, of which they were totally ignorant. So I left that line of inquiry too with the same sense of advantage that I had felt in the case of the politicians.

Last of all I turned to the skilled craftsmen. I knew quite well that I had practically no technical qualifications myself, and I was sure that I should find them full of impressive knowledge. In this I was not disappointed; they understood things which I did not, and to that extent they were wiser than I was. But, gentlemen, these professional experts seemed to share the same failing which I had noticed in the poets; I mean that on the strength of their technical proficiency they claimed a perfect understanding of every other subject, however important; and I felt that this error more than outweighed their positive wisdom. So I made myself spokesman for the oracle, and asked myself whether I would rather be as I was—neither wise with their wisdom nor stupid with their stupidity—or possess both qualities as they did. I replied through myself to the oracle that it was best for me to be as I was.

The effect of these investigations of mine, gentlemen, has been to arouse against me a great deal of hostility, and hostility of a particularly bitter and persistent kind, which has resulted in various malicious suggestions, including the description of me as a professor of wisdom. This is due to the fact that whenever I succeed in disproving another person's claim to wisdom in a given subject, the bystanders assume that I know everything about that subject myself. But the truth of the matter, gentlemen, is pretty certainly this: that real wisdom is the property of God, and this oracle is his way of telling us that human wisdom has little or no value. It seems to me that he is not referring literally to Socrates, but has merely taken my name as an example, as if he would say to us 'The wisest of you men is he who has realized, like Socrates, that in respect of wisdom he is really worthless.'

That is why I still go about seeking and searching in obedience to the divine command, if I think that anyone is wise, whether citizen or stranger; and when I think that any person is not wise, I try to help the cause of God by proving that he is not. This occupation has kept me too busy to do much either in politics or in my own affairs; in fact, my service to God has reduced me to extreme poverty.

There is another reason for my being unpopular. A number of young men with wealthy fathers and plenty of leisure have deliberately attached themselves to me because they enjoy hearing other people cross-questioned. These often take me as their model, and go on to try to question other persons; whereupon, I suppose, they find an unlimited number of people who think that they know something, but really know little or nothing. Consequently their victims become annoyed, not with themselves but with me; and they complain that there is a pestilential busybody called Socrates who fills young people's heads with wrong ideas. If you ask them what he does, and what he teaches that has this effect, they have no answer, not knowing what to say; but as they do not want to admit their confusion, they fall back on the stock charges against any philosopher: that he teaches his pupils about things in the heavens and below the earth, and to disbelieve in gods, and to make the weaker argument defeat the stronger. They would be very loath, I fancy, to admit the truth: which is that they are being convicted of pretending to knowledge when they are entirely ignorant. So, jealous, I suppose, for their own reputation, and also energetic and numerically strong, and provided with a plausible and carefully worked out case against me, these people have been dinning into your ears for a long time past their violent denunciations of myself. There you have the causes which led to the attack upon me by Meletus and Anytus and Lycon, Meletus being aggrieved on behalf of the poets, Anytus on behalf of the professional men and politicians, and Lycon on behalf of the orators. So, as I said at the beginning, I should be surprised if I were able, in the short time that I have, to rid your minds of a misconception so deeply implanted.

There, gentlemen, you have the true facts, which I present to you without any concealment or suppression, great or small. I am fairly certain that this plain speaking of mine is the cause of my unpopularity; and this really goes to prove that my statements are true, and that I have described correctly the nature and the grounds of the calumny which has been brought against me. Whether you inquire into them now or later, you will find the facts as I have just described them.

So much for my defense against the charges brought by the first group of my accusers. I shall now try to defend myself against Meletus—high-principled and patriotic as he claims to be—and after that against the rest.

Let us first consider their deposition again, as though it represented a fresh prosecution. It runs something like this: 'Socrates is guilty of corrupting the minds of the young and of believing in deities of his own invention instead of the gods recognized by the State.' Such is the charge; let us examine its points one by one.

First it says that I am guilty of corrupting the young. But I say, gentlemen, that Meletus is guilty of treating a serious matter with levity, since he summons people to stand their trial on frivolous grounds, and professes concern and keen anxiety in matters about which he has never had the slightest interest. I will try to prove this to your satisfaction.

Come now, Meletus, tell me this. You regard it as supremely important, do you not, that our young people should be exposed to the best possible influence? 'I do.' Very well, then; tell these gentlemen who it is that influences the young for the better. Obviously you must know, if you are so much interested. You have discovered the vicious influence, as you say, in myself, and you are now prosecuting me before these gentlemen; speak up and inform them who it is that has a good influence upon the young.—You see, Meletus, that you are tongue-tied and cannot answer. Do you not feel that this is discreditable, and a sufficient proof in itself of what I said, that you have no interest in the subject? Tell me, my friend, who is it that makes the young good? 'The laws.' That is not what I mean, my dear sir; I am asking you to name the *person* whose first business it is to know the laws. 'These gentlemen here, Socrates, the members of the jury.' Do you mean, Meletus, that they have the ability to educate the young, and to make them better? 'Certainly.' Does this apply to all jurymen, or only to some? 'To all of them.' Excellent! a generous supply of benefactors. Well, then, do these spectators who are present in court have an improving influence, or not? 'Yes, they do.' And what about the members of the Council? 'Yes, the Councilors too.' But surely, Meletus, the members of the Assembly do not corrupt the young? Or do all of them too exert an improving influence? 'Yes, they do.' Then it would seem that the whole population of Athens has a refining effect upon the young, except myself; and I alone demoralize them. Is that your meaning? 'Most emphatically, yes.' This is certainly a most unfortunate quality that you have detected in me. Well, let me put another question to you. Take the case of horses; do you believe that those who improve them make up the whole of mankind, and that there is only one person who has a bad effect on them? Or is the truth just the opposite, that the ability to improve them belongs to one person or to very few persons, who are horse-trainers, whereas most people, if they have to do with horses and make use of them, do them harm? Is not this the case, Meletus, both with horses and with all other animals? Of course it is, whether you and Anytus deny it or not. It would be a singular dispensation of fortune for our young people if there is only one person who corrupts them, while all the rest have a beneficial effect. But I need say no more; there is ample proof, Meletus, that you have never bothered your head about the young; and you make it perfectly clear that you have never taken the slightest interest in the cause for the sake of which you are now indicting me.

Here is another point. Tell me seriously, Meletus, is it better to live in a good or in a bad community? Answer my question, like a good fellow; there is nothing difficult about it. Is it not true that wicked people have a bad effect upon those with whom they are in the closest contact, and that good people have a good effect? 'Quite true.' Is there anyone who prefers to be harmed rather than benefited by his associates? Answer me, my good man; the law commands you to answer. Is there anyone who prefers to be harmed? 'Of course not.' Well, then, when you summon me before this court for corrupting the young and making their characters worse, do you mean that I do so intentionally or unintentionally? 'I mean intentionally.' Why, Meletus, are you at your age so much wiser than I am at mine? You have discovered that bad people always have a bad effect, and good people a good effect, upon their nearest neighbours; am I so hopelessly ignorant as not even to realize that by spoiling the character of one of my companions I shall run the risk of getting some harm from him? because nothing else would make me commit this grave offence intentionally. No, I do not believe it, Meletus, and I do not suppose that anyone else does. Either I have not a bad influence, or it is unintentional; so that in either case your accusation is false. And if I unintentionally have a bad influence, the correct procedure in cases of such involuntary misdemeanours is not to summon the culprit before this court, but to take him aside privately for instruction and reproof; because obviously if my eyes are opened, I shall stop doing what I do not intend to do. But you deliberately avoided my company in the past and refused to enlighten me, and now you bring me before this court, which is the place appointed for those who need punishment, not for those who need enlightenment.

It is quite clear by now, gentlemen, that Meletus, as I said before, has never shown any degree of interest in this subject. However, I invite you to tell us, Meletus, in what sense you make out that I corrupt the minds of the young. Surely the terms of your indictment make it clear that you accuse me of teaching them to believe in new deities instead of the gods recognized by the State; is not that the teaching of mine which you say has this demoralizing effect? 'That is precisely what I maintain.' Then I appeal to you, Meletus, in the name of these same gods about whom we are speaking, to explain yourself a little more clearly to myself and to the jury, because I cannot make out what your point is. Is it that I teach people to believe in some gods (which implies that I myself believe in gods, and am not a complete atheist, so that I am not guilty on that score), but in different gods from those recognized by the State so that your accusation rests upon the fact that they are different? Or do you assert that I believe in no gods at all, and teach others to do the same? 'Yes; I say that you disbelieve in gods altogether.' You surprise me, Meletus; what is your object in saying that? Do you suggest that I do not believe that the sun and moon are gods, as is the general belief of all mankind? 'He certainly does not, gentlemen of the jury, since he says that the sun is a stone and the moon a mass of earth.' Do you imagine that you are prosecuting Anaxagoras, my dear Meletus? Have you so poor an opinion of these gentlemen, and do you assume them to be so illiterate as not to know that the writings of Anaxagoras of Clazomenae are full of theories like these? and do you seriously suggest that it is from me that the young get these ideas, when they can buy them on occasion in the market-place for a drachma at most, and so have the laugh on Socrates if he claims them for his own, to say nothing of their being so silly? Tell me honestly, Meletus, is that your opinion of me? do I believe in no god? 'No, none at all; not in the slightest degree.' You are not at all convincing, Meletus; not even to yourself, I suspect. In my opinion, gentlemen, this man is a thoroughly selfish bully, and has brought this action against me out of sheer wanton aggressiveness and self-assertion. He seems to be devising a sort of intelligence test for me, saying to himself 'Will the infallible Socrates realize that I am contradicting myself for my own amusement, or shall I succeed in deceiving him and the rest of my audience?' It certainly seems to me that he is contradicting himself in this indictment, which might just as well run 'Socrates is guilty of not believing in the gods, but believing in the gods.' And this is pure flippancy.

I ask you to examine with me, gentlemen, the line of reasoning which leads me to this conclusion. You, Meletus, will oblige us by answering my questions. Will you all kindly remember, as I requested at the beginning, not to interrupt if I conduct the discussion in my customary way?

Is there anyone in the world, Meletus, who believes in human activities, and not in human beings? Make him answer, gentlemen, and don't let him keep on making these continual objections. Is there anyone who does not believe in horses, but believes in horses' activities? or who does not believe in musicians, but believes in musical activities? No, there is not, my worthy friend. If you do not want to answer, I will supply it for you and for these gentlemen too. But the next question you must answer: Is there anyone who believes in supernatural activities and not supernatural beings? 'No.' How good of you to give a bare answer under compulsion by the court! Well, do you assert that I believe and teach others to believe in supernatural activities? It does not matter whether they are new or old; the fact remains that I believe in them according to your statement; indeed you solemnly swore as much in your affidavit. But if I believe in supernatural activities, it follows inevitably that I also believe in supernatural beings. Is not that so? It is; I assume you assent, since you do not answer. Do we not hold that supernatural beings are either gods or the children of gods? Do you agree or not? 'Certainly.' Then if I believe in supernatural beings, as you assert, if these supernatural beings are gods in any sense, we shall reach the conclusion which I mentioned just now when I said that you were testing my intelligence for your own amusement, by stating first that I do not believe in gods, and then again that I do, since I believe in supernatural beings. If on the other hand these supernatural beings are bastard children of the gods by nymphs or other mothers, as they are reputed to be, who in the world would believe in the children of gods and not in the gods themselves? It would be as ridiculous as to believe in the young of horses or donkeys and not in horses and donkeys themselves. No, Meletus; there is no avoiding the conclusion that you brought this charge against me as a test of my wisdom, or else in despair of finding a genuine offence of which to accuse me. As for your prospect of convincing any living person with even a smattering of intelligence that belief in supernatural and divine activities does not imply belief in supernatural and divine activities does not imply belief in supernatural and divine beings, and *vice versa*, it is outside all the bounds of possibility.

As a matter of fact, gentlemen, I do not feel that it requires much defence to clear myself of Meletus' accusation; what I have said already is enough. But you know very well the truth of what I said in an earlier part of my speech, that I have incurred a great deal of bitter hostility; and this is what will bring about my destruction, if anything does; not Meletus nor Anytus, but the slander and jealousy of a very large section of the people. They have been fatal to a great many other innocent men, and I suppose will continue to be so; there is no likelihood that they will stop at me. But perhaps someone will say 'Do you feel no compunction, Socrates, at having followed a line of action which puts you in danger of the death-penalty?' I might fairly reply to him 'You are mistaken, my friend, if you think that a man who is worth anything ought to spend his time weighing up the prospects of life and death. He has only one thing to consider in performing any action; that is, whether he is acting rightly or wrongly, like a good man or a bad one. On your view the heroes who died at Troy would be poor creatures, especially the son of Thetis. He, if you remember, made so light of danger in comparison with incurring dishonour that when his goddess mother warned him, eager as he was to kill Hector, in some such words as these I fancy, "My son, if you avenge your comrade Patroclus' death and kill Hector, you will die yourself;

Next after Hector is thy fate prepared,"

— when he heard this warning, he made light of his death and danger, being much more afraid of an ignoble life and of failing to avenge his friends. "Let me die forthwith," said he, "when I have requited the villain, rather than remain here by the beaked ships to be mocked, a burden on the ground." Do you suppose that he gave a thought to death and danger?'

The truth of the matter is this, gentlemen. Where a man has once taken up his stand, either because it seems best to him or in obedience to his orders, there I believe he is bound to remain and face the danger, taking no account of death or anything else before dishonour.

This being so, it would be shocking inconsistency on my part, gentlemen, if, when the officers whom you chose to command me assigned me my position at Potidaea and Amphipolis and Delium, I remained at my post like anyone else and faced death, and yet afterwards, when God appointed me, as I supposed and believed, to the duty of leading the philosophic life, examining myself and others, I were then through fear of death or of any other danger to desert my post. That would indeed be shocking, and then I might really with justice be summoned into court for not believing in the gods, and disobeying the oracle, and being afraid of death, and thinking that I am wise when I am not. For let me tell you, gentlemen, that to be afraid of death is only another form of thinking that one is wise when one is not; it is to think that one knows what one does not know. No one knows with regard to death whether it is not really the greatest blessing that can happen to a man; but people dread it as though they were certain that it is the greatest evil; and this ignorance, which thinks that it knows what it does not, must surely be ignorance most culpable. This, I take it, gentlemen, is the degree, and this the nature of my advantage over the rest of mankind; and if I were to claim to be wiser than my neighbour in any respect, it would be in this: that not possessing any real knowledge of what comes after death,

I am also conscious that I do not possess it. But I do know that to do wrong and to disobey my superior, whether God or man, is wicked and dishonourable; and so I shall never feel more fear or aversion for something which, for all I know, may really be a blessing, than for those evils which I know to be evils.

Suppose, then, that you acquit me, and pay no attention to Anytus, who has said that either I should not have appeared before this court at all, or, since I have appeared here, I must be put to death, because if I once escaped your sons would all immediately become utterly demoralized by putting the teaching of Socrates into practice. Suppose that, in view of this, you said to me 'Socrates, on this occasion we shall disregard Anytus and acquit you, but only on one condition, that you give up spending your time on this quest and stop philosophizing. If we catch you going on in the same way, you shall be put to death.' Well, supposing, as I said, that you should offer to acquit me on these terms, I should reply 'Gentlemen, I am your very grateful and devoted servant, but I owe a greater obedience to God than to you; and so long as I draw breath and have my faculties, I shall never stop practicing philosophy and exhorting you and elucidating the truth for everyone that I meet. I shall go on saying, in my usual way, "My very good friend, you are an Athenian and belong to a city which is the greatest and most famous in the world for its wisdom and strength. Are you not ashamed that you give your attention to acquiring as much money as possible, and similarly with reputation and honour, and give no attention or thought to truth and understanding and the perfection of your soul?" And if any of you disputes this and professes to care about these things, I shall not at once let him go or leave him; no, I shall question him and examine him and test him; and if it appears that in spite of his profession he has made no real progress towards goodness, I shall reprove him for neglecting what is of supreme importance, and giving his attention to trivialities. I shall do this to everyone that I meet, young or old, foreigner or fellow-citizen; but especially to you my fellow-citizens, inasmuch as you are closer to me in kinship. This, I do assure you, is what my God commands; and it is my belief that no greater good has ever befallen you in this city than my service to my God; for I spend all my time going about trying to persuade you, young and old, to make your first and chief concern not for your bodies nor for your possessions, but for the highest welfare of your souls, proclaiming as I go 'Wealth does not bring goodness, but goodness brings wealth and every other blessing, both to the individual and to the State.' Now if I corrupt the young by this message, the message would seem to be harmful; but if anyone says that my message is different from this, he is talking nonsense. And so, gentlemen, I would say, 'You can please yourselves whether you listen to Anytus or not, and whether you acquit me or not; you know that I am not going to alter my conduct, not even if I have to die a hundred deaths.'

Order, please, gentlemen! Remember my request to give me a hearing without interruption; besides, I believe that it will be to your advantage to listen. I am going to tell you something else, which may provoke a storm of protest; but please restrain yourselves. I assure you that if I am what I claim to be, and you put me to death, you will harm yourselves more than me. Neither Meletus nor Anytus can do me any harm at all; they would not have the power, because I do not believe that the law of God permits a better man to be harmed by a worse. No doubt my accuser might put me to death or have me banished or deprived of civic rights; but even if he thinks, as he probably does (and others too, I dare say), that these are great calamities, I do not think so; I believe that it is far worse to do what he is doing now, trying to put an innocent man to death. For this reason, gentlemen, so far from pleading on my own behalf, as might be supposed, I am really pleading on yours, to save you from misusing the gift of God by condemning me. If you put me to death, you will not easily find anyone to take my place. It is literally true (even if it sounds rather comical) that God has specially appointed me to this city, as though it were a large thoroughbred horse which because of its great size is inclined to be lazy and needs the stimulation of some stinging fly. It seems to me that God has attached me to this city to perform the office of such a fly; and all day long I never cease to settle here, there, and everywhere, rousing, persuading, reproving every one of you. You will not easily find another like me, gentlemen, and if you take my advice you will spare my life. I suspect, however, that before long you will awake from your drowsing, and in your annoyance you will take Anytus' advice and finish me off with a single slap; and then you will go on sleeping till the end of your days, unless God in his care for you sends someone to take my place.

If you doubt whether I am really the sort of person who would have been sent to this city as a gift from God, you can convince yourselves by looking at it in this way. Does it seem natural that I should have neglected my own affairs and endured the humiliation of allowing my family to be neglected for all these years, while I busied myself all the time on your behalf, going like a father or an elder brother to see each one of you privately, and urging you to set your thoughts on goodness? If I had got any enjoyment from it, or if I had been paid for my good advice, there would have been some explanation for my conduct; but as it is you can see for yourselves that although my accusers unblushingly charge me with all sorts of other crimes, there is one thing that they have not had the impudence to pretend on any testimony, and that is that I have ever exacted or asked a fee from anyone. The witness that I can offer to prove the truth of my statement is, I think, a convincing one—my poverty.

It may seem curious that I should go round giving advice like this and busying myself in people's private affairs, and yet never venture publicly to address you as a whole and advise on matters of state. The reason for this is what you have often heard me say before on many other occasions: that I am subject to a divine or supernatural experience, which Meletus saw fit to travesty in his indictment. It began in my early childhood—a sort of voice which comes to me; and when it comes it always dissuades me from what I am proposing to do, and never urges me on. It is this that debars me from entering public life, and a very good thing too, in my opinion; because you may be quite sure, gentlemen, that if I had tried long ago to engage in politics, I should long ago have lost my life, without doing any good either to you or to myself. Please do not be offended if I tell you the truth. No man on earth who conscientiously opposes either you or any other organized democracy, and flatly prevents a great many wrongs and illegalities from taking place in the state to which he belongs, can possibly escape with his life. The true champion of justice, if he intends to survive even for a short time, must necessarily confine himself to private life and leave politics alone.

I will offer you substantial proofs of what I have said; not theories, but what you can appreciate better, facts. Listen while I describe my actual experiences, so that you may know that I would never submit wrongly to any authority through fear of death, but would refuse even at the cost of my life. It will be a commonplace story, such as you often hear in the courts; but it is true.

The only office which I have ever held in our city, gentlemen, was when I was elected to the Council. It so happened that our group was acting as the executive when you decided that the ten commanders who had failed to rescue the men who were lost in the naval engagement should be tried *en bloc*; which was illegal, as you all recognized later. On this occasion I was the only member of the executive who insisted that you should not act unconstitutionally, and voted against the proposal; and although your leaders were all ready to denounce and arrest me, and you were all urging them on at the top of your voices, I thought that it was my duty to face it out on the side of law and justice rather than support you, through fear of prison or death, in your wrong decision.

This happened while we were still under a democracy. When the oligarchy came into power, the Thirty Commissioners in their turn summoned me and four others to the Round Chamber and instructed us to go and fetch Leon of Salamis from his home for execution. This was of course only one of many instances in which they issued such instructions, their object being to implicate as many people as possible in their wickedness. On this occasion, however, I again made it clear not by my words but by my actions that death did not matter to me at all (if that is not too strong an expression); but that it mattered all the world to me that I should do nothing wrong or wicked. Powerful as it was, that government did not terrify me into doing a wrong action; when we came out of the Round Chamber the other four went off to Salamis and arrested Leon, and I went home. I should probably have been put to death for this, if the government had not fallen soon afterwards. There are plenty of people who will testify to these statements.

Do you suppose that I should have lived as long as I have if I had moved in the sphere of public life, and conducting myself in that sphere like an honourable man, had always upheld the cause of right, and conscientiously set this end above all other things? Not by a very long way, gentlemen; neither would any other man. You will find that throughout my life I have been consistent in any public duties that I have performed, and the same also in my personal dealings: I have never countenanced any action that was incompatible with justice on the part of any person, including those whom some people maliciously call my pupils. I have never set up as any man's teacher; but if anyone, young or old, is eager to hear me conversing and carrying out my private mission, I never grudge him the opportunity; nor do I charge a fee for talking to him, and refuse to talk without one; I am ready to answer questions for rich and poor alike, and I am equally ready if anyone prefers to listen to me and answer my questions. If any given one of these people becomes a good citizen or a bad one, I cannot fairly be held responsible, since I have never promised or imparted any teaching to anybody; and if anyone asserts that he has ever learned or heard from me privately anything which was not open to everyone else, you may be quite sure that he is not telling the truth.

But how is it that some people enjoy spending a great deal of time in my company? You have heard the reason, gentlemen; I told you quite frankly. It is because they enjoy hearing me examine those who think that they are wise when they are not; an experience which has its amusing side. This duty I have accepted, as I said, in obedience to God's commands given in oracles and dreams and in every other way that any other divine dispensation has ever impressed a duty upon man. This is a true statement, gentlemen, and easy to verify. If it is a fact that I am in the process of corrupting some of the young, and have succeeded already in corrupting others; and if it were a fact that some of the latter, being now grown up, had discovered that I had ever given them bad advice when they were young, surely they ought now to be coming forward to denounce and punish me; and if they did not like to do it themselves, you would expect some of their families—their fathers and brothers and other near relations—to remember it now, if their own flesh and blood had suffered any harm from me. Certainly a great many of them have found their way into this court, as I can see for myself: first Crito over there, my contemporary and near neighbour, the father of this young man Critobulus; and then Lysanias of Sphettus, the father of Aeschines here; and next Antiphon of Cephisia, over there, the father of Epigenes. Then besides there are all those whose brothers have been members of our circle: Nicostratus the son of Theozotides, the brother of Theodotus—but Theodotus is dead, so he cannot appeal to his brother—and Paralius here, the son of Demodocus; his brother was Theages. And here is Adimantus the son of Ariston, whose brother Plato is over there; and Aeantodorus, whose brother Apollodorus is here on this side. I can name many more besides, some of whom Meletus most certainly ought to have produced as witness in the course of his speech. If he forgot to do so then, let him do it now— I am willing to make way for him; let him state whether he has any such evidence to offer. On the contrary, gentlemen, you will find that they are all prepared to help me—the corrupter and evil genius of their nearest and dearest relatives, as Meletus and Anytus say. The actual victims of my corrupting influence might perhaps be excused for helping me; but as for the uncorrupted, their relations of mature age, what other reason can they have for helping me except the right and proper one, that they know Meletus is lying and I am telling the truth?

There, gentlemen: that, and perhaps a little more to the same effect, is the substance of what I can say in my defence. It may be that some one of you, remembering his own case, will be annoyed that whereas he, in standing his trial upon a less serious charge than this, made pitiful appeals to the jury with floods of tears, and had his infant children produced in court to excite the maximum of sympathy, and many of his relatives and friends as well, I on the contrary intend to do nothing of the sort, and that although I am facing (as it might appear) the utmost danger. It may be that one of you, reflecting on these facts, will be prejudiced against me, and being irritated by his reflections, will give his vote in anger. If one of you is so disposed—I do not expect it, but there is the possibility—I think that I should be quite justified in saying to him 'My dear sir, of course I have some relatives. To quote the very words of Homer, even I am not sprung "from an oak or from a rock," but from human parents, and consequently I have relatives; yes, and sons too, gentlemen, three of them, one almost grown up and the other two only children; but all the same I am not going to produce them here and beseech you to acquit me.'

Why do I not intend to do anything of this kind? Not out of perversity, gentlemen, not out of contempt for you; whether I am brave or not in the face of death has nothing to do with it; the point is that for my own credit and yours and for the credit of the state as a whole, I do not think that it is right for me to use any of these methods at my age and with my reputation—which may be true or it may be false, but at any rate the view is held that Socrates is different from the common run of mankind. Now if those of you who are supposed to be distinguished for wisdom or courage or any other virtue are to behave in this way, it would be a disgrace. I have often noticed that some people of this type, for all their high standing, go to extraordinary lengths when they come up for trial, which shows that they think it will be a dreadful thing to lose their lives; as though they would be immortal if you did not put them to death! In my opinion these people bring disgrace upon our city. Any of our visitors might be excused for thinking that the finest specimens of Athenian manhood, whom their fellow-citizens select on their merits to rule over them and hold other high positions, are no better than women. If you have even the smallest reputation, gentlemen, you ought not to descend to these methods; and if we do so, you must not give us licence. On the contrary, you must make it clear that anyone who stages these pathetic scenes and so brings ridicule upon our city is far more likely to be condemned than if he kept perfectly quiet.

But apart from all question of appearances, gentlemen, I do not think that it is right for a man to appeal to the jury or to get himself acquitted by doing so; he ought to inform them of the facts and convince them by argument. The jury does not sit to dispense justice as a favour, but to decide where justice lies; and the oath which they have sworn is not to show favour at their own discretion, but to return a just and lawful verdict. It follows that we must not develop in you, nor you allow to grow in yourselves, the habit of perjury; that would be sinful for us both. Therefore you must not expect me, gentlemen, to behave towards you in a way which I consider neither reputable nor moral nor consistent with my religious duty; and above all you must not expect it when I stand charged with impiety by Meletus here. Surely it is obvious that if I tried to persuade you and prevail upon you by my entreaties to go against your solemn oath, I should be teaching you contempt for religion and by my very defence I should be accusing myself of having no religious belief. But that is very far from the truth. I have a more sincere belief, gentlemen, than any of my accusers; and I leave it to you and to God to judge me as it shall be best for me and for yourselves.

(The verdict is 'Guilty', and Meletus proposes the penalty of death.)

There are a great many reasons, gentlemen, why I am not distressed by this result—I mean your condemnation of me—but the chief reason is that the result was not unexpected. What does surprise me is the number of votes cast on the two sides. I should never have believed that it would be such a close thing; but now it seems that if a mere thirty votes had gone the other way, I should have been acquitted. Even as it is, I feel that so far as Meletus' part is concerned I have been acquitted; and not only that, but anyone can see that if Anytus and Lycon had not come forward to accuse me, Meletus would actually have lost a thousand drachmae for not having obtained one-fifth of the votes.

However, we must face the fact that he demands the death-penalty. Very good. What alternative penalty shall I propose to you, gentlemen? Obviously it must be adequate. Well, what penalty do I deserve to pay or suffer, in view of what I have done?

I have never lived an ordinary quiet life. I did not care for the things that most people care about: making money, having a comfortable home, high military or civil rank, and all the other activities—political appointments, secret societies, party organizations—which go on in our city; I thought that I was really too strict in my principles to survive if I went in for this sort of thing. So instead of taking a course which would have done no good either to you or to me, I set myself to do you individually in private what I hold to be the greatest possible service: I tried to persuade each one of you not to think of more practical advantages than of his mental and moral well-being, or in general to think more of advantage than of well-being in the case of the state or of anything else. What do I deserve for behaving in this way? Some reward, gentlemen, if I am bound to suggest what I really deserve; and what is more, a reward which would be appropriate for myself. Well, what is appropriate for a poor man who is a public benefactor and who requires leisure for giving you moral encouragement? Nothing could be more appropriate for such a person than free maintenance at the State's expense. He deserves it much more than any victor in the races at Olympia, whether he wins with a single horse or a pair or a team of four. These people give you the semblance of success, but I give you the reality; they do not need maintenance, but I do. So if I am to suggest an appropriate penalty which is strictly in accordance with justice, I suggest free maintenance by the State.

Perhaps when I say this I may give you the impression, as I did in my remarks about exciting sympathy and making passionate appeals, that I am showing a deliberate perversity. That is not so, gentlemen; the real position is this. I am convinced that I never wrong anyone intentionally, but I cannot convince you of this, because we have had so little time for discussion. If it was your practice, as it is with other nations, to give not one day but several to the hearing of capital trials, I believe that you might have been convinced; but under present conditions it is not easy to dispose of grave allegations in a short space of time. So being convinced that I do no wrong to anybody, I can hardly be expected to wrong myself by asserting that I deserve something bad, or by proposing a corresponding penalty. Why should I? For fear of suffering this penalty proposed by Meletus, when, as I said, I do not know whether it is a good thing or a bad? Do you expect me to choose something which I know very well is bad by making my counter-proposal? Imprisonment? Why should I spend my days in prison, in subjection to the periodically appointed officers of the law? A fine, with imprisonment until it is paid? In my case the effect would be just the same, because I have no money to pay a fine. Or shall I suggest banishment? You would very likely accept the suggestion.

I should have to be desperately in love with life to do that, gentlemen. I am not so blind that I cannot see that you, my fellow-citizens, have come to the end of your patience with my discussions and conversations; you have found them too irksome and irritating, and now you are trying to get rid of them. Will any other people find them easy to put up with? That is most unlikely, gentlemen. A fine life I should have if I left this country at my age and spent the rest of my days trying one city after another and being turned out every time! I know very well that wherever I go the young people will listen to my conversation just as they do here; and if I try to keep them off, they will make their elders drive me out, while if I do not, the fathers and other relatives will drive me out of their own accord for the sake of the young.

Perhaps someone may say 'But surely, Socrates, after you have left us you can spend the rest of your life in quietly minding your own business.' This is the hardest thing of all to make some of you understand. If I say that this would be disobedience to God, and that is why I cannot 'mind my own business', you will not believe that I am serious. If on the other hand I tell you that to let no day pass without discussing goodness and all the other subjects about which you hear me talking and examining both myself and others is really the very best thing that a man can do, and that life without this sort of examination is not worth living, you will be even less inclined to believe me. Nevertheless that is how it is, gentlemen, as I maintain; though it is not easy to convince you of it. Besides, I am not accustomed to think of myself as deserving punishment. If I had money, I would have suggested a fine that I could afford, because that would not have done me any harm. As it is, I cannot, because I have none; unless of course you like to fix the penalty at what I could pay. I suppose I could probably afford a hundred drachmae. I suggest a fine of that amount.

One moment, gentlemen. Plato here, and Crito and Critobulus and Apollodorus, want me to propose three thousand drachmae on their security. Very well, I agree to this sum, and you can rely upon these gentlemen for its payment.

(The jury decides for the death-penalty.)

Well, gentlemen, for the sake of a very small gain in time you are going to earn the reputation—and the blame from those who wish to disparage our city—of having put Socrates to death, 'that wise man'— because they will say I am wise even if I am not, these people who want to find fault with you. If you had waited just a little while, you would have had your way in the course of nature. You can see that I am well on in life and near to death. I am saying this not to all of you but to those who voted for my execution, and I have something else to say to them as well.

No doubt you think, gentlemen, that I have been condemned for lack of the arguments which I could have used if I had thought it right to leave nothing unsaid or undone to secure my acquittal. But that is very far from the truth. It is not a lack of arguments that has caused my condemnation, but a lack of effrontery and impudence, and the fact that I have refused to address you in the way which would give you most pleasure. You would have liked to hear me weep and wail, doing and saying all sorts of things which I regard as unworthy of myself, but which you are used to hearing from other people. But I did not think then that I ought to stoop to servility because I was in danger, and I do not regret now the way in which I pleaded my case; I would much rather die as the result of this defence than live as the result of the other sort. In a court of law, just as in warfare, neither I nor any other ought to use his wits to escape death by any means. In battle it is often obvious that you could escape being killed by giving up your arms and throwing yourself upon the mercy of your pursuers; and in every kind of danger there are plenty of devices for avoiding death if you are unscrupulous enough to stick at nothing. But I suggest, gentlemen, that the difficulty is not so much to escape death; the real difficulty is to escape from doing wrong, which is far more fleet of foot. In this present instance I, the slow old man, have been overtaken by the slower of the two, but my accusers, who are clever and quick, have been overtaken by the faster: by iniquity. When I leave this court I shall go away condemned by you to death, but they will go away convicted by Truth herself of depravity and wickedness. And they accept their sentence even as I accept mine. No doubt it was bound to be so, and I think that the result is fair enough.

Having said so much, I feel moved to prophesy to you who have given your vote against me; for I am now at that point where the gift of prophecy comes most readily to men: at the point of death. I tell you, my executioners, that as soon as I am dead, vengeance shall fall upon you with a punishment far more painful than your killing of me. You have brought about my death in the belief that through it you will be delivered from submitting your conduct to criticism; but I say that the result will be just the opposite. You will have more critics, whom up till now I have restrained without your knowing it; and being younger they will be harsher to you and will cause you more annoyance. If you expect to stop denunciation of your wrong way of life by putting people to death, there is something amiss with your reasoning. This way of escape is neither possible nor creditable; the best and easiest way is not to stop the mouths of others, but to make yourselves as good men as you can. This is my last message to you who voted for my condemnation.

As for you who voted for my acquittal, I should very much like to say a few words to reconcile you to the result, while the officials are busy and I am not yet on my way to the place where I must die. I ask you, gentlemen, to spare me these few moments; there is no reason why we should not exchange fancies while the law permits. I look upon you as my friends, and I want you to understand the right way of regarding my present position.

Gentlemen of the jury—for *you* deserve to be so called—I have had a remarkable experience. In the past the prophetic voice to which I have become accustomed has always been my constant companion, opposing me even in quite trivial things if I was going to take the wrong course. Now something has happened to me, as you can see, which might be thought and is commonly considered to be a supreme calamity; yet neither when I left home this morning, nor when I was taking my place here in the court, nor at any point in any part of my speech did the divine sigh oppose me. In other discussions it has often checked me in the middle of a sentence; but this time it has never opposed me in any part of this business in anything that I have said or done. What do I suppose to be the explanation? I will tell you. I suspect that this thing that has happened to me is a blessing, and we are quite mistaken in supposing death to be an evil. I have good grounds for thinking this, because my accustomed sign could not have failed to oppose me if what I was doing had not been sure to bring some good result.

We should reflect that there is much reason to hope for a good result on other grounds as well. Death is one of two things. Either it is annihilation, and the dead have no consciousness of anything; or, as we are told, it is really a change: a migration of the soul from this place to another. Now if there is no consciousness but only a dreamless sleep, death must be a marvelous gain. I suppose that if anyone were told to pick out the night on which he slept so soundly as not even to dream, and then to compare it with all the other nights and days of his life, and then were told to say, after due consideration, how many better and happier days and nights than this he had spent in the course of his life—well, I think that the Great King himself, to say nothing of any private person, would find these days and nights easy to count in comparison with the rest. If death is like this, then, I call it gain; because the whole of time, if you look at it in this way, can be regarded as no more than one single night. If on the other hand death is a removal from here to some other place, and if what we are told is true, that all the dead are there, what greater blessing could there be than this, gentlemen? If on arrival in the other world, beyond the reach of our so-called justice, one will find there the true judges who are said to preside in those courts, Minos and Rhadamanthys and Aeacus and Triptolemus and all those other half-divinities who were upright in their earthly life, would that be an unrewarding journey? Put it in this way: how much would one of you give to meet Orpheus and Musaeus, Hesiod and Homer? I am willing to die ten times over if this account is true. It would be a specially interesting experience for me to join them there, to meet Palamedes and Ajax the son of Telamon and any other heroes of the old days who met their death through an unfair trial, and to compare my fortunes with theirs—it would be rather amusing, I think—; and above all I should like to spend my time there, as here, in examining and searching people's minds, to find out who is really wise among them, and who only thinks that he is. What would one not give, gentlemen, to be able to question the leader of that great host against Troy, or Odysseus, or Sisyphus, or the thousands of other men and women whom one could mention, to talk and mix and argue with whom would be unimaginable happiness? At any rate I presume that they do not put one to death there for such conduct; because apart from the other happiness in which their world surpasses ours, they are now immortal for the rest of time, if what we are told is true.

You too, gentlemen of the jury, must look forward to death with confidence, and fix your minds on this one belief, which is certain: that nothing can harm a good man either in life or after death, and his fortunes are not a matter of indifference to the gods. This present experience of mine has not come about mechanically; I am quite clear that the time had come when it was better for me to die and be released from my distractions. That is why my sign never turned me back. For my own part I bear no grudge at all against those who condemned me and accused me, although it was not with this kind intention that they did so, but because they thought that they were hurting me; and that is culpable of them. However, I ask them to grant me one favour. When my sons grow up, gentlemen, if you think that they are putting money or anything else before goodness, take your revenge by plaguing them as I plagued you; and if they fancy themselves for no reason, you must scold them just as I scolded you, for neglecting the important things and thinking that they are good for something when they are good for nothing. If you do this, I shall have had justice at your hands, both I myself and my children.

Now it is time that we were going, I to die and you to live; but which of us has the happier prospects is unknown to anyone but God.

—Translated by Hugh Tredennick

From the *Republic*, Book VII:

The "Allegory of the Cave"

"Next, then," I said, "take the following parable of education and ignorance as a picture of the condition of our nature. Imagine mankind as dwelling in an underground cave with a long entrance open to the light across the whole width of the cave; in this they have been from childhood, with necks and legs fettered, so they have to stay where they are. They cannot move their heads round because of the fetters, and they can only look forward, but light comes to them from fire burning behind them higher up at a distance. Between the fire and the prisoners is a road above their level, and along it imagine a low wall has been built, as puppet showmen have screens in front of their people over which they work their puppets."

"I see," he said.

"See, then, bearers carrying along this wall all sorts of articles which they hold projecting above the wall, statues of men and other living things made of stone or wood and all kinds of stuff, some of the bearers speaking and some silent, as you might expect."

"What a remarkable image," he said, "and what remarkable prisoners!"

"Just like ourselves," I said. "For, first of all, tell me this: What do you think such people would have seen of themselves and each other except their shadows, which the fire cast on the opposite wall of the cave?"

"I don't see how they could see anything else," said he, "if they were compelled to keep their heads unmoving all their lives!"

"Very well, what of the things being carried along? Would not this be the same?"

"Of course it would."

"Suppose the prisoners were able to talk together, don't you think that when they named the shadows which they saw passing they would believe they were naming things?"

"Necessarily."

"Then if their prison had an echo from the opposite wall, whenever one of the passing bearers uttered a sound, would they not suppose that the passing shadow must be making the sound? Don't you think so?"

"Indeed I do," he said.

"If so," said I, "such persons would certainly believe that there were no realities except those shadows of handmade things."

"So it must be," he said.

"Now consider," said I, "what their release would be like, and their cure from these fetters and their folly; let us imagine whether it might naturally be something like this. One might be released, and compelled suddenly to stand up and turn his neck round, and to walk and look towards the firelight; all this would hurt him, and he would be too much dazzled to see distinctly those things whose shadows he had seen before. What do you think he would say, if someone told him that what he saw before was foolery, but now he saw more rightly, being a bit nearer reality and turned towards what was a little more real? What if he were shown each of the passing things, and compelled by questions to answer what each one was? Don't you think he would be puzzled, and believe what he saw before was more true than what was shown to him now?"

"Far more," he said.

"Then suppose he were compelled to look towards the real light, it would hurt his eyes, and he would escape by turning them away to the things which he was able to look at, and these he would believe to be clearer than what was being shown to him."

"Just so," said he.

"Suppose, now," said I, "that someone should drag him thence by force, up the rough ascent, the steep way up, and never stop until he could drag him out into the light of the sun, would he not be distressed and furious at being dragged; and when he came into the light, the brilliance would fill his eyes and he would not be able to see even one of the things now called real?"

"That he would not," said he, "all of a sudden."

"He would have to get used to it, surely, I think, if he is to see the things above. First he would most easily look at shadows, after that images of mankind and the rest in water, lastly the things themselves. After this he would find it easier to survey by night the heavens themselves and all that is in them, gazing at the light of the stars and moon, rather than by day the sun and sun's light."

"Of course."

"Last of all, I suppose, the sun; he could look on the sun itself by itself in its own place, and see what it is like, not reflections of it in water or as it appears in some alien setting."

"Necessarily," said he.

"And only after all this he might reason about it, how this is he who provides seasons and years, and is set over all there is in the visible region, and he is in a manner the cause of all things which they saw."

"Yes, it is clear," said he, "that after all that, he would come to this last."

"Very good. Let him be reminded of his first habitation, and what was wisdom in that place, and of his fellow-prisoners there: don't you think he would bless himself for the change, and pity them?"

"Yes, indeed."

"And if there were honours and praises among them and prizes for the one who saw the passing things most sharply and remembered best which of them used to come before and which after and which together, and from these was best able to prophesy accordingly what was going to come—do you believe he would set his desire on that, and envy those who were honoured men or potentates among them? Would he not feel as Homer says, and heartily desire rather to be serf of some landless man of earth and to endure anything in the world, rather than to opine as they did and to live in that way?"

"Yes indeed," said he, "he would rather accept anything than live like that."

"Then again," I said, "just consider; if such a one should go down again and sit on his old seat, would he not get his eyes full of darkness coming in suddenly out of the sun?"

"Very much so," said he.

"And if he should have to compete with those who had been always prisoners, by laying down the law about those shadows while he was blinking before his eyes were settled down—and it would take a good long time to get used to things— wouldn't they all laugh at him and say he had spoiled his eyesight by going up there, and it was not worth-while so much as to try to go up? And would they not kill anyone who tried to release them and take them up, if they could somehow lay hands on him and kill him?"

"That they would!" said he.

"Then we must apply this image, my dear Glaucon," said I, "to all we have been saying. The world of our sight is like the habitation in prison, the firelight there to the sunlight here, the ascent and the view of the upper world is the rising of the soul into the world of mind; put it so and you will not be far from my own surmise, since that is what you want to hear; but God knows if it is really true. At least, what appears to me is, that in the world of the known, last of all is the idea of the good, and with what toil to be seen! And seen, this must be inferred to be the cause of all right and beautiful things for all, which gives birth to light and the king of light in the world of sight, and, in the world of mind, herself the queen produces truth and reason; and she must be seen by one who is to act with reason publicly or privately."

"I believe as you do," he said, "in so far as I am able."

"Then believe also, as I do," said I, "and do not be surprised, that those who come thither are not willing to have part in the affairs of men, but their souls ever strive to remain above; for that surely may be expected if our parable fits the case."

"Quite so," he said.

"Well then," said I, "do you think it surprising if one leaving divine contemplation and passing to the evils of men is awkward and appears to be a great fool, while he is still blinking—not yet accustomed to the darkness around him, but compelled to struggle in law courts or elsewhere about shadows of justice, or the images which make the shadows, and to quarrel about notions of justice in those who have never seen justice itself?"

"Not surprising at all," said he.

"But any man of sense," I said, "would remember that the eyes are double confused from two different causes, both in passing from light to darkness and from darkness to light; and believing that the same things happen with regard to the soul also, whenever he sees a soul confused and unable to discern anything he would not just laugh carelessly; he would examine whether it had come out of a more brilliant life, and if it were darkened by the strangeness; or whether it had come out of greater ignorance into a more brilliant light, and if it were dazzled with the brighter illumination. Then only would he congratulate the one soul upon its happy experience and way of life, and pity the other; but if he must laugh, his laugh would be a less downright laugh than his laughter at the soul which came out of the light above."

"That is fairly put," said he.

"Then if this is true," I said, "our belief about these matters must be this, that the nature of education is not really such as some of its professors say it is; as you know, they say that there is not understanding in the soul, but they put it in, as if they were putting sight into blind eyes."

"They do say so," said he.

"But our reasoning indicates," I said, "that this power is already in the soul of each, and is the instrument by which each learns; thus if the eye could not see without being turned with the whole body from the dark towards the light, so this instrument must be turned round with the whole soul away from the world of becoming until it is able to endure the sight of being and the most brilliant light of being: and this we say is the good, don't we?"

"Yes."

"Then this instrument," said I, "must have its own art, for the circumturning or conversion, to show how the turn can be most easily and successfully made; not an art of putting sight into an eye, which we say has it already, but since the instrument has not been turned aright and does not look where it ought to look—that's what must be managed."

"So it seems," he said.

"Now most of the virtues which are said to belong to the soul are really something near to those of the body; for in fact they are not already there, but they are put later into it by habits and practices; but the virtue of understanding everything really belongs to something certainly more divine, as it seems, for it never loses its power, but becomes useful and helpful or, again, useless and harmful, by the direction in which it is turned. Have you not noticed men who are called worthless but clever, and how keen and sharp is the sight of their petty soul, and how it sees through the things towards which it is turned? Its sight is clear enough, but it is compelled to be the servant of vice, so that the clearer it sees the more evil it does."

"Certainly," said he.

"Yet if this part of such a nature," said I, "had been hammered at from childhood, and all those leaden weights of the world of becoming knocked off—the weights, I mean, which grow into the soul from gorging and gluttony and such pleasures, and twist the soul's eye downwards—if, I say, it had shaken these off and been turned round towards what is real and true, that same instrument of those same men would have seen those higher things most clearly, just as now it sees those towards which it is turned."

"Quite likely," said he.

"Very well," said I, "isn't it equally likely, indeed, necessary, after what has been said, that men uneducated and without experience of truth could never properly supervise a city, nor can those who are allowed to spend all their lives in education right to the end? The first have no single object in life, which they must always aim at in doing everything they do, public or private; the second will never do anything if they can help it, believing they have already found mansions abroad in the Islands of the Blest."

"True," said he.

"Then it is the task of us founders," I said, "to compel the best natures to attain that learning which we said was the greatest, both to see the good, and to ascend that ascent; and when they have ascended and properly seen, we must never allow them what is allowed now."

"What is that, pray?" he asked.

"To stay there," I said, "and not be willing to descend again to those prisoners, and to share their troubles and their honours, whether they are worth having or not."

"What!" said he, "are we to wrong them and make them live badly, when they might live better?"

"You have forgotten again, my friend," said I, "that the law is not concerned how any one class in a city is to prosper above the rest; it tries to contrive prosperity in the city as a whole, fitting the citizens into a pattern by persuasion and compulsion, making them give of their help to one another wherever each class is able to help the community. The law itself creates men like this in the city, not in order to allow each one to turn by any way he likes, but in order to use them itself to the full for binding the city together."

"True," said he, "I did forget."

"Notice then, Glaucon," I said, "we shall not wrong the philosophers who grow up among us, but we shall treat them fairly when we compel them to add to their duties the care and guardianship of the other people. We shall tell them that those who grow up philosophers in other cities have reason in taking no part in public labours there; for they grow up there of themselves, though none of the city governments wants them; a wild growth has its rights, it owes nurture to no one, and need not trouble to pay anyone for its food. But you we have engendered, like king bees in hives, as leaders and kings over yourselves and the rest of the city; you have been better and more perfectly educated than the others, and are better able to share in both ways of life. Down you must go then, in turn, to the habitation of the others, and accustom yourselves to their darkness; for when you have grown accustomed you will see a thousand times better than those who live there, and you will know what the images are and what they are images of, because you have seen the realities behind just and beautiful and good things. And so our city will be managed wide awake for us and for you, not in a dream, as most are now, by people fighting together for shadows, and quarreling to be rulers, as if that were a great good. But the truth is more or less that the city where those who are to rule are least anxious to be rulers is of necessity best managed and has least faction in it: while the city which gets rulers who want it most is worst managed."

"Certainly," said he.

"Then will our fosterlings disobey us when they hear this? Will they refuse to help, each group in its turn, in the labours of the city, and want to spend most of their time dwelling in the pure air?"

"Impossible," said he, "for we shall only be laying just commands on just men. No, but undoubtedly each man of them will go to the ruler's place as to a grim necessity, exactly the opposite of those who now rule in cities."

"For the truth, is, my friend," I said, "that only if you can find for your future rulers a way of life better than ruling, is it possible for you to have a well-managed city; since in that city alone those will rule who are truly rich, not rich in gold, but in that which is necessary for a happy man, the riches of a good and wise life: but if beggared and hungry, for want of goods of their own, they hasten to public affairs, thinking that they must snatch goods for themselves from there, it is not possible. Then rule becomes a thing to be fought for; and a war of such a kind, being between citizens and within them, destroys both them and the rest of the city also."

—Translated by W.H.D. Rouse

ARISTOTLE

The philosopher Aristotle (384-323 B.C.) is such a towering figure in Western thought that medieval scholars referred to him merely as "the Philosopher." Aristotle's thought was characterized by an encyclopedic range and a clarity of argument that profoundly affected the course of Western philosophy, as well as Jewish and Arabic thought. In contrast to Plato's search for ideal forms, Aristotle sought to describe and analyze the world that he observed around him.

In his *Nicomachean Ethics*, Aristotle defines *eudaimonia* ("happiness"), which he considers to be the proper aim of human action. In the selection here, the philosopher rigorously distinguishes happiness from pleasure and possessions, seeking to define the human quality closest to "the good." In the remainder of the *Ethics*, Aristotle explains that the virtuous human being tends always to choose a mean between two extremes of human action.

From the *Nichomachean Ethics*, Book 1 : On Happiness

Let us now turn back again to the good which is the object of our search, and ask what it can possibly be; because it appears to vary with the action or art. It is one thing in medicine and another in strategy, and similarly in all the other sciences. What, then, is the good of each particular one? Surely it is that for the sake of which everything else is done. In medicine this is health; in strategy, victory; in architecture, a building—different things in different arts, but in every action and pursuit it is the *end*, since it is for the sake of this that everything else is done. Consequently if there is any one thing that is the end of all actions, this will be the practical good—or goods, if there are more than one. Thus while changing its ground the argument has reached the same conclusion as before.

We must try, however, to make our meaning still clearer. Since there are evidently more ends than one, and of these we choose some (e.g., wealth or musical instruments or tools generally) as means to something else, it is clear that not all of them are final ends, whereas the supreme good is obviously something final. So if there is only one final end, this will be the good of which we are in search; and if there are more than one, it will be the most final of these. Now we call an object pursued for its own sake more final than one pursued because of something else, and one which is never choosable because of another more final than those which are choosable because of it as well as for their own sakes; and that which is always choosable for its own sake and never because of something else we call final without any qualification.

Well, happiness more than anything else is thought to be just such an end, because we always choose it for itself, and never for any other reason. It is different with honour, pleasure, intelligence and good qualities generally. We do choose them partly for themselves (because we should choose each one of them irrespectively of any consequences); but we choose them also for the sake of our happiness, in the belief that they will be instrumental in promoting it. On the other hand nobody chooses happiness for *their* sake, or in general for any other reason.

The same conclusion seems to follow from another consideration. It is a generally accepted view that the perfect good is self-sufficient. By self-sufficient we mean not what is sufficient for oneself alone living a solitary life, but something that includes parents, wife and children, friends and fellow-citizens in general; for man is by nature a social being. (We must set some limit to these, for if we extend the application to grandparents and grandchildren and friends of friends it will proceed to infinity; but we must consider this point later.) A self-sufficient thing, then, we take to be one which by itself makes life desirable and in no way deficient; and we believe that happiness is such a thing. What is more, we regard it as the most desirable of all things, not reckoned as one item among many; if it were so reckoned, happiness would obviously be more desirable by the addition of even the least good, because the addition makes the sum of goods greater, and the greater of two goods is always more desirable. Happiness, then, is found to be something perfect and self-sufficient, being the end to which our actions are directed.

But presumably to say that happiness is the supreme good seems a platitude, and some more distinctive account of it is still required. This might perhaps be achieved by grasping what is the function of man. If we take a flautist or a sculptor or any artist—or in general any class of men who have a specific function or activity—his goodness and proficiency is considered to lie in the performance of that function; and the same will be true of man, assuming that man has a function. But is it likely that whereas joiners and shoemakers have certain functions or activities, man as such has none, but has been left by nature a functionless being? Just as we can see that eye and hand and foot and everyone of our members has some function, should we not assume that in like manner a human being has a function over and above these particular functions? What, then, can this possibly be? Clearly life is a thing shared also by plants, and we are looking for man's *proper* function; so we must exclude from our definition the life that consists in nutrition and growth. Next in order would be a sort of sentient life; but this too we see is shared by horses and cattle and animals of all kinds. There remains, then, a practical life of the rational part. (This has two aspects: one amenable to reason, the other possessing it and initiating thought.) As this life also has two meanings, we must lay down that we intend here life determined by activity, because this is accepted as the stricter sense. Now if the function of man is an activity of the soul in accordance with, or implying, a rational principle; and if we hold that the function of an individual and of a good individual of the same kind—e.g., of a harpist and of a good harpist, and so on generally—is generically the same, the latter's distinctive excellence being attached to the name of the function (because the function of the harpist is to play the harp, but that of the good harpist is to play it well); and if we assume that the function of man is a kind of life, viz., an activity or series of actions of the soul, implying a rational principle; and if the function of a good man is to perform these well and rightly; and if every function is performed well when performed in accordance with its proper excellence: if all this is so, the conclusion is that the good for man is an activity of soul in accordance with virtue, or if there are more kinds of virtue than one, in accordance with the best and most perfect kind....

Now our definition is in harmony with those who say that happiness is virtue, or a particular virtue; because an activity in accordance with virtue implies virtue. But presumably it makes no little difference whether we think of the supreme good as consisting in the *possession* or in the *exercise* of virtue: in a state of mind or in an activity. For it is possible for the *state* to be present in a person without effecting any good result (e.g., if he is asleep or quiescent in some other way), but not for the *activity:* he will necessarily act, and act well. Just as at the Olympic Games it is not the best-looking or the strongest men present that are crowned with wreaths, but the competitors (because it is from them that the winners come), so it is those who *act* that rightly win the honours and rewards in life.

Moreover, the life of such people is in itself pleasant. For pleasure is an experience of the soul, and each individual finds pleasure in that of which he is said to be fond. For example, a horse gives pleasure to one who is fond of horses, and a spectacle to one who is fond of sight-seeing. In the same way just acts give pleasure to a lover of justice, and virtuous conduct generally to the lover of virtue. Now most people find that the things which give them pleasure conflict; because they are not pleasant by nature; but lovers of beauty find pleasure in things that are pleasant by nature, and virtuous actions are of this kind, so that they are pleasant not only to this type of person but also in themselves. So their life does not need to have pleasure attached to it as a sort of accessory, but contains its own pleasure in itself. Indeed, we may go further and assert that anyone who does not delight in fine actions is not even a good man; for nobody would say that a man is just unless he enjoys acting justly, nor liberal unless he enjoys liberal actions, and similarly in all the other cases. If this is so, virtuous actions must be pleasurable in themselves. What is more, they are both good and fine, and each in the highest degree, assuming that the good man is right in his judgment of them; and his judgment is as we have described. So happiness is the best, the finest, the most pleasurable thing of all; and these qualities are not separated as the inscription at Delos suggests:

Justice is loveliest, and health is best,
But sweetest to obtain is heart's desire.

All these attributes belong to the best activities; and it is these, or the one that is best of them, that we identify with happiness.

Nevertheless it seems clear that happiness needs the addition of external goods, as we have said; for it is difficult if not impossible to do fine deeds without any resources. Many can only be done by the help of friends, or wealth, or political influence. There are also certain advantages, such as good ancestry or good children, or personal beauty, the lack of which mars our felicity; for a man is scarcely happy if he is very ugly to look at, or of low birth, or solitary and childless; and presumably even less so if he has children or friends who are quite worthless, or if he had good ones who are now dead. So, as we said, happiness seems to require this sort of prosperity too; which is why some identify it with good fortune, although others identify it with virtue.

—Translated by J.A.K. Thomson

3

The Romans

As is true in the Roman arts, the development of a Latin literature and philosophy dates from the Roman's first contact with Greek civilization in the second century B.C. Virtually every learned Roman author, including writers of all the selections here, composed with a Greek example clearly in mind.

Roman literature is conventionally divided into a Golden or Classic Age (ca. 100 B.C.–A.D. 14) and a Silver Age (A.D. 14–150). The Golden Age encompasses the first significant Roman authors, including Julius Caesar and Cicero, reaching its high point in the poetry of Virgil and Ovid, author of the *Metamorphoses*, and the history of Livy. The Silver Age is generally seen as a period of some decline and is marked by the satirical poetry of Petronius and Juvenal.

Though they often lack the ancient Greeks' profoundly philosophical view of life, the greatest Roman works express an inimitable spirit of practicality and worldliness. This is true in minor works like Catullus's poetry, in which the bitterness of unrequited love coexists with a sense of the absurdity of passion. The great hero Aeneas stoically accepts and dutifully carries out the task of founding the Latin race, instead of dying tragically in defense of Troy. The Greek tradition has no equivalent to Marcus Aurelius, the introspective emperor who mingles his philosophy with the daily exercise of power.

Roman authors are also important for their role as the principal conduit of classical ideas and literature to the Middle Ages and Renaissance. For virtually a thousand years, European civilization was isolated from Greece and largely ignorant of the original writings of Greek poets and philosophers. The Romans' assimilation of Greek models helped preserve the classical spirit for many centuries after Rome's great empire had fallen.

CATULLUS

The poet Catullus (ca. 84–ca. 54 B.C.) was a fashionable literary figure of the late Roman Republic, an acquaintance of Julius Caesar and Cicero. Often in imitation of Hellenistic poets, Catullus wrote learned occasional poems, characterized by his use of colloquial language in traditionally elevated poetic settings. His most famous poems concern his love affair with a woman he calls Lesbia (most likely the wife of a Roman public official). These poems frankly reveal Catullus's passion and his growing doubts and bitterness. Written when traditional values were being challenged by Rome's new power and prosperity, Catullus's lyrics anticipate the literate decadence of much later Roman poets like Petronius.

For analysis and interpretation:

1. Describe the poetic tone of Catullus's passionate enthusiasm. How do you expect this tone might change as love fades?

2. Evaluate the frank decadence and sensualism of Catullus's poetry. How does it compare to other examples of literary hedonism, such as the poem from the *Carmina Burana* (Chapter 5)?

1

My Lesbia, let us live and love
And not care tuppence for old men
Who sermonise and disapprove.
Suns when they sink can rise again,
But we, when our brief light has shone,
Must sleep the long night on and on.
Kiss me: a thousand kisses, then
A hundred more, and now a second
Thousand and hundred, and now still
Hundreds and thousands more, until
The thousand thousands can't be reckoned
And we've lost track of the amount
And nobody can work us ill
With the evil eye by keeping count.

2

Fabullus, if the gods are kind,
In a few days you'll be wined and dined
At my house—if it's understood
You bring the feast with you: good food,
Good wine, a pretty girl, salt wit,

And lots of laughs to garnish it.
Those are the terms of my fine dinner,
Sweet friend, for the old cobweb-spinner
Is busy in my purse. My side
Of the bargain will be to provide
The most delicious of all presents
Imaginable, love's pure essence—
The ointment which was my girl's gift
From Venus and the Loves. Once sniffed,
You'll beg the gods to metamorphose
Fabullus into one huge nose!

3

Yesterday, to while time away,
Licinius, we agreed to play
A naughty game of epigrams, using
My tablets. Scribbling verses, choosing
Any old metre, each one taking
Turns, we had fun, drinking and making
Jokes. And I left so laughter-lit
By your incendiary wit
That food gave me no appetite
And, open-eyed, I spent all night
Bed-wandering in delirium
And longing for the light to come,
To talk and be with you. Half-dead
At last, dog-weary on my bed,
I wrote this so that you could read,
Sweet friend, how desperate is my need.
Now, apple of my eye, don't tease me,
By playing proud. Humour me, please me,
Otherwise Nemesis will inflict
Punishment; she's a very strict
Goddess, not to be lightly tricked.

—Translated by James Michie

VIRGIL

No ancient poet has been more esteemed in the Western tradition than Virgil (70–19 B.C.), no epic poem more widely read than Virgil's *Aeneid*. The story of Aeneas's escape from a burning Troy and his voyage to Italy contains all the essential heroic elements that Virgil gleaned from his models, the *Iliad* and *Odyssey*. However, Virgil's Aeneas is a purely Roman hero in his central aim: he struggles, not for the individual glory of heroic fame, but for the higher purpose of founding the race that will rule the world.

Virgil opens with the line, "I sing of warfare and a man at war," a great warrior, like Homer's Achilles, who undertakes a great voyage, like Odysseus. Aeneas has left his ruined homeland to found a new race of heroes in Italy, as directed by the gods. The jealous goddess Juno, however, guides his fleet off course to Carthage in northern Africa. Here, in a scene reminiscent of Odysseus before the Phaecians, Aeneas narrates his adventures to a rapt audience.

As the poem recounts in Book IV, the Carthaginian queen Dido is fired by passion for the Trojan, and the two begin a liaison that distracts Aeneas for a year's time. The dalliance with Dido is the epic's greatest test of Aeneas's devotion to duty, more so than the later battle with Italy's native tribes. Aeneas's dutiful submission to his destiny pales in comparison to the self-immolating heat of Dido's passion.

For analysis and interpretation:

1. Explain the reasons why Dido hesitates to pursue Aeneas and her sister Anna urges her to proceed.

2. How are the conflicting purposes of the gods reflected in the mixed emotions of the story's human characters?

3. How can Dido be seen as a tragic hero, in the mold of Sophocles' Oedipus?

The Aeneid: ## Book I

I sing of warfare and a man at war.
From the sea-coast of Troy in early days
He came to Italy by destiny,
To our Lavinian western shore,
A fugitive, this captain, buffeted
Cruelly on land as on the sea
By blows from powers of the air—behind them
Baleful Juno in her sleepless rage.
And cruel losses were his lot in war,
Till he could found a city and bring home
His gods to Latium, land of the Latin race,
The Alban lords, and the high walls of Rome.
Tell me the causes now, O Muse, how galled
In her divine pride, and how sore at heart
From her old wound, the queen of gods compelled him—
A man apart, devoted to his mission—
To undergo so many perilous days
And enter on so many trials. Can anger

Black as this prey on the minds of heaven?
Tyrian settlers in that ancient time
Held Carthage, on the far shore of the sea,
Set against Italy and Tiber's mouth,
A rich new town, warlike and trained for war.
And Juno, we are told, cared more for Carthage
Than for any walled city of the earth,
More than for Samos, even. There her armor
And chariot were kept, and, fate permitting,
Carthage would be the ruler of the world.
So she intended, and so nursed that power.
But she had heard long since
That generations born of Trojan blood
Would one day overthrow her Tyrian walls,
And from that blood a race would come in time
With ample kingdoms, arrogant in war,
For Libya's ruin: so the Parcae spun.
In fear of this, and holding in memory
The old war she had carried on at Troy
For Argos' sake (the origins of that anger,
That suffering, still rankled: deep within her,
Hidden away, the judgment Paris gave,
Snubbing her loveliness; the race she hated;
The honors given ravished Ganymede),
Saturnian Juno, burning for it all,
Buffeted on the waste of sea those Trojans
Left by the Greeks and pitiless Achilles,
Keeping them far from Latium. For years
They wandered as their destiny drove them on
From one sea to the next: so hard and huge
A task it was to found the Roman people. . .

The Aeneid:
Book IV

The queen, for her part, all that evening ached
With longing that her heart's blood fed, a wound
Or inward fire eating her away.
The manhood of the man, his pride of birth,
Came home to her time and again; his looks,
His words remained with her to haunt her mind,
And desire for him gave her no rest.
                        When Dawn

Swept earth with Phoebus' torch and burned away
Night-gloom and damp, this queen, far gone and ill,
Confided to the sister of her heart:
"My sister Anna, quandaries and dreams
Have come to frighten me—such dreams!
                          Think what a stranger
Yesterday found lodging in our house:
How princely, how courageous, what a soldier.
I can believe him in the line of gods,
And this is no delusion. Tell-tale fear
Betrays inferior souls. What scenes of war
Fought to the bitter end he pictured for us!
What buffetings awaited him at sea!
Had I not set my face against remarriage
After my first love died and failed me, left me
Barren and bereaved—and sick to death
At the mere thought of torch and bridal bed—
I could perhaps give way in this one case
To frailty. I shall say it: since that time
Sychaeus, my poor husband, met his fate,
And blood my brother shed stained our hearth gods,
This man alone has wrought upon me so
And moved my soul to yield. I recognize
The signs of the old flame, of old desire.
But O chaste life, before I break your laws,
I pray that Earth may open, gape for me
Down to its depth, or the omnipotent
With one stroke blast me to the shades, pale shades
Of Erebus and the deep world of night!
That man who took me to himself in youth
Has taken all my love; may that man keep it,
Hold it forever with him in the tomb."

At this she wept and wet her breast with tears.
But Anna answered:
                   "Dearer to your sister
Than daylight is, will you wear out your life,
Young as you are, in solitary mourning,
Never to know sweet children, or the crown
Of joy that Venus brings? Do you believe
This matters to the dust, to ghosts in tombs?
Granted no suitors up to now have moved you,
Neither in Libya nor before, in Tyre—
Iarbas you rejected, and the others,

Chieftains bred by the land of Africa
Their triumphs have enriched—will you contend
Even against a welcome love? Have you
Considered in whose lands you settled here?
On one frontier the Gaetulans, their cities,
People invincible in war—with wild
Numidian horseman, and the offshore banks,
The Syrtës; on the other, desert sands,
Bone-dry, where fierce Barcaean nomads range.
Or need I speak of future wars brought on
From Tyre, and the menace of your brother?
Surely by dispensation of the gods
And backed by Juno's will, the ships from Ilium
Held their course this way on the wind
                                        Sister,
What a great city you'll see rising here,
And what a kingdom, from this royal match!
With Trojan soldiers as companions in arms
By what exploits will Punic glory grow!
Only ask the indulgence of the gods,
Win them with offerings, give your guests ease,
And contrive reasons for delay, while winter
Gales rage, drenched Orion storms at sea,
And their ships, damaged still, face iron skies."

This counsel fanned the flame, already kindled,
Giving her hesitant sister hope, and set her
Free of scruple. Visiting the shrines
They begged for grace at every altar first,
Then put choice rams and ewes to ritual death
For Ceres Giver of Laws, Father Lyaeus,
Phoebus, and for Juno most of all
Who has the bonds of marriage in her keeping.
Dido herself, splendidly beautiful,
Holding a shallow cup, tips out the wine
On a white shining heifer, between the horns,
Or gravely in the shadow of the gods
Approaches opulent altars. Through the day
She brings new gifts, and when the breasts are opened
Pores over organs, living still, for signs.
Alas, what darkened minds have soothsayers!
What good are shrines and vows to maddened lovers?
The inward fire eats the soft marrow away,
And the internal wound bleeds on in silence.

Unlucky Dido, burning, in her madness
Roamed through all the city, like a doe
Hit by an arrow shot from far away
By a shepherd hunting in the Cretan woods—
Hit by surprise, nor could the hunter see
His flying steel had fixed itself in her;
But though she runs for life through copse and glade
The fatal shaft clings to her side.
                                   Now Dido
Took Aeneas with her among her buildings,
Showed her Sidonian wealth, her walls prepared,
And tried to speak, but in mid-speech grew still.
When the day waned she wanted to repeat
The banquet as before, to hear once more
In her wild need the throes of Ilium,
And once more hung on the narrator's words.
Afterward, when all the guests were gone,
And the dim moon in turn had quenched her light,
And setting stars weighed weariness to sleep,
Alone she mourned in the great empty hall
Alone pressed her body on the couch he left:
She heard him still, though absent—heard and saw him.
Or she would hold Ascanius in her lap,
Enthralled by him, the image of his father,
As though by this ruse to appease a love
Beyond all telling.
                              Towers, half-built, rose
No farther; men no longer trained in arms
Or toiled to make harbors and battlements
Impregnable. Projects were broken off,
Laid over, and the menacing huge walls
With cranes unmoving stood against the sky.

As soon as Jove's dear consort saw the lady
prey to such illness, and her reputation
Standing no longer in the way of passion,
Saturn's daughter said to Venus:
                                   "Wondrous!
Covered yourself with glory, have you not,
You and you-boy, and won such prizes, too.
Divine power is something to remember
If by collusion of two gods one mortal
Woman is brought low.
                              I am not blind.

Your fear of our new walls has not escaped me,
Fear and mistrust of Carthage at her height.
But how far will it go? What do you hope for,
Being so contentious? Why do we not
Arrange eternal peace and formal marriage?
You have your heart's desire: Dido in love,
Dido consumed with passion to her core.
Why not, then, rule this people side by side
With equal authority? And let the queen
Wait on her Phrygian lord, let her consign
Into your hand her Tyrians as a dowry."

Now Venus knew this talk was all pretence,
All to divert the future power from Italy
To Libya; and she answered:
                "Who would be
So mad, so foolish as to shun that prospect
Or prefer war with you? That is, provided
Fortune is on the side of your proposal.
The fates here are perplexing: would one city
Satisfy Jupiter's will for Tyrians
And Trojan exiles? Does he approve
A union and mingling of these races?
You are his consort: you have every right
To sound him out. Go on, and I'll come, too."

But regal Juno pointedly replied:
"That task will rest with me. Just now, as to
The need of the moment and the way to meet it,
Listen, and I'll explain in a few words.
Aeneas and Dido in her misery
Plan hunting in the forest, when the Titan
Sun comes up with rays to light the world.
While beaters in excitement ring the glens
My gift will be a black raincloud, and hail,
A downpour, and I'll shake heaven with thunder.
The company will scatter, lost in gloom,
As Dido and the Trojan captain come
To one same cavern. I shall be on hand,
And if I can be certain you are willing,
There I shall marry them and call her his.
A wedding, this will be."
                Then Cytherëa,
Not disinclined, nodded to Juno's plea,
And smiled at the stratagem now given away.

Dawn came up meanwhile from the Ocean stream,
And in the early sunshine from the gates
Picked huntsmen issued: wide-meshed nets and snares,
Broad spearheads for big game, Massylian horseman
Trooping with hounds in packs keen on the scent.
But Dido lingered in her hall, as Punic
Nobles waited, and her mettlesome hunter
Stood nearby, cavorting in gold and scarlet,
Champing his foam-flecked bridle. At long last
The queen appeared with courtiers in a crowd,
A short Sidonian cloak edged in embroidery
Caught about her, at her back a quiver
Sheathed in gold, her hair tied up in gold,
And a brooch of gold pinning her scarlet dress.
Phrygians came in her company as well,
And Iulus, joyous at the scene. Resplendent
Above the rest, Aeneas walked to meet her,
To join his retinue with hers. He seemed—
Think of the lord Apollo in the spring
When he leaves wintering in Lycia
By Xanthus torrent, for his mother's isle
Of Delos, to renew the festival;
Around his altars Cretans, Dryopës,
And painted Agathyrsans raise a shout,
But the god walks the Cynthian ridge alone
And smoothes his hair, binds it in fronded laurel,
Braids it in gold; and shafts ring on his shoulders.
So elated and swift, Aenas walked
With sunlit grace upon him.
                              Soon the hunters,
Riding in company to high pathless hills,
Saw mountain goats shoot down from a rocky peak
And scamper on the ridges; toward the plain
Deer left the slopes, herding in clouds of dust
In flight across the open lands. Alone,
The boy Ascanius, delightedly riding
His eager horse amid the lowland vales,
Outran both goats and deer. Could he only meet
Amid the harmless game some foaming boar,
Or a tawny lion down from the mountainside!
Meanwhile in heaven began a rolling thunder,
And soon the storm broke, pouring rain and hail.
Then Tyrians and Trojans in alarm—
With Venus' Dardan grandson—ran for cover

Here and there in the wilderness, as freshets
Coursed from the high hills.
                              Now to the self-same cave
Came Dido and the captain of the Trojans.
Primal Earth herself and Nuptial Juno
Opened the ritual, torches of lightning blazed,
High Heaven became witness to the marriage,
And nymphs cried out wild hymns from a mountain top.
    That day was the first cause of death, and first
Of sorrow. Dido had no further qualms
As to impressions given and set abroad;
She thought no longer of a secret love
But called it marriage. Thus, under that name,
She hid her fault.
                    Now in no time at all
Through all the African cities Rumor goes—
Nimble as quicksilver among evils. Rumor
Thrives on motion, stronger for the running,
Lowly at first through fear, then rearing high,
She treads the land and hides her head in cloud.
As people fable it, the Earth, her mother,
Furious against the gods, bore a late sister
To the giants Coeus and Enceladus,
Giving her speed on foot and on the wing:
Monstrous, deformed, titanic. Pinioned, with
An eye beneath for every body feather,
And, strange to say, as many tongues and buzzing
Mouths as eyes, as many pricked-up ears,
By night she flies between the earth and heaven
Shrieking through darkness, and she never turns
Her eye-lids down to sleep. By day she broods,
On the alert, on rooftops or on towers,
Bringing great cities fear, harping on lies
And slander evenhandedly with truth.
In those days Rumor took an evil joy
At filling countrysides with whispers, whispers,
Gossip of what was done, and never done:
How this Aeneas landed, Trojan born,
How Dido in her beauty graced his company,
Then how they reveled all the winter long
Unmindful of the realm, prisoners of lust.
These tales the scabrous goddess put about
On men's lips everywhere. Her twisting course

Took her to King Iarbas, whom she set
Ablaze with anger piled on top of anger.
Son of Jupiter Hammon by a nymph,
A ravished Garamantean, this prince
Had built the god a hundred giant shrines,
A hundred altars, each with holy fires.
Alight by night and day, sentries on watch,
The ground enriched by victims' blood, the doors
Festooned with flowering wreaths. Before his altars
King Iarbas, crazed by the raw story,
Stood, they say, amid the Presences,
With supplicating hands, pouring out prayer:
"All powerful Jove, to whom the feasting Moors
At ease on colored couches tip their wine,
Do you see this? Are we then fools to fear you
Throwing down your bolts? Those dazzling fires
Of lightning, are they aimless in the clouds
And rumbling thunder meaningless? This woman
Who turned up in our country and laid down
A tiny city at a price, to whom
I gave a beach to plow—and on my terms—
After refusing to marry me has taken
Aeneas to be master in her realm.
And now Sir Paris with his men, half-men,
His chin and perfumed hair tied up
In a Maeonian bonnet, takes possession.
As for ourselves, here we are bringing gifts
Into these shrines—supposedly your shrines—
Hugging that empty fable."
                              Pleas like this
From the man clinging to his altars reached
The ears of the Almighty. Now he turned
His eyes upon the queen's town and the lovers
Careless of their good name; then spoke to Mercury,
Assigning him a mission:
                              "Son, bestir yourself,
Call up the Zephyrs, take to your wings and glide.
Approach the Dardan captain where he tarries
Rapt in Tyrian Carthage, losing sight
Of future towns the fates ordain. Correct him,
Carry my speech to him on the running winds:
No son like this did his enchanting mother
Promise to us, nor such did she deliver

Twice from peril at the hands of Greeks.
He was to be the ruler of Italy,
Potential empire, armorer of war;
To father men from Teucer's noble blood
And bring the whole world under law's dominion.
If glories to be won by deeds like these
Cannot arouse him, if he will not strive
For his own honor, does he begrudge his son,
Ascanius, the high strongholds of Rome?
What has he in mind? What hope, to make him stay
Amid a hostile race, and lose from view
Ausonian progeny, Lavinian lands?
The man should sail: that is the whole point.
Let this be what you tell him, as from me."
He finished and fell silent. Mercury
Made ready to obey the great command
Of his great father, and he first tied on
The golden sandals, winged, that high in air
Transport him over seas or over land
Abreast of gale winds; then he took the wand
With which he summons pale souls out of Orcus
And ushers others to the undergloom,
Lulls men to slumber or awakens them,
And opens dead men's eyes. This wand in hand,
He can drive winds before him, swimming down
Along the stormcloud. Now aloft, he saw
The craggy flanks and crown of patient Atlas,
Giant Atlas, balancing the sky
Upon his peak—his pine-forested head
In vapor cowled, beaten by wind and rain.
Snow lay upon his shoulders, rills cascaded
Down his ancient chin and beard a-bristle,
Caked with ice. Here Mercury of Cyllenë
Hovered first on even wings, then down
He plummeted to sea-level and flew on
Like a low-flying gull that skims the shallows
And rocky coasts where fish ply close inshore.
So, like a gull between the earth and sky,
The progeny of Cyllenë, on the wing
From his maternal grandsire, split the winds
To the sands bars of Libya
                              Alighting tiptoe
On the first hutments, there he found Aeneas

Laying foundations for new towers and homes.
He noted well the swordhilt the man wore,
Adorned with yellow jasper; and the cloak
Aglow with Tyrian dye upon his shoulders—
Gifts of the wealthy queen, who had inwoven
Gold thread in the fabric. Mercury
Took him to task at once:
                              "Is it for you
To lay the stones for Carthage's high walls,
Tame husband that you are, and build their city?
Oblivious of your own world, your own kingdom!
From bright Olympus he that rules the gods
And turns the earth and heaven by his power—
He and no other sent me to you, told me
To bring this message on the running winds:
What have you in mind? What hope, wasting your days
In Libya? If future history's glories
Do not affect you, if you will not strive
For your own honor, think of Ascanius,
Think of the expectations of your heir,
Iulus, to whom the Italian realm, the land
Of Rome, are due."
                      And Mercury, as he spoke,
Departed from the visual field of mortals
To a great distance, ebbed in subtle air.
Amazed, and shocked to the bottom of his soul
By what his eyes had seen, Aeneas felt
His hackles rise, his voice choke in his throat.
As the sharp admonition and command
From heaven had shaken him awake, he now
Burned only to be gone, to leave that land
Of the sweet life behind. What can he do? How tell
The impassioned queen and hope to win her over?
What opening shall he choose? This way and that
He let his mind dart, testing alternatives,
Running through every one. And as he pondered
This seemed the better tactic: he called in
Mnestheus, Sergestus and stalwart Serestus,
Telling them:
                  "Get the fleet ready for sea,
But quietly, and collect the men on shore.
Lay in ship stores and gear."
                                  As to the cause

For a change of plan, they were to keep it secret,
Seeing the excellent Dido had no notion,
No warning that such love could be cut short;
He would himself look for the right occasion,
The easiest time to speak, the way to do it.
The Trojans to a man gladly obeyed.

The queen, for her part, felt some plot afoot
Quite soon—for who deceives a woman in love?
She caught wind of a change, being in fear
Of what had seemed her safety. Evil Rumor,
Shameless as before, brought word to her
In her distracted state of ships being rigged
In trim for sailing. Furious, at her wits' end,
She traversed the whole city, all aflame
With rage, like a Bacchantë driven wild
By emblems shaken, when the mountain revels
Of the odd year possess her, when the cry
Of Bacchus rises and Cithaeron calls
All through the shouting night. Thus it turned out
She was the first to speak and charge Aeneas:

"You even hoped to keep me in the dark
As to this outrage, did you, two-faced man,
And slip away in silence? Can our love
Not hold you, can the pledge we gave not hold you,
Can Dido not, now sure to die in pain?
Even in winter weather must you toil
With ships, and fret to launch against high winds
For the open seas? Oh, heartless!
                                    Tell me now,
If you were not in search of alien lands
And new strange homes, if ancient Troy remained,
Would ships put out for Troy on these big seas?
Do you go to get away from me? I beg you,
By these tears, by your own right hand, since I
Have left my wretched self nothing but that—
Yes, by the marriage that we entered on,
If ever I did well and you were grateful
Or found some sweetness in a gift from me,
Have pity now on a declining house!
Put this plan by, I beg you, if a prayer
Is not yet out of place.
Because of you, Libyans and nomad kings

Detest me, my own Tyrians are hostile;
Because of you, I lost my integrity
And that admired name by which alone
I made my way once toward the stars.
                                        To whom
Do you abandon me, a dying woman,
Guest that you are—the only name now left
From that of husband? Why do I live on?
Shall I, until my brother Pygmalion comes
To pull my walls down? Or the Gaetulan
Iarbas leads me captive? If at least
There were a child by you for me to care for,
A little one to play in my courtyard
And give me back Aeneas, in spite of all,
I should not feel so utterly defeated,
Utterly bereft."
                        She ended there.
The man by Jove's command held fast his eyes
And fought down the emotion in his heart.
At length he answered:
                        "As for myself, be sure
I never shall deny all you can say,
Your majesty, of what you meant to me.
Never will the memory of Elissa
Stale for me, while I can still remember
My own life, and the spirit rules my body.
As to the event, a few words. Do not think
I meant to be deceitful and slip away.
I never held the torches of a bridegroom,
Never entered upon the pact of marriage.
If Fate permitted me to spend my days
By my own lights, and make the best of things
According to my wishes, first of all
I should look after Troy and the loved relics
Left me of my people. Priam's great hall
Should stand again; I should have restored the tower
Of Pergamum for Trojans in defeat.
But now it is the rich Italian land
Apollo tells me I must make for: Italy,
Named by his oracles. There is my love;
There is my country. If, as a Phoenician,
You are so given to the charms of Carthage,
Libyan city that it is, then tell me,

Why begrudge the Teucrians new lands
For homesteads in Ausonia? Are we not
Entitled, too, to look for realms abroad?
Night never veils the earth in damp and darkness,
Fiery stars never ascend the east,
But in my dreams my father's troubled ghost
Admonishes and frightens me. Then, too,
Each night thoughts come of young Ascanius,
My dear boy wronged, defrauded of his kingdom,
Hesperian lands of destiny. And now
The gods' interpreter, sent by Jove himself—
I swear it by your head and mine—has brought
Commands down through the racing winds! I say
With my own eyes in full daylight I saw him
Entering the building! With my very ears
I drank his message in! So please, no more
Of these appeals that set us both afire.
I sail for Italy not of my own free will."

During all this she had been watching him
With face averted, looking him up and down
In silence, and she burst out raging now:

"No goddess was your mother. Dardanus
Was not the founder of your family.
Liar and cheat! Some rough Caucasian cliff
Begot you on flint. Hyrcanian tigresses
Tendered their teats to you. Why should I palter?
Why still hold back for more indignity?
Sigh, did he, while I wept? Or look at me?
Or yield a tear, or pity her who loved him?
What shall I say first, with so much to say?
The time is past when either supreme Juno
Or the Saturnian father viewed these things
With justice. Faith can never be secure.
I took the man in, thrown up on this coast
In dire need, and in my madness then
Contrived a place for him in my domain,
Rescued his lost fleet, saved his shipmates' lives.
Oh, I am swept away burning by furies!
Now the prophet Apollo, now his oracles,
Now the gods' interpreter, if you please,
Sent down by Jove himself, brings through the air
His formidable commands! What fit employment

For heaven's high powers! What anxieties
To plague serene immortals! I shall not
Detain you or dispute your story. Go,
Go after Italy on the sailing winds,
Look for your kingdom, cross the deepsea swell!
If divine justice counts for anything,
I hope and pray that on some grinding reef
Midway at sea you'll drink your punishment
And call and call on Dido's name!
From far away I shall come after you
With my black fires, and when cold death has parted
Body from soul I shall be everywhere
A shade to haunt you! You will pay for this,
Unconscionable! I shall hear! The news will reach me
Even among the lowest of the dead!"

At this abruptly she broke off and ran
In sickness from his sight and the light of day,
Leaving him at a loss, alarmed, and mute
With all he meant to say. The maids in waiting
Caught her as she swooned and carried her
To bed in her marble chamber.
                                        Duty-bound,
Aeneas, though he struggled with desire
To calm and comfort her in all her pain,
To speak to her and turn her mind from grief,
And though he sighed his heart out, shaken still
With love of her, yet took the course heaven gave him
And went back to the fleet. Then with a will
The Teucrians fell to work and launched the ships
Along the whole shore: slick with tar each hull
Took to the water. Eager to get away,
The sailors brought oar-boughs out of the woods
With leaves still on, and oaken logs unhewn.
Now you could see them issuing from the town
To the water's edge in streams, as when, aware
Of winter, ants will pillage a mound of spelt
To store it in their granary; over fields
The black battalion moves, and through the grass
On a narrow trail they carry off the spoil;
Some put their shoulders to the enormous weight
Of a trundled grain, while some pull stragglers in
And castigate delay; their to-and-fro
Of labor makes the whole track come alive.

At that sight, what were your emotions, Dido?
Sighing how deeply, looking out and down
From your high tower on the seething shore
Where all the harbor filled before your eyes
With bustle and shouts! Unconscionable Love,
To what extremes will you not drive our hearts!
She now felt driven to weep again, again
To move him, if she could, by supplication,
Humbling her pride before her love—to leave
Nothing untried, not to die needlessly.

"Anna, you see the arc of waterfront
All in commotion: they come crowding in
From everywhere. Spread canvas calls for wind,
The happy crews have garlanded the stems.
If I could brace myself for this great sorrow,
Sister, I can endure it, too. One favor,
Even so, you may perform for me.
Since that deserter chose you for his friend
And trusted you, even with private thoughts,
Since you alone know when he may be reached,
Go, intercede with our proud enemy.
Remind him that I took no oath at Aulis
With Danaans to destroy the Trojan race;
I sent no ship to Pergamum. Never did I
Profane his father Anchisës' dust and shade.
Why will he not allow my prayers to fall
On his unpitying ears? Where is he racing?
Let him bestow one last gift on his mistress:
This, to await fair winds and easier flight.
Now I no longer plead the bond he broke
Of our old marriage, nor do I ask that he
Should live without his dear love, Latium,
Or yield his kingdom. Time is all I beg,
Mere time, a respite and a breathing space
For madness to subside in, while my fortune
Teaches me how to take defeat and grieve.
Pity your sister. This is the end, this favor—
To be repaid with interest when I die."

She pleaded in such terms, and such, in tears,
Her sorrowing sister brought him, time and again.
But no tears moved him, no one's voice would he
Attend to tractably. The fates opposed it;
God's will blocked the man's once kindly ears.

And just as when the north winds from the Alps
This way and that contend among themselves
To tear away an oaktree hale with age,
The wind and tree cry, and the buffeted trunk
Showers high foliage to earth, but holds
On bedrock, for the roots go down as far
Into the underworld as cresting boughs
Go up in heaven's air: just so this captain,
Buffeted by a gale of pleas
This way and that way, dinned all the day long,
Felt their moving power in his great heart,
And yet his will stood fast; tears fell in vain.

On Dido in her desolation now
Terror grew at her fate. She prayed for death,
Being heartsick at the mere sight of heaven.
That she more surely would perform the act
And leave the daylight, now she saw before her
A thing one shudders to recall: on altars
Fuming with incense where she placed her gifts,
The holy water blackened, the spilt wine
Turned into blood and mire. Of this she spoke
To no one, not to her sister even. Then, too,
Within the palace was a marble shrine
Devoted to her onetime lord, a place
She held in wondrous honor, all festooned
With snowy fleeces and green festive boughs.
From this she now thought voices could be heard
And words could be made out, her husband's words,
Calling her, when midnight hushed the earth;
And lonely on the rooftops the night owl
Seemed to lament, in melancholy notes,
Prolonged to a doleful cry. And then, besides,
The riddling words of seers in ancient days,
Foreboding sayings, made her thrill with fear.
In nightmare, fevered, she was hunted down
By pitiless Aeneas, and she seemed
Deserted always, uncompanioned always,
On a long journey, looking for her Tyrians
In desolate landscapes—
                                    as Pentheus gone mad
Sees the oncoming Eumenidës and sees
A double sun and double Thebes appear,
Or as when, hounded on the stage, Orestës

Runs from a mother armed with burning brands,
With serpents hellish black,
And in the doorway squat the Avenging Ones.

So broken in mind by suffering, Dido caught
Her fatal madness and resolved to die.
She pondered time and means, then visiting
Her mournful sister, covered up her plan
With a calm look, a clear and hopeful brow.

"Sister, be glad for me! I've found a way
To bring him back or free me of desire.
Near to the Ocean boundary, near sundown,
The Aethiops' farthest territory lies,
Where giant Atlas turns the sphere of heaven
Studded with burning stars. From there
A priestess of Massylian stock has come;
She had been pointed out to me: custodian
Of that shrine named for daughters of the west,
Hesperidës; and it is she who fed
The dragon, guarding well the holy boughs
With honey dripping slow and drowsy poppy.
Chanting her spells she undertakes to free
What hearts she wills, but to inflict on others
Duress of sad desires; to arrest
The flow of rivers, make the stars move backward,
Call up the spirits of deep Night. You'll see
Earth shift and rumble underfoot and ash trees
Walk down mountainsides. Dearest, I swear
Before the gods and by your own sweet self,
It is against my will that I resort
For weaponry to magic powers. In secret
Build up a pyre in the inner court
Under the open sky, and place upon it
The arms that faithless man left in my chamber,
All his clothing, and the marriage bed
On which I came to grief—solace for me
To annihilate all vestige of the man,
Vile as he is: my priestess shows me this."

While she was speaking, cheek and brow grew pale.
But Anna could not think her sister cloaked
A suicide in these unheard-of rites;
She failed to see how great her madness was

And feared no consequence more grave
Than at Sychaeus' death. So, as commanded,
She made the preparations. For her part,
The queen, seeing the pyre in her inmost court
Erected huge with pitch-pine and sawn ilex,
Hung all the place under the sky with wreaths
And crowned it with funeral cypress boughs.
On the pyre's top she put a sword he left
With clothing, and an effigy on a couch,
Her mind fixed now ahead on what would come.
Around the pyre stood altars, and the priestess,
Hair unbound, called in a voice of thunder
Upon three hundred gods, on Erebus,
On Chaos, and on triple Hecatë,
Three-faced Diana. Then she sprinkled drops
Purportedly from the fountain of Avernus.
Rare herbs were brought out, reaped at the new moon
By scythes of bronze, and juicy with a milk
Of dusky venom; then the rare love-charm
Or caul torn from the brow of a birthing foal
And snatched away before the mother found it.
Dido herself with consecrated grain
In her pure hands, as she went near the altars,
Freed one foot from sandal straps, let fall
Her dress ungirdled, and, now sworn to death,
Called on the gods and stars that knew her fate.
She prayed then to whatever power may care
In comprehending justice for the grief
Of lovers bound unequally by love.

The night had come, and weary in every land
Men's bodies took the boon of peaceful sleep.
The woods and the wild seas had quieted
At that hour when the stars are in mid-course
And every field is still; cattle and birds
With vivid wings that haunt the limpid lakes
Or nest in thickets in the country places
All were asleep under the silent night.
Not, though, the agonized Phoenician queen:
She never slackened into sleep and never
Allowed the tranquil night to rest
Upon her eyelids or within her heart.
Her pain redoubled; love came on again,

Devouring her, and on her bed she tossed
In a great surge of anger.
                                    So awake,
She pressed these questions, musing to herself:

"Look now, what can I do? Turn once again
To the old suitors, only to be laughed at—
Begging a marriage with Numidians
Whom I disdained so often? Then what? Trail
The Ilian ships and follow like a slave
Commands of Trojans? Seeing them so agreeable,
In view of past assistance and relief,
So thoughtful their unshaken gratitude?
Suppose I wished it, who permits or takes
Aboard their proud ships one they so dislike?
Poor lost soul, do you not yet grasp or feel
The treachery of the line of Laömedon?
What then? Am I to go alone, companion
Of the exultant sailors in their flight?
Or shall I set out in their wake, with Tyrians,
With all my crew close at my side, and send
The men I barely tore away from Tyre
To sea again, making them hoist their sails
To more sea-winds? No: die as you deserve,
Give pain quietus with a steel blade.
                                            Sister,
You are the one who gave way to my tears
In the beginning, burdened a mad queen
With sufferings, and thrust me on my enemy.
It was not given me to lead my life
Without new passion, innocently, the way
Wild creatures live, and not to touch these depths.
The vow I took to the ashes of Sychaeus
Was not kept."
                        So she broke out afresh
In bitter mourning. On his high stern deck
Aeneas, now quite certain of departure,
Everything ready, took the boon of sleep.
In dream the figure of the god returned
With looks reproachful as before: he seemed
Again to warn him, being like Mercury
In every way, in voice, in golden hair,

And in the bloom of youth.
      "Son of the goddess,
Sleep away this crisis, can you still?
Do you not see the dangers growing round you,
Madman, from now on? Can you not hear
The offshore westwind blow? The woman hatches
Plots and drastic actions in her heart,
Resolved on death now, whipping herself on
To heights of anger. Will you not be gone
In flight, while flight is still within your power?
Soon you will see the offing boil with ships
And glare with torches; soon again
The waterfront will be alive with fires,
If Dawn comes while you linger in this country.
Ha! Come, break the spell! Woman's a thing
Forever fitful and forever changing."

At this he merged into the darkness. Then
As the abrupt phantom filled him with fear,
Aeneas broke from sleep and roused his crewmen:
"Up, turn out now! Oarsmen, take your thwarts!
Shake out sail! Look here, for the second time
A god from heaven's high air is goading me
To hasten our break away, to cut the cables.
Holy one, whatever god you are,
We go with you, we act on your command
Most happily! Be near, graciously help us,
Make the stars in heaven propitious ones!"

He pulled his sword aflash out of its sheath
And struck at the stern hawser. All the men
Were gripped by his excitement to be gone,
And hauled and hustled. Ships cast off their moorings,
And an array of hulls hid inshore water
As oarsmen churned up foam and swept to sea.

Soon early Dawn, quitting the saffron bed
Of old Tithonus, cast new light on earth,
And as air grew transparent, from her tower
The queen caught sight of ships on the seaward reach
With sails full and the wind astern. She knew
The waterfront now empty, bare of oarsmen.
Beating her lovely breast three times, four times,
And tearing her golder hair,
      "O Jupiter,"

She said, "will this man go, will he have mocked
My kingdom, stranger that he was and is?
Will they not snatch up arms and follow him
From every quarter of the town? and dockhands
Tear our ships from moorings? On! Be quick
With torches! Give out arms! Unship the oars!
What am I saying? Where am I? What madness
Takes me out of myself? Dido, poor soul,
Your evil doing has come home to you.
Then was the right time, when you offered him
A royal scepter. See the good faith and honor
Of one they say bears with him everywhere
The hearthgods of his country! One who bore
His father, spent with age, upon his shoulders!
Could I not then have torn him limb from limb
And flung the pieces on the sea? His company,
Even Ascanius could I not have minced
And served up to his father at a feast?
The luck of battle might have been in doubt—
So let it have been! Whom had I to fear,
Being sure to die? I could have carried torches
Into his camp, filled passage ways with flame,
Annihilated father and son and followers
And given my own life on top of all!
O Sun, scanning with flame all works of earth,
And thou, O Juno, witness and go-between
Of my long miseries; and Hecatë,
Screeched for at night at crossroads in the cities;
And thou, avenging Furies, and all gods
On whom Elissa dying may call: take notice,
Overshadow this hell with your high power,
As I deserve, and hear my prayer!
If by necessity that impious wretch
Must find his haven and come safe to land,
If so Jove's destinies require, and this,
His end in view, must stand, yet all the same
When hard beset in war by a brave people,
Forced to go outside his boundaries
And torn from Iulus, let him beg assistance,
Let him see the unmerited deaths of those
Around and with him, and accepting peace
On unjust terms, let him not, even so,
Enjoy his kingdom or the life he longs for,

But fall in battle before his time and lie
Unburied on the sand! This I implore,
This is my last cry, as my last blood flows.
Then, O my Tyrians, besiege with hate
His progeny and all his race to come:
Make this your offering to my dust. No love,
No pact must be between our peoples; No,
But rise up from my bones, avenging spirit!
Harry with fire and sword the Dardan countrymen
Now, or hereafter, at whatever time
The strength will be afforded. Coast with coast
In conflict, I implore, and sea with sea,
And arms with arms: may they contend in war,
Themselves and all the children of their children!"

Now she took thought of one way or another,
At the first chance, to end her hated life,
And briefly spoke to Barcë, who had been
Sychaeus' nurse; her own an urn of ash
Long held in her ancient fatherland.
                              "Dear nurse,
Tell Sister Anna to come here, and have her
Quickly bedew herself with running water
Before she brings our victims for atonement.
Let her come that way. And you, too, put on
Pure wool around your brows. I have a mind
To carry out that rite to Stygian Jove
That I have readied here, and put an end
To my distress, committing to the flames
The pyre of that miserable Dardan."

At this with an old woman's eagerness
Barcë hurried away. And Dido's heart
Beat wildly at the enormous thing afoot.
She rolled her bloodshot eyes, her quivering cheeks
Were flecked with red as her sick pallor grew
Before her coming death. Into the court
She burst her way, then at her passion's height
She climbed the pyre and bared the Dardan sword—
A gift desired once, for no such need.
Her eyes now on the Trojan clothing there
And the familiar bed, she paused a little,
Weeping a little, mindful, then lay down
And spoke her last words:
                              "Remnants dear to me

While god and fate allowed it, take this breath
And give me respite from these agonies.
I lived my life out to the very end
And passed the stages Fortune had appointed.
Now my tall shade goes to the under world.
I built a famous town, saw my great walls,
Avenged my husband, made my hostile brother
Pay for his crime. Happy, alas, too happy,
If only the Dardanian keels had never
Beached on our coast." And here she kissed the bed.
"I die unavenged," she said, " but let me die.
This way, this way, a blessed relief to go
Into the undergloom. Let the cold Trojan,
Far at sea, drink in this conflagration
And take with him the omen of my death!"

Amid these words her household people saw her
Crumpled over the steel blade, and the blade
Aflush with red blood, drenched her hands. A scream
Pierced the high chambers. Now through the shocked city
Rumor went rioting, as wails and sobs
With women's outcry echoed in the palace
And heaven's high air gave back the beating din,
As though all Carthage or old Tyre fell
To storming enemies, and, out of hand,
Flames billowed on the roofs of men and gods.
Her sister heard the trembling, faint with terror,
Lacerating her face, beating her breast,
Ran through the crowd to call the dying queen:

"It came to this, then, sister? You deceived me?
The pyre meant this, altars and fires meant this?
What shall I mourn first, being abandoned? Did you
Scorn your sister's company in death?
You should have called me out to the same fate!
The same blade's edge and hurt, at the same hour,
Should have taken us off. With my own hands
Had I to build this pyre, and had I to call
Upon our country's gods, that in the end
With you placed on it there, O heartless one,
I should be absent? You have put to death
Yourself and me, the people and the fathers
Bred in Sidon, and your own new city.
Give me fresh water, let me bather her wound
And catch upon my lips any last breath

Hovering over hers."
                Now she had climbed
The topmost steps and took her dying sister
Into her arms to cherish, with a sob,
Using her dress to stanch the dark blood flow.
But Dido trying to lift her heavy eyes
Fainted again. Her chest-wound whistled air.
Three times she struggled up on one elbow
And each time fell back on the bed. Her gaze
Went wavering as she looked for heaven's light
And groaned at finding it. Almighty Juno,
Filled with pity for this long ordeal
And difficult passage, now sent Iris down
Out of Olympus to set free
The wrestling spirit from the body's hold.
For since she died, not at her fated span
Nor as she merited, but before her time
Enflamed and driven mad, Proserpina
Had not yet plucked from her the golden hair,
Delivering her to Orcus of the Styx.
So humid Iris through bright heaven flew
On saffron-yellow wings, and in her train
A thousand hues shimmered before the sun.
At Dido's head she came to rest.
                    "This token
Sacred to Dis I bear away as bidden
And free you from your body."
                  Saying this,
She cut a lock of hair. Along with it
Her body's warmth fell into dissolution,
And out into the winds her life withdrew.

—Translated by Robert Fitzgerald

LUCRETIUS

The Roman philosopher Lucretius (98–ca. 55 B.C.) is known only by his philosophical poem *De rerum natura (On the Nature of the Universe)*, the most complete exposition of philosophical materialism preserved from classical times. Following the teachings of the Hellenistic philosopher Epicurus, Lucretius explains that nature is governed solely by mechanical laws and the gods have no power over humans, either during or after life. Lucretius's views contradicted Plato's teachings on the immortality of the soul, as well as the classical poets' contention that the gods actively supervise human affairs.

Despite his own reassurances that death is mere nothingness, Lucretius considers in Book III the human reluctance to face the inevitability of death. In the selection here, the voice of Nature queries humanity about its curious attachment to life.

For analysis and interpretation:

1. Summarize Lucretius's argument on the fate of the human body and soul after death.

2. What counsel might Lucretius have given to Socrates as he faced the death sentence in an Athenian court?

3. Respond to Nature's chiding voice and explain humans' fear of death according to your own beliefs.

From *On the Nature of the Universe*, Book III

From all this it follows that *death is nothing to us* and no concern of ours, since our tenure of the mind is mortal. In days of old, we felt no disquiet when the hosts of Carthage poured in to battle on every side—when the whole earth, dizzied by the convulsive shock of war, reeled sickeningly under the high ethereal vault, and between realm and realm the empire of mankind by land and sea trembled in the balance. So, when we shall be no more—when the union of body and spirit that engenders us has been disrupted—to us, who shall then be nothing, nothing by any hazard will happen any more at all. Nothing will have power to stir our senses, not though earth be fused with sea and sea with sky.

If any feeling remains in mind or spirit after it has been torn from our body, that is nothing to us, who are brought into being by the wedlock of body and spirit, conjoined and coalesced. Or even if the matter that composes us should be reassembled by time after our death and brought back into its present state—if the light of life were given to us anew—even that contingency would still be no concern of ours once the chain of our identity had been snapped. We who are now are not concerned with ourselves in any previous existence: the sufferings of those selves do not touch us. When you look at the immeasurable extent of time gone by and the multiform movements of matter, you will readily credit that these same atoms that compose us now must many a time before have entered into the selfsame combinations as now. But our mind cannot recall this to remembrance. For between then and now is interposed a breach in life, and all the atomic motions have been wandering far astray from sentience.

If the future holds travail and anguish in store, the self must be in existence, when that time comes, in order to experience it. But from this fate we are redeemed by death, which denies existence to the self that might have suffered these tribulations. Rest assured, therefore, that we have nothing to fear in death. One who no longer is cannot suffer, or differ in any way from one who has never been born, when once this mortal life has been usurped by death the immortal.

When you find a man treating it as a grievance that after death he will either moulder in the grave or fall a prey to flames or to the jaws of predatory beasts, be sure that his utterance does not ring true. Subconsciously his heart is stabbed by a secret dread, however loudly the man himself may disavow the belief that after death he will still experience sensation. I am convinced that he does not grant the admission he professes, nor the grounds of it; he does not oust and pluck himself root and branch out of life, but all unwittingly makes something of himself linger on. When a living man confronts the thought that after death his body will be mauled by birds and beasts of prey, he is filled with self-pity. He does not banish himself from the scene nor distinguish sharply enough between himself and that abandoned carcass. He visualizes that object as himself and infects it with his own feelings as an onlooker. That is why he is aggrieved at having been created mortal. He does not see that in real death there will be no other self alive to mourn his own decease—no other self standing by to flinch at the agony he suffers lying there being mangled, or indeed being cremated. For if it is really a bad thing after death to be mauled and crunched by ravening jaws, I cannot see why it should not be disagreeable to roast in the scorching flames of a funeral pyre, or to lie embalmed in honey, stifled and stiff with cold, on the surface of a chilly slab, or to be squashed under a crushing weight of earth.

'Now it is all over. Now the happy home and the best of wives will welcome you no more, nor winsome children rush to snatch the first kiss at your coming and touch your heart with speechless joy. No chance now to further your fortune or safeguard your family. Unhappy man,' they cry, 'unhappily cheated by one treacherous day out of all the uncounted blessings of life!' But they do not go on to say: 'And now no repining for these lost joys will oppress you anymore.' If they perceived this clearly with their minds and acted according to the words, they would free their breasts from a great load of grief and dread.

'Ah yes! *You* are at peace now in the sleep of death, and so you will stay to the end of time. Pain and sorrow will never touch you again. But to *us*, who stood weeping inconsolably while you were consumed to ashes on the dreadful pyre—to us no day will come that will lift the undying sorrow from our hearts.' Ask the speaker, then, what is so heart-rending about this. If something returns to sleep and peace, what reason is that for pining in inconsolable grief?

Here, again, is the way men often talk from the bottom of their hearts when they recline at a banquet, goblet in hand and brows decked with garlands: 'How all too short are these good times that come to us poor creatures! Soon they will be past and gone, and there will be no recalling them.' You would think the crowning calamity in store for them after death was to be parched and shriveled by a tormenting thirst or oppressed by some other vain desire. But even in sleep, when mind and body alike are at rest, no one misses himself or sighs for life. If such sleep were prolonged to eternity, no longing for ourselves would trouble us. And yet the vital atoms in our limbs cannot be far removed from their sensory motions at a time when a mere jolt out of sleep enables a man to pull himself together. Death, therefore, must be regarded, so far as we are concerned, as having much less existence than sleep, if anything can have less existence than what we perceive to be nothing. For death is followed by a far greater dispersal of the seething mass of matter: once that icy breach in life has intervened, there is no more waking.

Suppose that Nature herself were suddenly to find a voice and round upon one of us in these terms: 'What is your grievance, mortal, that you give yourself up to this whining and repining? Why do you weep and wail over death? If the life you have lived till now has been a pleasant thing—if all its blessings have not leaked away like water poured into a cracked pot and run to waste unrelished—why then, you silly creature, do you not retire as a guest who has had his fill of life and take your care-free rest with a quiet mind? Or, if all your gains have been poured profitless away and life has grown distasteful, why do you seek to swell the total? The new can but turn out as badly as the old and perish as unprofitably. Why not rather make an end of life and labour? Do you expect me to invent some new contrivance for your pleasure? I tell you, there is none. All things are always the same. If your body is not yet withered with age, nor your limbs decrepit and flagging, even so there is nothing new to look forward to—not though you should outlive all living creatures, or even though you should never die at all.' What are we to answer, except that Nature's rebuttal is justified and the plea she puts forward is a true one?

But suppose it is some man of riper years who complains—some dismal greybeard who frets unconscionably at his approaching end. Would she not have every right to protest more vehemently and repulse him in stern tones: 'Away with your tears, old reprobate! Have done with your grumbling! You are withering now after tasting all the joys of life. But, because you are always pining for what is not and unappreciative of the things at hand, your life has slipped away unfulfilled and unprized. Death has stolen upon you unawares, before you are ready to retire from life's banquet filled and satisfied. Come now, put away all that is unbecoming to your years and compose your mind to make way for others. You have no choice.' I cannot question but she would have right on her side; her censure and rebuke would be well merited. The old is always thrust aside to make way for the new, and one thing must be built out of the wreck of another. There is no murky pit of Hell awaiting anyone. There is need of matter, so that later generations may arise; when they have lived out their span, they will all follow you. Bygone generations have taken your road, and those to come will take it no less. So one thing will never cease to spring from another. To none is life given in freehold; to all on lease. Look back at the eternity that passed before we were born, and mark how utterly it counts to us as nothing. This is a mirror that Nature holds up to us, in which we may see the time that shall be after we are dead. Is there anything terrifying in the sight—anything depressing—anything that is not more restful than the soundest sleep?

—Translated by R. E. Latham

MARCUS AURELIUS

The emperor and Stoic philosopher Marcus Aurelius (A.D. 121–180) ruled near the end of the two centuries of Roman peace and order inaugurated by Caesar Augustus. During his last ten years, usually while on military campaigns against relentless invaders, Marcus kept a diary of philosophical musings and self-examination that we know as the *Meditations*. Like most Stoics, Marcus believed that the universe was governed by a divine law of reason and that he should strive to live reasonably and responsibly, while accepting events beyond his control.

In the selection here, Marcus muses on his duty as a Roman, the world order, the nature of death, and the impermanence of all things. The *Meditations* do not systematically develop the Stoic philosophy, but rather apply it in random reflections to the practical problems of an emperor's daily life.

For analysis and interpretation:

1. Evaluate Marcus's advice to himself as "a Roman and a man." How does it compare to the advice you would give yourself in a similar vein?

2. Explain what errors lead the soul to become "a tumor upon the universe," according to Marcus.

3. Compare Marcus's reflections on death to the beliefs of Lucretius, expressed in *On the Nature of the Universe*. In what ways do these proponents of different philosophies agree?

From *The Meditations*, Book II

4. Remember how long you have delayed, how often the gods have appointed the day of your redemption and you have let it pass. Now, if ever, you must realize of what kind of ordered universe you are a part, of what kind of governor of that universe you are an emanation, that a time limit has now been set for you and that if you do not use it to come out into the light, it will be lost, and you will be lost, and there will be no further opportunity.

5. Firmly, as a Roman and a man should, think at all times how you can perform the task at hand with precise and genuine dignity, sympathy, independence, and justice, making yourself free from all other preoccupations. This you will achieve if you perform every action as if it was the last of your life, if you rid yourself of all aimless thoughts, of all emotional opposition to the dictates of reason, of all pretense, selfishness and displeasure with your lot. You see how few are the things a man must overcome to enable him to live a smoothly flowing and godly life; for even the gods will require nothing further from the man who keeps to these beliefs.

6. You shame yourself, my soul, you shame yourself, and you will have no further opportunity to respect yourself; the life of every man is short and yours is almost finished while you do not respect yourself but allow your happiness to depend upon the souls of others.

7. Do external circumstances to some extent distract you? Give yourself leisure to acquire some further good knowledge and cease to wander aimlessly. Then one must guard against another kind of wandering, for those who are exhausted by life, and have no aim at which to direct every impulse and generally every impression, are foolish in their deeds as well as in their words.

8. A man is not easily found to be unhappy because he takes no thought for what happens in the soul of another; it is those who do not attend to the disturbances of their own soul who are inevitably in a state of unhappiness.

9. Always keep this thought in mind: what is the essential nature of the universe

and what is my own essential nature? How is the one related to the other, being so small a part of so great a Whole? And remember that no one can prevent your deeds and your words being in accord with nature.

10. Theophrastus speaks as a philosopher when, in comparing sins as a man commonly might, he states that offenses due to desire are worse than those due to anger, for the angry man appears to be in the grip of pain and hidden pangs when he discards Reason, whereas he who sins through desire, being overcome by pleasure, seems more licentious and more effeminate in his wrongdoing. So Theophrastus is right, and speaks in a manner worthy of philosophy, when he says that one who sins through pleasure deserves more blame than one who sins through pain. The latter is more like a man who was wronged first and compelled by pain to anger; the former starts on the path to sin of his own accord, driven to action by desire.

11. It is possible to depart from life at this moment. Have this thought in mind whenever you act, speak, or think. There is nothing terrible in leaving the company of men, if the gods exist, for they would not involve you in evil. If, on the other hand, they do not exist or do not concern themselves with human affairs, then what is life to me in a universe devoid of gods or of Providence? But they do exist and do care for humanity, and have put it altogether within a man's power not to fall into real evils. And if anything else were evil they would have seen to it that it be in every man's power not to fall into it. As for that which does not make a man worse, how could it make the life of man worse?

Neither through ignorance nor with knowledge could the nature of the Whole have neglected to guard against this or correct it; nor through lack of power or skill could it have committed so great a wrong, namely that good and evil should come to the good and the evil alike, and at random. True, death and life, good and ill repute, toil and pleasure, wealth and poverty, being neither good nor bad, come to the good and the bad equally. They are therefore neither blessings nor evils.

12. How swiftly all things vanish; in the universe the bodies themselves, and in time the memories of them. Of what kind are all the objects of sense, especially those which entice us by means of pleasure, frighten us by means of pain, or are shouted about in vainglory; how cheap they are, how contemptible, sordid, corruptible and dead— upon this our intellectual faculty should fix its attention. Who are these men whose voice and judgment make or break reputations? What is the nature of death? When a man examines it in itself, and with his share of intelligence dissolves the imaginings which cling to it, he conceives it to be no other than a function of nature, and to fear a natural function is to be only a child. Death is not only a function of nature but beneficial to it.

How does man reach god, with what part of himself, and in what condition must that part be?

13. Nothing is more wretched than the man who runs around in circles busying himself with all kinds of things—investigating things below the earth, as the saying goes—always looking for signs of what his neighbors are feeling and thinking. He does not realize that it is enough to be concerned with the spirit within oneself and genuinely to serve it. This service consists in keeping it free from passions, aimlessness, and discontent with its fate at the hands of gods and men. What comes from the gods must be revered because of their goodness; what comes from men must be welcomed because

of our kinship, although sometimes these things are also pitiful in a sense, because of men's ignorance of good and evil, which is no less a disability than to be unable to distinguish between black and white.

14. Even if you were to live three thousand years of three times ten thousand, remember nevertheless that no one can shed another life than this which he is living, nor live another life than this which he is shedding, so that the longest and the shortest life come to the same thing. The present is equal for all, and that which is being lost is equal, and that which is being shed is thus shown to be but a moment. No one can shed that which is past, nor what is still to come: for how could he be deprived of what he does not possess?

Therefore remember these two things always: first, that all things as they come round again have been the same from eternity, and it makes no difference whether you see the same things for a hundred years, or for two hundred years, or for an infinite time; second, that the longest-lived or the shortest-lived sheds the same thing at death, for it is the present moment only of which he will be deprived, if indeed only the present moment is his, and no man can discard what he does not have.

15. "All is but thinking so." The retort to the saying of Monimus the Cynic is obvious, but the usefulness of the saying is also obvious, if one accepts the essential meaning of it insofar as it is true.

16. The human soul violates itself most of all when it becomes, as far as it can, a separate tumor or growth upon the universe; for to be discontented with anything that happens is to rebel against that Nature which embraces, in some part of itself, all other natures. The soul violates itself also whenever it turns away from a man and opposes him to do him harm, as do the souls of angry men; thirdly, whenever it is overcome by pleasure or pain; fourthly, whenever it acts a part and does or says anything falsely and hypocritically; fifthly, when it fails to direct any action or impulse to a goal, but acts at random, without purpose, whereas even the most trifling actions must be directed toward the end; and this end, for reasonable creatures, is to follow the reason and the law of the most honored commonwealth and constitution.

17. In human life time is but a point, reality a flux, perception indistinct, the composition of the body subject to easy corruption, the soul a spinning top, fortune hard to make out, fame confused. To put it briefly: physical things are but a flowing stream, things of the soul dreams and vanity; life is but a struggle and the visit to a strange land, posthumous fame but a forgetting.

What then can help us on our way? One thing only: philosophy. This consists in guarding our inner spirit inviolate and unharmed, stronger than pleasures and pains, never acting aimlessly, falsely or hypocritically, independent of the actions or inaction of others, accepting all that happens or is given as coming from whence one came oneself, and at all times awaiting death with contented mind as being only the release of the elements of which every creature is composed. If it is nothing fearful for the elements themselves that one should continually change into another, why should anyone look with suspicion upon the change and dissolution of all things? For this is in accord with nature, and nothing evil is in accord with nature.

—Translated by G. M. A. Grube

4

Christianity and Islam

In the period 400 to 750, the transition between the classical age and the Middle Ages, Greco-Roman civilization was threatened by barbarian invasions and its own internal tensions. In response to this decline, Christianity established itself as a unifying force, able to preserve urban life by its ethical teachings and institutional authority. The sacred writings of Christianity were woven together with classical learning to produce a new fabric of governing ideas in the West.

The advent of Islam in seventh-century Arabia was equally remarkable and epochal in its consequences. Galvanized by Muhammad's revelation of a demanding but merciful God, Muslim fighters conquered the southern Mediterranean world from Spain to Syria and pushed eastward into south Asia. Islamic faith in the lyrical Arabic pronouncements of the Qur'an did not hinder Arabic scholars in their study of classical learning and progress in science and philosophy.

Both Christianity and Islam were rooted in the religious faith of the ancient Israelites, whose minor political role in the ancient world was far outstripped by the influence of their religious ideas. With story and history, the Hebrew scriptures elaborated a subtle concept of an all-powerful God who expected his people to treat each other with kindness and generosity.

Reflecting the Israelites' evolving faith, the Hebrew Bible recounts the lives of the early Hebrews and their unique covenant with God. From the creation stories to the lives of the patriarchs, the Hebrew scriptures describe a God who acts in history and commands the faith and obedience of followers like Abraham and Job.

Whereas the Hebrew Bible grew from stories told over a thousand years, the new faith of Christianity founded its sacred scriptures in the century after the death of its central figure, Jesus of Nazareth. The gospels of the New Testament professed Jesus as the messiah and recounted his miraculous deeds. As summarized in the Sermon on the Mount, Jesus' teaching obliged his followers to reject a world governed by power, family, and material wealth. Jesus' call for a "kingdom of God" can well be measured against Buddha's insights and Muhammad's demand for a righteous life. In his *Confessions*, Augustine gives a vivid account of his own spiritual and intellectual struggle against the temptations of the late Roman world, culminating in his conversion to Christianity while reading the letters of Paul.

In contrast to the Christian scriptures, the Muslim Qur'an speaks with one voice: the voice of God himself, as transmitted through his prophet Muhammad. In the tradition of the Hebrew Bible and New Testament, the Qur'an defines the nature of an omnipotent and merciful God, who calls his servants to treat each other with justice and respect. Like its counterparts, the Qur'an continues to inspire and guide believers today.

THE HEBREW CREATION

The Genesis creation stories rival the great myths of Mesopotamia in their scope, majesty, and profound human truth. Like the myths of Egypt and Mesopotamia, they address fundamental questions about the nature of the universe and humans' relation to the divine. They also illustrate an evolving belief. The story of Adam and Eve (Genesis 2:4–3:24), what scholars call the J story (attributed to the Jahwist author), is actually the older of the two stories. Its geography is more specific and localized while God's creation of humanity is a physical act and is followed by the highly symbolic drama of the first sin. The seven days of creation (Genesis 1:1–2:3), attributed to the P or "priestly" source, offers a more universally conceived creating God, who majestically calls the universe into existence by only his voice. These stories are the foundation of Western beliefs about humans' role in the world, the nature of free will, and the existence of evil and suffering.

For analysis and interpretation:

1. What does the P story (seven days of creation) imply about the hierarchy of being in God's creation? What is humanity's place and responsibility in this hierarchy?

2. Compare the endings of the two stories. How do these endings support different conceptions of the nature of humanity and humanity's relation to God?

3. What part do human freedom and intelligence play in both stories?

The Hebrew Bible:
The Creation Stories

Genesis 1:1–3:24

1 In the beginning God created the heavens and the earth. The earth was without form and void, and darkness was upon the face of the deep; and the Spirit of God was moving over the face of the waters.

3 And God said, "Let there be light"; and there was light. And God saw that the light was good; and God separated the light from the darkness. God called the light Day, and the darkness he called Night. And there was evening and there was morning, one day.

6 And God said, "Let there be a firmament in the midst of the waters, and let it separate the waters from the waters." And God made the firmament and separated the waters which were under the firmament from the waters which were above the firmament. And it was so. And God called the firmament Heaven. And there was evening and there was morning, a second day.

9 And God said, "Let the waters under the heavens be gathered together into one place, and let the dry land appear." And it was so. God called the dry land Earth, and the waters that were gathered together he called Seas. And God saw that it was good. And God said, "Let the earth put forth vegetation, plants yielding seed, and fruit trees bearing fruit in which is their seed, each according to its kind, upon the earth." And it was so. The earth brought forth vegetation, plants yielding seed according to their own kinds, and trees bearing fruit in which is their seed, each according to its kind. And God saw that it was good. And there was evening and there was morning, a third day.

14 And God said, "Let there be lights in the firmament of the heavens to separate the day from the night; and let them be for signs and for seasons and for days and years, and let them be lights in the firmament of the heavens to give light upon the earth." And it was so. And God made the two great lights, the greater light to rule the day, and the lesser to rule the night; he made the stars also. And God set them in the firmament of the heavens to give light upon the earth, to rule over the day and over the night, and to separate the light from the darkness. And God saw that it was good. And there was evening and there was morning, a fourth day.

20 And God said, "Let the waters bring forth swarms of living creatures and let birds fly above the earth across the firmament of the heavens." So God created the great sea monsters and every living creature that moves, with which the waters swarm, according to their kinds, and every winged bird according to its kind. And God saw that it was good. And God blessed them, saying, "Be fruitful and multiply and fill the waters in the seas and let birds multiply on the earth." And there was evening and there was morning, a fifth day.

24 And God said, "Let the earth bring forth living creatures according to their kinds: cattle and creeping things and beasts of the earth according to their kinds." And it was so. And God made the beasts of the earth according to their kinds and the cattle according to their kinds, and everything that creeps upon the ground according to its kind. And God saw that it was good.

26 Then God said, "Let us make man in our image, after our likeness; and let them have dominion over the fish of the sea, and over the birds of the air, and over the cattle, and over all the earth, and over every creeping thing that creeps upon the earth." So God created man in his own image, in the image of God he created him; male and female he created them. And God blessed them, and God said to them, "Be fruitful and multiply, and fill the earth and subdue it; and have dominion over the fish of the sea and over the birds of the air and over every living thing that moves upon the earth." And God said, "Behold, I have given you every plant yielding seed which is upon the face of all the earth, and every tree with seed in its fruit; you shall have them

for food. And to every beast of the earth, and to every bird of the air, and to everything that creeps on the earth, everything that has the breath of life, I have given every green plant for food." And it was so. And God saw everything that he had made, and behold it was very good. And there was evening and there was morning, a sixth day.

2 Thus the heavens and the earth were finished, and all the host of them. And on the seventh day God finished his work which he had done, and he rested on the seventh day from all his work which he had done. So God blessed the seventh day and hallowed it, because on it God rested from all his work which he had done in creation.

4 These are the generations of the heavens and the earth when they were created. In the day that the LORD God made the earth and the heavens, when no plant of the field was yet in the earth and no herb of the field had yet sprung up—for the LORD God had not caused it to rain upon the earth, and there was no man to till the ground; but a mist went up from the earth and watered the whole face of the ground — then the LORD God formed man of dust from the ground, and breathed into his nostrils the breath of life; and man became a living being. And the LORD God planted a garden in Eden, in the east; and there he put the man whom he had formed. And out of the ground the LORD God made to grow every tree that is pleasant to the sight and good for food, the tree of life also in the midst of the garden, and the tree of the knowledge of good and evil.

10 A river flowed out of Eden to water the garden, and there it divided and became four rivers. The name of the first is Pi´shon; it is the one which flows around the whole land of Hav´i•lah, where there is gold; and the gold of that land is good; bdellium and onyx stone are there. The name of the second river is Gi´hon; it is the one which flows around the whole land of Cush. And the name of the third river is Ti´gris, which flows east of Assyria. And the fourth river is the Euphra´tes.

15 The LORD God took the man and put him in the garden of Eden to till it and keep it. And the LORD God commanded the man, saying, "You may freely eat of every tree of the garden; but of the tree of the knowledge of good and evil you shall not eat, for in the day that you eat of it you shall die."

18 Then the LORD God said, "It is not good that the man should be alone; I will make him a helper fit for him." So out of the ground the LORD God formed every beast of the field and every bird of the air, and brought them to the man to see what he would call them; and whatever the man called every living creature, that was its name. The man gave names to all cattle, and to the birds of the air, and to every beast of the field; but for the man there was not found a helper fit for him. So the LORD God caused a deep sleep to fall upon the man, and while he slept took one of his ribs and closed up its place with flesh; and the rib which the LORD God had taken from the man he made into a woman and brought her to the man. Then the man said,

> "This at last is bone of my bones
> and flesh of my flesh;
> she shall be called Woman
> because she was taken out of Man."

24 Therefore a man leaves his father and his mother and cleaves to his wife, and they become one flesh. And the man and his wife were both naked, and were not ashamed.

3 Now the serpent was more subtle than any other wild creature that the LORD God had made. He said to the woman, "Did God say, 'You shall not eat of any tree of the garden'?" And the woman said to the serpent, "We may eat of the fruit of the trees of the garden; but God said, 'You shall not eat of the fruit of the tree which is in the midst of the garden, neither shall you touch it, lest you die.'" But the serpent said to the woman, "You will not die. For God knows that when you eat of it your eyes will be opened, and you will be like God, knowing good and evil." So when the woman saw that the tree was good for food, and that it was a delight to the eyes, and that the tree was to be desired to make one wise, she took of its fruit and ate; and she also gave some to her husband, and he ate. Then the eyes of both were opened, and they knew that they were naked; and they sewed fig leaves together and made themselves aprons.

8 And they heard the sound of the LORD God walking in the garden in the cool of the day, and the man and his wife hid themselves from the presence of the LORD God among the trees of the garden. But the LORD God called to the man, and said to him, "Where are you?" And he said, "I heard the sound of thee in the garden and I was afraid, because I was naked; and I hid myself." He said, "Who told you that you were naked? Have you eaten of the tree of which I commanded you not to eat?" The man said, "The woman whom thou gavest to be with me, she gave me fruit of the tree, and I ate." Then the LORD God said to the woman, "What is this that you have done?" The woman said, "The serpent beguiled me, and I ate."

14 The LORD God said to the serpent,
"Because you have done this,
  cursed are you above all cattle,
  and above all wild animals;
upon your belly you shall go,
  and dust you shall eat
  all the days of your life.
I will put enmity between you and the woman,
  and between your seed and her seed;
  he shall bruise your head,
  and you shall bruise his heel."
To the woman he said,
"I will greatly multiply your pain in childbearing;
in pain you shall bring forth children,
yet your desire shall be for your husband,
and he shall rule over you."
And to Adam he said,
  "Because you have listened to the voice of your wife,
  and have eaten of the tree
of which I commanded you,
  'You shall not eat of it,'
cursed is the ground because of you;

in toil you shall eat of it all the days of your life;
thorns and thistles it shall bring forth to you;
and you shall eat the plants of the field.
In the sweat of your face
you shall eat bread
till you return to the ground,
for out of it you were taken;
you are dust,
and to dust you shall return."

20 The man called his wife's name Eve, because she was the mother of all living. And the LORD God made for Adam and for his wife garments of skins, and clothed them.

22 Then the LORD God said, "Behold, the man has become like one of us, knowing good and evil; and now, lest he put forth his hand and take also of the tree of life, and eat, and live forever"—therefore the LORD God sent him forth from the garden of Eden, to till the ground from which he was taken. He drove out the man; and at the east of the garden of Eden he placed the cherubim, and a flaming sword which turned every way, to guard the way to the tree of life.

ABRAHAM AND HIS SONS

Abraham was founder of the Israelite nation and the first of the great patriarchs of the Hebrew tradition. Though they are ordinary men, these patriarchs are commanded by God to lead his chosen people, according to God's often inscrutable will. In Abraham's case, God has promised the shepherd his descendants will occupy the land between Egypt and the Euphrates. Because Abraham's wife Sarah is childless, God instructs Abraham to conceive a son with the servant-woman Hagar, who bears a son named Ishmael. Later, when the aged Sarah conceives by divine miracle and bears Isaac, the patriarch banishes Hagar and Ishmael. In keeping with God's promise, however, Arabic tradition holds that the exiled Ishmael settled in Arabia and fathered the Arabic nation, making all Arabs descendants of Abraham.

Blessed with his son Isaac, however, Abraham hears God's fearsome command to sacrifice the boy. The story of this sacrifice is one of the Hebrew Bible's most memorable dramas.

For analysis and interpretation:

1. The existentialist philosopher Sören Kierkegaard based an entire work on Abraham's thoughts as he obeyed the command to sacrifice his son. What might have been Abraham's thoughts and feelings as he journeyed to the mountain and prepared the sacrifice?

2. Evaluate God's command to Abraham as a test of faith and obedience. What does this episode say about the nature of the Hebrew conception of God?

The Hebrew Bible:
Ishmael

Genesis 21:1–21

21 The LORD visited Sarah as he had said, and the LORD did to Sarah as he had promised. And Sarah conceived, and bore Abraham a son in his old age at the time of which God had spoken to him. Abraham called the name of his son who was born to him, whom Sarah bore him, Isaac. And Abraham circumcised his son Isaac when he was eight days old, as God had commanded him. Abraham was a hundred years old when his son Isaac was born to him. And Sarah said, "God has made laughter for me; every one who hears will laugh over me." And she said, "Who would have said to Abraham that Sarah would suckle children? Yet I have borne him a son in his old age."

8 And the child grew, and was weaned; and Abraham made a great feast on the day that Isaac was weaned. But Sarah saw the son of Hāgàr the Egyptian, whom she had borne to Abraham, playing with her son Isaac. So she said to Abraham, "Cast out this slave woman with her son; for the son of this slave woman shall not be heir with my son Isaac." And the thing was very displeasing to Abraham on account of his son. But God said to Abraham, "Be not displeased because of the lad and because of your slave woman; whatever Sarah says to you, do as she tells you, for through Isaac shall your descendants be named. And I will make a nation of the son of the slave woman also, because he is your offspring." So Abraham rose early in the morning, and took bread and a skin of water, and gave it to Hāgàr, putting it on her shoulder, along with the child, and sent her away. And she departed, and wandered in the wilderness of Beersheba.

15 When the water in the skin was gone, she cast the child under one of the bushes. Then she went, and sat down over against him a good way off, about the distance of a bowshot; for she said, "Let me not look upon the death of the child." And as she sat over against him, the child lifted up his voice and wept. And God heard the voice of the lad; and the angel of god called to Hāgàr from heaven, and said to her, "What troubles you, Hāgàr ? Fear not; for God has heard the voice of the lad where he is. Arise, lift up the lad, and hold him fast with your hand; for I will make him a great nation." Then God opened her eyes, and she saw a well of water; and she went, and filled the skin with water, and gave the lad a drink. And God was with the lad, and he grew up; he lived in the wilderness, and became an expert with the bow. He lived in the wilderness of Pâran; and his mother took a wife for him from the land of Egypt.

The Hebrew Bible:
Abraham and Isaac

Genesis 22:1–19

22 After these things God tested Abraham, and said to him "Abraham!" And he said, "Here am I." He said, "Take your son, your only son Isaac, whom you love, and go to the land of Mŏrīåh, and offer him there as a burnt offering upon one of the mountains of which I shall tell you." So Abraham rose early in the morning, saddled his ass, and took two of his young men with him, and his son Isaac; and he cut the wood for the burnt offering, and arose and went to the place of which God had told him. On the third day Abraham lifted up his eyes and saw the place afar off. Then Abraham said to his young men, "Stay here with the ass; I and the lad will go yonder and worship, and come again to you." And Abraham took the wood of the burnt offering, and laid it on Isaac his son; and he took in his hand the fire and the knife. So they went both of them together. And Isaac said to his father Abraham, "My father!" And he said, "Here am I, my son." He said, "Behold, the fire and the wood; but where is the lamb for a burnt offering?" Abraham said, "God will provide himself the lamb for a burnt offering, my son." So they went both of them together.

9 When they came to the place of which God had told him, Abraham built an altar there, and laid the wood in order, and bound Isaac his son, and laid him on the altar, upon the wood. Them Abraham put forth his hand, and took the knife to slay his son. But the angel of the LORD called to him from heaven, and said, "Abraham, Abraham!" And he said, "Here am I." He said, "Do not lay your hand on the lad or do anything to him; for now I know that you fear God, seeing you have not withheld your son, your only son, from me." And Abraham lifted up his eyes and looked, and behold, behind him was a ram, caught in a thicket by his horns; and Abraham went and took the ram, and offered it up as a burnt offering instead of his son. So Abraham called the name of that place The LORD will provide; as it is said to this day, "On the mount of the LORD it shall be provided."

15 And the angel of the LORD called to Abraham a second time from heaven, and said, "By myself I have sworn, says the LORD, because you have done this, and have not withheld your son, your only son, I will indeed bless you, and I will multiply your descendants as the stars of heaven and as the sand which is on the seashore. And your descendants shall possess the gate of their enemies, and by your descendants shall all the nations of the earth bless themselves, because you have obeyed my voice." So Abraham returned to his young men, and they arose and went together to Beersheba; and Abraham dwelt at Beersheba.

JOB

The story of Job is recognized as a literary masterpiece of the Hebrew Bible, with its touching account of Job's suffering and awesome description of God's power. The prologue and the epilogue, which may be later additions to the original text, offer a scenario that rationalizes Job's inexplicable fate. Omitted in this selection are Job's long conversations with the three counselors, who seek to reassure him with conventional Hebrew wisdom. Finally, after demanding that God account for his suffering, Job is answered by a God who belittles his complaint and reminds him of God's incomprehensible power.

For analysis and interpretation:

1. Paraphrase God's answer to Job's demand for a justification of his suffering.

2. How might your understanding of the Book of Job change if the prologue and epilogue were omitted?

3. How would you explain the purpose of Job's suffering?

The Hebrew Bible:
Job

Job 1–3, 38–42

1 There was a man in the land of Uz, whose name was Job; and that man was blameless and upright, one who feared God, and turned away from evil. There were born to him seven sons and three daughters. He had seven thousand sheep, three thousand camels, five hundred yoke of oxen, and five hundred she-asses, and very many servants; so that this man was the greatest of all the people of the east. His sons used to go and hold a feast in the house of each on his day; and they would send and invite their three sisters to eat and drink with them. And when the days of the feast had run their course, Job would send and sanctify them, and he would rise early in the morning and offer burnt offerings according to the number of them all; for Job said, "It may be that my sons have sinned, and cursed God in their hearts." Thus Job did continually.

6 Now there was a day when the sons of God came to present themselves before the LORD, and Satan also came among them. The LORD said to Satan, "Whence have you come?" Satan answered the LORD, "From going to and fro on the earth, and from walking up and down on it." And the LORD said to Satan, "Have you considered my servant Job, that there is none like him on the earth, a blameless and upright man, who fears God and turns away from evil?" Then Satan answered the LORD, "Does Job fear God for nought? Hast thou not put a hedge about him and his house and all that he has, on every side? Thou hast blessed the work of his hands, and his possessions have increased in the land. But put forth thy hand now, and touch all that he has, and he will curse thee to thy face." And the LORD said to Satan, "Behold, all that he has is in your power; only upon himself do not put forth your hand." So Satan went forth from the presence of the LORD.

13 Now there was a day when his sons and daughters were eating and drinking wine in their eldest brother's house; and there came a messenger to Job, and said, "The oxen were plowing and the asses feeding beside them; and the Sà•bēàns fell upon them and took them, and slew the servants with the edge of the sword; and I alone have escaped to tell you." While he was yet speaking, there came another, and said, "The fire of God fell from heaven and burned up the sheep and the servants, and consumed them; and I alone have escaped to tell you." While he was yet speaking, there came another, and said, "The Chal•dē´àns formed three companies, and made a raid upon the camels and took them, and slew the servants with the edge of the sword; and I alone have escaped to tell you." While he was yet speaking, there came another, and said, "Your sons and daughters were eating and drinking wine in their eldest brother's house; and behold, a great wind came across the wilderness, and struck the four corners of the house, and it fell upon the young people, and they are dead; and I alone have escaped to tell you."

20 Then Job arose, and rent his robe, and shaved his head, and fell upon the ground, and worshiped. And he said, "Naked I came from my mother's womb, and naked shall I return; the LORD gave, and the LORD has taken away; blessed be the name of the LORD."

22 In all this Job did not sin or charge God with wrong.

2 Again there was a day when the sons of God came to present themselves before the LORD, and Satan also came among them to present himself before the LORD. And the LORD said to Satan, "Whence have you come?" Satan answered the LORD, "From going to and fro on the earth, and from walking up and down on it." And the LORD said to Satan, "Have you considered my servant Job, that there is none like him on the earth, a blameless and upright man, who fears God and turns away from evil? He still holds fast his integrity, although you moved against him, to destroy him without cause." Then Satan answered the LORD, "Skin for skin! All that a man has he will give for his life. But put forth thy hand now, and touch his bone and his flesh, and he will curse thee to thy face." And the LORD said to Satan, "Behold, he is in your power; only spare his life."

7 So Satan went forth from the presence of the LORD, and afflicted Job with loathsome sores from the sole of his foot to the crown of his head. And he took a potsherd with which to scrape himself, and sat among the ashes.

Then his wife said to him, "Do you still hold fast your integrity? Curse God, and die." But he said to her, "You speak as one of the foolish women would speak. Shall we receive good at the hand of God, and shall we not receive evil?" In all this Job did not sin with his lips.

11 Now when Job's three friends heard of all this evil that had come upon him, they came each from his own place. E•lĭ´´phaz the Tē´mà•nīte, Bil´dad the Shü´hīte, and Zō´ph´är the Nā´à•mà•thīte. They made an appointment together to come to condole with him and comfort him. And when they saw him from afar, they did not recognize him; and they raised their voices and wept; and they rent their robes and sprinkled dust upon their heads toward heaven. And they sat with him on the ground seven days and seven nights, and no one spoke a word to him, for they saw that his suffering was very great.

3 After this Job opened his mouth and cursed the day of his birth. And Job said:
"Let the day perish wherein I was born,
and the night which said,
'A man-child is conceived.'
Let that day be darkness!
May God above not seek it,
nor light shine upon it.
Let gloom and deep darkness claim it.
Let clouds dwell upon it;
let the blackness of the day terrify it.
That night—let thick darkness seize it!
let it not rejoice among the days of the year,
let it not come into the number of the months.
Yea, let that night be barren;
let no joyful cry be heard in it.
Let those curse it who curse the day,
who are skilled to rouse up Leviathan.
Let the stars of its dawn be dark;
let it hope for light, but have none,
nor see the eyelids of the morning;
because it did not shut the doors of my mother's womb,
nor hide trouble from my eyes.

"Why did I not die at birth,
come forth from the womb and expire?
Why did the knees receive me?
Or why the breasts, that I should suck?
For then I should have lain down and been quiet;
I should have slept; then I should have been at rest,
with kings and counselors of the earth
who rebuilt ruins for themselves,
or with princes who had gold,
who filled their houses with silver.
Or why was I not as a hidden untimely birth,
as infants that never see the light?
There the wicked cease from troubling,
and there the weary are at rest.
There the prisoners are at ease together;
they hear not the voice of the taskmaster.
The small and the great are there,
and the slave is free from his master.

"Why is light given to him that is in misery,
and life to the bitter in soul,

who long for death, but it comes not,
and dig for it more than for hid treasures;
who rejoice exceedingly,
and are glad, when they find the grave?
Why is light given to a man whose way is hid,
whom God has hedged in?
For my sighing comes as my bread,
and my groanings are poured out like water.
For the thing that I fear comes upon me,
and what I dread befalls me.
I am not at ease, nor am I quiet;
I have no rest; but trouble comes."

*   *   *   *   *

38 Then the LORD answered Job out of the whirlwind:
"Who is this that darkens counsel by words without knowledge?
Gird up your loins like a man,
I will question you, and you shall declare to me.

"Where were you when I laid the foundation of the earth?
Tell me, if you have understanding.
Who determined its measurements—surely you know!
Or who stretched the line upon it?
On what were its bases sunk,
or who laid its cornerstone,
when the morning stars sang together,
and all the sons of God shouted for joy?

"Or who shut in the sea with doors,
when it burst forth from the womb;
when I made clouds its garment,
and thick darkness its swaddling band,
and prescribed bounds for it,
and set bars and doors,
and said, 'Thus far shall you come, and no farther,
and here shall your proud waves
be stayed'?

'Have you commanded the morning since your days began,
and caused the dawn to know its place,
that it might take hold of the skirts of the earth,
and the wicked be shaken out of it?
It is changed like clay under the seal,
and it is dyed like a garment.
From the wicked their light is withheld,

and their uplifted arm is broken,

"Have you entered into the springs of the sea,
or walked in the recesses of the deep?
Have the gates of death been revealed to you,
or have you seen the gates of deep darkness?
Have you comprehended the expanse of the earth?
Declare, if you know all this.

"Where is the way to the dwelling of light,
and where is the place of darkness,
that you may take it to its territory
and that you may discern the paths to its home?
You know, for you were born then,
and the number of your days is great!

"Have you entered the storehouses of the snow,
or have you seen the storehouses of the hail,
which I have reserved for the time of trouble,
for the day of battle and war?
What is the way to the place where the light is distributed,
or where the east wind is scattered upon the earth?

"Who has cleft a channel for the torrents of rain,
and a way for the thunderbolt,
to bring rain on a land where no man is,
on the desert in which there is no man;
to satisfy the waste and desolate land,
and to make the ground put forth grass?

"Has the rain a father,
or who has begotten the drops of dew?
From whose womb did the ice come forth,
and who has given birth to the hoarfrost of heaven?
The waters become hard like stone,
and the face of the deep is frozen.

"Can you bind the chains of the Plēiadēs,
or loose the cords of Ō•rī´òn?
Can you lead forth the Mazzā•roth in their season,
or can you guide the Bear with its children?
Do you know the ordinances of the heavens?
Can you establish their rule on the earth?

"Can you lift up your voice to the clouds,
That a flood of waters may cover you?
Can you send forth lightnings, that they may go

and say to you, 'Here we are'?
Who has put wisdom in the clouds,
or given understanding to the mists?
Who can number the clouds by wisdom?
Or who can tilt the waterskins of the heavens,
when the dust runs into a mass
and the clods cleave fast together?

"Can you hunt the prey for the lion,
or satisfy the appetite of the young lions,
when they crouch in their dens,
or lie in wait in their covert?
Who provides for the raven its prey
when its young ones cry to God,
and wander about for lack of food?

39 "Do you know when the mountain goats bring forth?
Do you observe the calving of the hinds?
Can you number the months that they fulfil,
and do you know the time when they bring forth,
when they crouch, bring forth their offspring,
and are delivered of their young?
Their young ones become strong,
they grow up in the open;
they go forth, and do not return to them.

"Who has let the wild ass go free?
Who has loosed the bonds of the swift ass,
to whom I have given the steppe for his home,
and the salt land for his dwelling place?
He scorns the tumult of the city;
he hears not the shouts of the driver.
He ranges the mountains as his pasture,
and he searches after every green thing.

"Is the wild ox willing to serve you?
Will he spend the night at your crib?
Can you bind him in the furrow with ropes,
or will he harrow the valleys after you?
Will you depend on him because his strength is great,
and will you leave to him your labor?
Do you have faith in him that he will return,
and bring your grain to your threshing floor?

"The wings of the ostrich wave proudly;
but are they the pinions and plumage of love?

For she leaves her eggs to the earth,
and lets them be warmed on the ground,
forgetting that a foot may crush them,
and that the wild beast may trample them.
She deals cruelly with her young,
as if they were not hers;
though her labor be in vain, yet she has no fear;
because God has made her forget wisdom,
and given her no share in understanding.
When she rouses herself to flee,
she laughs at the horse and his rider.

"Do you give the horse his might?
Do you clothe his neck with strength?
Do you make him leap like the locust?
His majestic snorting is terrible.
He paws in the valley, and exults in his strength;
he goes out to meet the weapons.
He laughs at fear, and is not dismayed;
he does not turn back from the sword.
Upon him rattle the quiver,
the flashing spear and the javelin.
With fierceness and rage he swallows the ground;
he cannot stand still at the sound of the trumpet.
When the trumpet sounds, he says 'Aha!'
He smells the battle from afar,
the thunder of the captains, and the shouting.

"Is it by your wisdom that the hawk soars,
and spreads his wings toward the south?
Is it at your command that the eagle mounts up,
and makes his nest on high?
On the rock he dwells and makes his home
in the fastness of the rocky crag.
Thence he spies out the prey;
his eyes behold it afar off.
His young ones suck up blood;
and where the slain are, there is he."

40 And the LORD said to Job;
"Shall a faultfinder contend with the Almighty?
He who argues with God, let him answer it."
Then Job answered the LORD:
"Behold, I am of small account; what shall I answer thee?

I lay my hand on my mouth.
I have spoken once, and I will not answer;
twice, but I will proceed no further."

Then the LORD answered Job out of the whirlwind:
"Gird up your loins like a man;
I will question you, and you declare to me.
Will you even put me in the wrong?
Will you condemn me that you may be justified?
Have you an arm like God,
and can you thunder with a voice like his?
Deck yourself with majesty and dignity;
clothe yourself with glory and splendor.
Pour forth the overflowings of your anger,
and look on every one that is proud, and abase him.
Look on every one that is proud, and bring him low;
and tread down the wicked where they stand.
Hide them all in the dust together;
bind their faces in the world below.
Then will I also acknowledge to you,
That your own right hand can give you victory.

"Behold, Bē´hè•móth,
which I made as I made you;
he eats grass like an ox.
Behold, his strength in his loins,
and his power in the muscles of his belly.
He makes his tail stiff like a cedar;
the sinews of his thighs are knit together.
His bones are tubes of bronze,
his limbs like bars of iron.

"He is the first of the works of God;
let him who made him bring near his sword!
For the mountains yield food for him
where all the wild beasts play.
Under the lotus plants he lies,
in the covert of the reeds and in the marsh.
For his shade the lotus trees cover him;
the willows of the brook surround him.
Behold, if the river is turbulent he is not frightened;
he is confident though Jordan rushes against his mouth.
Can one take him with hooks,
or pierce his nose with a snare?

41 "Can you draw out Le•vī´àthàn with a fishhook,
or press down his tongue with a cord?
Can you put a rope in his nose,
or pierce his jaw with a hook?
Will he make many supplications to you?
Will he speak to you soft words?
Will he make a covenant with you
to take him for your servant for ever?

Will you play with him as with a bird,
or will you put him on leash for your maidens?
Will traders bargain over him?
Will they divide him up among the merchants?
Can you fill his skin with harpoons,
or his head with fishing spears?
Lay hands on him;
think of the battle; you will not do it again!
Behold, the hope of a man is disappointed;
he is laid low even at the sight of him.
No one is so fierce that he dares to stir him up.
Who then is he that can stand before me?
Who has given to me, that I should repay him?
Whatever is under the whole heaven is mine.

"I will not keep silence concerning his limbs,
or his mighty strength, or his goodly frame.
Who can strip off his outer garment?
Who can penetrate his double coat of mail?
Who can open the doors of his face?
Round about his teeth is terror.
His back is made of rows of shields,
shut up closely as with a seal.
One is so near to another
that no air can come between them.
They are joined one to another;
they clasp each other and cannot be separated.
His sneezings flash forth light,
and his eyes are like the eyelids of the dawn.
Out of his mouth go flaming torches;
sparks of fire leap forth.
Out of his nostrils comes forth smoke,
as from a boiling pot and burning rushes.

His breath kindles coals,
and a flame comes forth from his mouth.
In his neck abides strength
and terror dances before him.
The folds of his flesh cleave together,
firmly cast upon him and immovable.
His heart is hard as a stone,
hard as the nether millstone.
When he raises himself up the mighty are afraid;
at the crashing they are beside themselves.
Though the sword reaches him, it does not avail;
nor the spear, the dart, or the javelin.
He counts iron as a straw,
and bronze as rotten wood.
The arrow cannot make him flee;
for him slingstones are turned to stubble.
Clubs are counted as stubble;
he laughs at the rattle of javelins.
His underparts are like sharp potsherds;
he spreads himself like a threshing sledge on the mire.
He makes the deep boil like a pot;
he makes the sea like a pot of ointment.
Behind him he leaves a shining wake;
one would think the deep to be hoary.
Upon earth there is not his like,
a creature without fear.
He beholds everything that is high;
he is king over all the sons of pride."

42 Then Job answered the LORD:
"I know that thou canst do all things,
and that no purpose of thine can be thwarted.
'Who is this that hides counsel without knowledge?'
Therefore I have uttered what I did not understand,
things too wonderful for me,
which I did not know.
'Hear, and I will speak;
I will question you, and you declare to me.'
I had heard of thee by the hearing of the ear,
but now my eye sees thee;
therefore I despise myself,
and repent in dust and ashes."

7 After the LORD had spoken these words to Job, the LORD said to E•li′phaz the
Te′ma•nite: "My wrath is kindled against you and against your two friends; for you have
not spoken of me what is right, as my servant Job has. Now therefore take seven bulls and
seven rams, and go to my servant Job, and offer up for yourselves a burnt offering; and
my servant Job shall pray for you, for I will accept his prayer not to deal with you according to your folly; for you have not spoken of me what is right, as my servant Job has."
So E•li′phaz the Te′ma•nite and Bil′dad the Shu′hite and Zo′phar the Na′a•ma•thite
went and did what the LORD had told them; and the LORD accepted Job's prayer.

10 And the LORD restored the fortunes of Job, when he had prayed for his friends;
and the LORD gave Job twice as much as he had before. Then came to him all his brothers
and sisters and all who had known him before, and ate bread with him in his house; and
they showed him sympathy and comforted him for all the evil that the LORD had brought
upon him; and each of them gave him a piece of money and a ring of gold. And the LORD
blessed the latter days of Job more than his beginning; and he had fourteen thousand sheep,
six thousand camels, a thousand yoke of oxen, and a thousand she-asses. He had also sev-
en sons and three daughters. And he called the name of the first Je•mi′•mah; and the name
of the second Ke•zi′ah; and the name of the third Ker′en-hap′puch. And in all the land
there were no women so fair as Job's daughters; and their father gave them inheritance
among their brothers. And after this Job lived a hundred and forty years, and saw his sons,
and his sons' sons, four generations. And Job died, an old man, and full of days.

THE NEW TESTAMENT

The New Testament, the sacred writings of Christianity, testifies to the new
covenant established by Jesus between God and his faithful. At the heart of the
New Testament are the gospels (from the Latin *evangelium*, or "good news"), accounts of Jesus' life and teachings that are also professions of the authors' faith.
The first gospels (including probably the gospel of Mark) were recorded by about
A.D. 70; by about A.D. 100, all four of the canonical gospels were in circulation.
Though they shared common sources, the gospel writers are distinct in their in-
terests. Luke emphasizes the Davidic ancestry of Jesus, and so tells the familiar
story of Jesus' birth in Bethlehem, city of David. Matth ·v stresses Jesus' ethical
teaching; his "Sermon on the Mount" may be a compilation of sayings from an
earlier gospel source. The "Parable of the Prodigal Son" graphically illustrates the
gospels' vision of a merciful and forgiving God.

For analysis and interpretation:

    1. Explain the appeal of a god born under the humble circumstances of Luke's sto-
ry of Jesus' birth.

    2. Evaluate the ethical teachings of the Sermon on the Mount, comparing them to
the teachings of Confucius, Buddha, and the Roman emperor Marcus Aurelius.

    3. Compare the parable of the prodigal son to the Genesis account of Abraham and
Isaac. What do the stories reveal about the ancient Hebrew and Christian views of God?

The New Testament:
The Birth of Jesus
Luke 2:1–20

2 In those days a decree went out from Caesar Augustus that all the world should be enrolled. This was the first enrollment, when Qui•rin´i–us was governor of Syria. And all went to be enrolled, each to his own city. And Joseph also went up from Galilee, from the city of Nazareth, to Judea, the city of David, which is called Bethlehem, because he was of the house and lineage of David, to be enrolled with Mary his betrothed, who was with child. And while they were there, the time came for her to be delivered. And she gave birth to her first-born son and wrapped him in swaddling cloths, and laid him in a manger, because there was no place for them in the inn.

8 And in that region there were shepherds out in the field, keeping watch over their flock by night. And an angel of the Lord appeared to them, and the glory of the Lord shone around them, and they were filled with fear. And the angel said to them, "Be not afraid; for behold, I bring you good news of a great joy which will come to all the people; for to you is born this day in the city of David a Savior, who is Christ the Lord. And this will be a sign for you: you will find a babe wrapped in swaddling cloths and lying in a manger." And suddenly there was with the angel a multitude of the heavenly host praising God and saying,

> "Glory to God in the highest,
> and on earth peace among men
> with whom he is pleased!"

15 When the angels went away from them into heaven, the shepherds said to one another, "Let us go over to Bethlehem and see this thing that has happened, which the Lord has made known to us." And they went with haste, and found Mary and Joseph, and the babe lying in a manger. And when they saw it they made known the saying which had been told them concerning this child; and all who heard it wondered at what the shepherds told them. But Mary kept all these things, pondering them in her heart. And the shepherds returned, glorifying and praising God for all they had heard and seen, as it had been told them.

The New Testament:
The Sermon on the Mount
Matthew 5–7

5 Seeing the crowds, he went up on the mountain, and when he sat down his disciples came to him. And he opened his mouth and taught them, saying:

3 "Blessed are the poor in spirit, for theirs is the kingdom of heaven.

4 "Blessed are those who mourn, for they shall be comforted.

5 "Blessed are the meek, for they shall inherit the earth.

6 "Blessed are those who hunger and thirst for righteousness, for they shall be satisfied.

7 "Blessed are the merciful, for they shall obtain mercy.

8 "Blessed are the pure in heart, for they shall see God.

9 "Blessed are the peacemakers, for they shall be called sons of God.

10 "Blessed are those who are persecuted for righteousness' sake, for theirs is the kingdom of heaven.

11 "Blessed are you when men revile you and persecute you and utter all kinds of evil against you falsely on my account. Rejoice and be glad, for your reward is great in heaven, for so men persecuted the prophets who were before you.

13 "You are the salt of the earth; but if salt has lost its taste, how shall its saltness be restored? It is no longer good for anything except to be thrown out and trodden under foot by men.

14 "You are the light of the world. A city set on a hill cannot be hid. Nor do men light a lamp and put it under a bushel, but on a stand, and it gives light to all in the house. Let your light so shine before men, that they may see your good works and give glory to your Father who is in heaven.

17 "Think not that I have come to abolish the law and the prophets; I have come not to abolish them but to fulfil them. For truly, I say to you, till heaven and earth pass away, not an iota, not a dot, will pass from the law until all is accomplished. Whoever then relaxes one of the least of these commandments and teaches men so, shall be called least in the kingdom of heaven; but he who does them and teaches them shall be called great in the kingdom of heaven. For I tell you, unless your righteousness exceeds that of the scribes and Pharisees, you will never enter the kingdom of heaven.

21 "You have heard that it was said to the men of old, 'You shall not kill; and whoever kills shall be liable to judgment.' But I say to you that every one who is angry with his brother shall be liable to judgment; whoever insults his brother shall be liable to the council, and whoever says 'You fool!' shall be liable to the hell of fire. So if you are offering your gift at the altar, and then remember that your brother has something against you, leave your gift there before the altar and go; first be reconciled to your brother, and then come and offer your gift. Make friends quickly with your accuser, while you are going with him to court, lest your accuser hand you over to the judge, and the judge to the guard, and you be put in prison; truly, I say to you, you will never get out till you have paid the last penny.

27 "You have heard that it was said 'You shall not commit adultery.' But I say to you that every one who looks at a woman lustfully has already committed adultery with her in his heart. If your right eye causes you to sin, pluck it out and throw it away; it is better that you lose one of your members than that your whole body be thrown into hell. And if your right hand causes you to sin, cut it off and throw it away; it is better that you lose one of your members than that your whole body go into hell.

31 "It was also said 'Whoever divorces his wife, let him give her a certificate of divorce.' But I say to you that every one who divorces his wife, except on the ground of unchastity, makes her an adulteress; and whoever marries a divorced woman commits adultery.

33 "Again you have heard that it was said to the men of old, 'You shall not swear falsely, but shall perform to the Lord what you have sworn.' But I say to you, Do not swear at all, either by heaven, for it is the throne of God, or by the earth, for it is his footstool, or by Jerusalem, for it is the city of the great King. And do not swear by your head, for you cannot make one hair white or black. Let what you say be simply 'Yes' or 'No'; anything more than this comes from evil.

38 "You have heard that it was said, 'And eye for an eye and a tooth for a tooth.' But I say to you, Do not resist one who is evil. But if any one strikes you on the right cheek, turn to him the other also; and if any one would sue you and take your coat, let him have your cloak as well; and if any one forces you to go one mile, go with him two miles. Give to him who begs from you, and do not refuse him who would borrow from you.

43 "You have heard that it was said 'You shall love your neighbor and hate your enemy.' But I say to you, Love your enemies and pray for those who persecute you, so that you may be sons of your Father who is in heaven; for he makes his sun rise on the evil and on the good, and sends rain on the just and on the unjust. For if you love those who love you, what reward have you? Do not even the tax collectors do the same? And if you salute only your brethren, what more are you doing than others? Do not even the Gentiles do the same? You, therefore, must be perfect, as your heavenly Father is perfect.

6 "Beware of practicing your piety before men in order to be seen by them; for then you will have no reward from your Father who is in heaven.

2 "Thus, when you give alms, sound no trumpet before you, as the hypocrites do in the synagogues and in the streets, that they may be praised by men. Truly, I say to you, they have their reward. But when you give alms, do not let your left hand know what your right hand is doing, so that your alms may be in secret; and your Father who sees in secret will reward you.

5 "And when you pray, you must not be like the hypocrites; for they love to stand and pray in the synagogues and at the street corners, that they may be seen by men. Truly, I say to you, they have their reward. But when you pray, go into your room and shut the door and pray to your Father who is in secret; and your Father who sees in secret will reward you.

7 "And in praying do not heap up empty phrases as the Gentiles do; for they think that they will be heard for their many words. Do not be like them, for your Father knows what you need before you ask him. Pray then like this:

> Our Father who art in heaven,
> Hallowed be thy name.
> Thy kingdom come,
> Thy will be done.
> On earth as it is in heaven.
> Give us this day our daily bread;
> And forgive us our debts,
> As we also have forgiven our debtors;
> And lead us not into temptation,
> But deliver us from evil.

14 For if you forgive men their trespasses, your heavenly Father also will forgive you; but if you do not forgive men their trespasses, neither will your Father forgive your trespasses.

16 "And when you fast, do not look dismal like the hypocrites, for they disfigure their faces that their fasting may be seen by men. Truly, I say to you, they have their reward. But when you fast, anoint your head and wash your face, that your fasting may not be seen by men but by your Father who is in secret; and your Father who sees in secret will reward you.

19 "Do not lay up for yourselves treasures on earth, where moth and rust consume and where thieves break in and steal, but lay up for yourselves treasures in heaven, where neither moth nor rust consumes and where thieves do not break in and steal. For where your treasure is, there will your heart be also.

22 "The eye is the lamp of the body. So, if your eye is sound, your whole body will be full of light; but if your eye is not sound, your whole body will be full of darkness. If then the light in you is darkness, how great is the darkness!

24 "No one can serve two masters; for either he will hate the one and love the other, or he will be devoted to the one and despise the other. You cannot serve God and mammon.

25 "Therefore I tell you, do not be anxious about your life, what you shall eat or what you shall drink, nor about your body, what you shall put on. Is not life more than food, and the body more than clothing? Look at the birds of the air: they neither sow nor reap nor gather into barns, and yet your heavenly Father feeds them. Are you not of more value than they? And which of you by being anxious can add one cubit to his span of life? And why are you anxious about clothing? Consider the lilies of the field, how they grow; they neither toil nor spin; yet I tell you, even Solomon in all his glory was not arrayed like one of these. But if God so clothes the grass of the field, which today is alive and tomorrow is thrown into the oven, will he not much more clothe you, O men of little faith? Therefore do not be anxious, saying, 'What shall we eat?' or 'What shall we drink?' or 'What shall we wear?' For the Gentiles seek all these things; and your heavenly Father knows that you need them all. But seek first his kingdom and his righteousness, and all these things shall be yours as well.

34 "Therefore do not be anxious about tomorrow, for tomorrow will be anxious for itself. Let the day's own trouble be sufficient for the day.

7 "Judge not, that you be not judged. For with the judgment you pronounce you will be judged, and the measure you give will be the measure you get. Why do you see the speck that is in your brother's eye, but do not notice the log that is in your own eye? Or how can you say to your brother, 'Let me take the speck out of your eye,' when there is the log in your own eye? You hypocrite, first take the log out of your own eye, and then you will see clearly to take the speck out of your brother's eye.

6 "Do not give dogs what is holy; and do not throw your pearls before swine, lest they trample them under foot and turn to attack you.

7 "Ask, and it will be given you; seek, and you will find; knock, and it will be opened to you. For every one who asks receives, and he who seeks finds, and to him who knocks it will be opened. Or what man of you, if his son asks him for bread, will give him a stone? Or if he asks for a fish, will give him a serpent? If you then, who are evil, know how to give good gifts to your children, how much more will your Father who is in heaven give good things to those who ask him! So whatever you wish that men would do to you, do so to them; for this is the law and the prophets.

13 "Enter by the narrow gate; for the gate is wide and the way is easy that leads to destruction, and those who enter by it are many. For the gate is narrow and the way is hard that leads to life, and those who find it are few.

15 "Beware of false prophets, who come to you in sheep's clothing but inwardly are ravenous wolves. You will know them by their fruits. Are grapes gathered from thorns, or figs from thistles? So, every sound tree bears good fruit, but the bad tree bears evil fruit. A sound tree cannot bear evil fruit, nor can a bad tree bear good fruit. Every tree that does not bear good fruit is cut down and thrown into the fire. Thus you will know them by their fruits.

21 "Not every one who says to me, 'Lord, Lord,' shall enter the kingdom of heaven, but he who does the will of my Father who is in heaven. On that day many will say to me, 'Lord, Lord, did we not prophesy in your name, and cast out demons in your name, and do many mighty works in your name?' And then will I declare to them, 'I never knew you; depart from me, you evildoers.'

24 "Every one then who hears these words of mine and does them will be like a wise man who built his house upon the rock; and the rain fell, and the floods came, and the winds blew and beat upon that house, but it did not fall, because it had been founded on the rock. And every one who hears these words of mine and does not do them will be like a foolish man who built his house upon the sand; and the rain fell, and the floods came, and the winds blew and beat against that house, and it fell; and great was the fall of it."

28 And when Jesus finished these sayings, the crowds were astonished at his teaching, for he taught them as one who had authority, and not as their scribes.

The New Testament: The Prodigal Son

Luke 15:11–32

11 And he said, "There was a man who had two sons; and the younger of them said to his father, 'Father, give me the share of property that falls to me.' And he divided his living between them. Not many days later, the younger son gathered all he had and took his journey into a far country, and there he squandered his property in loose living. And when he had spent everything, a great famine arose in that country, and he began to be in want. So he went and joined himself to one of the citizens of that country, who sent him into his fields to feed swine. And he would gladly have

fed on the pods that the swine ate; and no one gave him anything. But when he came to himself he said, 'How many of my father's hired servants have bread enough and to spare, but I perish here with hunger! I will arise and go to my father, and I will say to him, "Father, I have sinned against heaven and before you; I am no longer worthy to be called your son; treat me as one of your hired servants."' And he arose and came to his father. But while he was yet at a distance, his father saw him and had compassion, and ran and embraced him and kissed him. And the son said to him, 'Father, I have sinned against heaven and before you; I am no longer worthy to be called your son.' But the father said to his servants, 'Bring quickly the best robe, and put it on him; and put a ring on his hand, and shoes on his feet; and bring the fatted calf and kill it, and let us eat and make merry; for this my son was dead, and is alive again; he was lost, and is found.' And they began to make merry.

25 "Now his elder son was in the field; and as he came and drew near to the house, he heard music and dancing. And he called one of the servants and asked what this meant. And he said to him, 'Your brother has come, and your father has killed the fatted calf, because he has received him safe and sound.' But he was angry and refused to go in. His father came out and entreated him, but he answered his father, 'Lo, these many years I have served you, and I never disobeyed your command; yet you never gave me a kid, that I might make merry with my friends. But when this son of yours came, who has devoured your living with harlots, you killed for him the fatted calf! And he said to him, 'Son, you are always with me, and all that is mine is yours. It was fitting to make merry and be glad, for this your brother was dead, and is alive; he was lost and is found.'"

AUGUSTINE

Augustine (354–430) was born into a time of historical crisis, with the late Roman world beset by barbarian invasions and a decaying imperial government. Educated in classical philosophy, converted to Christianity in middle life, Augustine laid the philosophical foundations of medieval Christianity while working to establish the Church as the preeminent institutional authority in Western society.

The motivation for Augustine's determined leadership lay in his experiences as a child and young man, which he set down in his *Confessions*, the first autobiography in the ancient world. Augustine recalls, often with bitter regret, the sins of his youth, while marveling at the mercy and providence of a God who, he believes, had marked him for salvation. The account of his youthful transgressions reflects Augustine's belief that humans are born with a disposition to sin which can only be overcome through the merciful grace of God.

For analysis and interpretation:

1. Augustine has a powerful sense of God's personal concern for him, an undeserving sinner. Compare Augustine's experience of God's concern to stories from the Hebrew Bible and Christian gospels.

2. Evaluate Augustine's account of the pear-tree. Do you agree that humans often do wrong purely for the pleasure of doing wrong?

3. For what reasons does Augustine believe the pleasures and ambitions of his youth were vain and sinful? How does his conversion alter his view of his true purpose in life?

From the *Confessions*

Who will grant me to rest content in you? To whom shall I turn for the gift of your coming into my heart and filling it to the brim, so that I may forget all the wrong I have done and embrace you alone, my only source of good?

Why do you mean so much to me? Help me to find words to explain. Why do I mean so much to you, that you should command me to love you? And if I fail to love you, you are angry and threaten me with great sorrow, as if not to love you were not sorrow enough in itself. Have pity on me and help me, O Lord my God. Tell me why you mean so much to me. *Whisper in my heart, I am here to save you.* Speak so that I may hear your words. My heart has ears ready to listen to you, Lord. Open them wide and *whisper in my heart, I am here to save you.* I shall hear your voice and make haste to clasp you to myself. Do not hide your face away from me, for I would gladly meet my death to see it, since not to see it would be death indeed.

My soul is like a house, small for you to enter, but I pray you to enlarge it. It is in ruins, but I ask you to remake it. It contains much that you will not be pleased to see: this I know and do not hide. But who is to rid it of these things? There is not one but you to whom I can say: *if I have sinned unwittingly, do you absolve me. Keep me ever your own servant, far from pride. I trust, and trusting I find words to utter.* Lord, you know that this is true. For have I not *made my transgression known to you?* Did you not *remit the guilt of my sin?* I do not wrangle with you for judgment, for you are Truth itself, and I have no wish to delude myself, for fear that my malice should be self-betrayed. No, I do not wrangle with you, for, *if you, Lord, will keep record of our iniquities, Master, who has strength to bear it?*

*   *   *   *   *

It is certain, O Lord, that theft is punished by your law, the law that is written in men's hearts and cannot be erased however sinful they are. For no thief can bear that another thief should steal from him, even if he is rich and the other is driven to it by want. Yet I was willing to steal, and steal I did, although I was not compelled by any lack, unless it were the lack of a sense of justice or a distaste for what was right and a greedy love of doing wrong. For of what I stole I already had plenty, and much better at that, and I had no wish to enjoy the things I coveted by stealing, but only to enjoy the theft itself and the sin. There was a pear-tree near our vineyard, loaded with fruit that was attractive neither to look at nor to taste. Late one night a band of ruffians, myself included, went off to shake down the fruit and carry it away, for we had continued our games out of doors until well after dark, as was our pernicious habit. We took away an enormous quantity of pears, not to eat them ourselves, but simply to throw them to the pigs. Perhaps we ate some of them, but our real pleasure consisted in doing something that was forbidden.

Look into my heart, O God, the same heart on which you took pity when it was in the depths of the abyss. Let my heart now tell you what prompted me to do wrong for no purpose, and why it was only my own love of mischief that made me do it. The evil in me was foul, but I loved it. I loved my own perdition and my own faults, not the things for which I committed wrong, but the wrong itself. My soul was vicious and broke away from your safe keeping to seek its own destruction, looking for no profit in disgrace but only for disgrace itself.

*   *   *   *   *

I went to Carthage, where I found myself in the midst of a hissing cauldron of lust. I had not yet fallen in love, but I was in love with the idea of it, and this feeling that something was missing made me despise myself for not being more anxious to satisfy the need. I began to look around for some object for my love, since I badly wanted to love something. I had no liking for the safe path without pitfalls, for although my real need was for you, my God, who are the food of the soul, I was not aware of this hunger. I felt no need for the food that does not perish, not because I had had my fill of it, but because the more I was starved of it the less palatable it seemed. Because of this my soul fell sick. It broke out in ulcers and looked about desperately for some material, worldly means of relieving the itch which they caused. But material things, which have no soul, could not be true objects for my love. To love and to have my love returned was my heart's desire, and it would be all the sweeter if I could also enjoy the body of the one who loved me.

So I muddied the stream of friendship with the filth of lewdness and clouded its clear waters with hell's black river of lust. And yet, in spite of this rank depravity, I was vain enough to have ambitions of cutting a fine figure in the world. I also fell in love, which was a snare of my own choosing. My God, my God of mercy, how good you were to me, for you mixed much bitterness in that cup of pleasure! My love was returned and finally shackled me in the bonds of its consummation. In the midst of my joy I was caught up in the coils of trouble, for I was lashed with the cruel, fiery rods of jealousy and suspicion, fear, anger, and quarrels.

*   *   *   *   *

I was much attracted by the theatre, because the plays reflected my own unhappy plight and were tinder to my fire. Why is it that men enjoy feeling sad at the sight of tragedy and suffering on the stage, although they would be most unhappy if they had to endure the same fate themselves? Yet they watch the plays because they hope to be made to feel sad, and the feeling of sorrow is what they enjoy. What miserable delirium this is! The more a man is subject to such suffering himself, the more easily he is moved by it in the theatre. Yet when he suffers himself, we call it misery: when he suffers out of sympathy with others, we call it pity. But what sort of pity can we really feel for an imaginary scene on the stage? The audience is not called upon to offer help but only to feel sorrow, and the more they are pained the more they applaud the author. Whether this human agony is based on fact or is simply imaginary, if it is acted so badly that the audience is not moved to sorrow, they leave the theatre in a disgruntled and critical mood; whereas, if they are made to feel pain, they stay to the end watching happily.

This shows that sorrow and tears can be enjoyable. Of course, everyone wants to be happy; but even if no one likes being sad, is there just the one exception that, because we enjoy pitying others, we welcome their misfortunes, without which we could not pity them? If so, it is because friendly feelings well up in us like the waters of a spring. But what course do these waters follow? Where do they flow? Why do they trickle away to join that stream of boiling pitch, the hideous flood of lust? For by their own choice they lose themselves and become absorbed in it. They are diverted from their true course and deprived of their original heavenly calm.

*   *   *   *   *

I was eager for fame and wealth and marriage, but you only derided these ambitions. They caused me to suffer the most galling difficulties, but the less you allowed me to find pleasure in anything that was not yourself, the greater, I know, was your goodness to me. Look into my heart, O Lord, for it was your will that I should remember these things and confess them to you. I pray now that my soul may cling to you, for it was you who released it from the deadly snare in which it was so firmly caught. It was in a state of misery and you probed its wound to the quick, pricking it on to leave all else and turn to you to be healed, to turn to you who are above all things and without whom nothing could exist.

My misery was complete and I remember how, one day, you made me realize how utterly wretched I was. I was preparing a speech in praise of the Emperor, intending that it should include a great many lies which would certainly be applauded by an audience who knew well enough how far from the truth they were. I was greatly preoccupied by this task and my mind was feverishly busy with its harassing problems. As I walked along one of the streets in Milan I noticed a poor beggar who must, I suppose, have had his fill of food and drink, since he was laughing and joking. Sadly I turned to my companions and spoke to them of all the pain and trouble which is caused by our own folly. My ambitions had placed a load of misery on my shoulders and the further I carried it the heavier it became, but the only purpose of all the efforts we made was to reach the goal of peaceful happiness. This beggar had already reached it ahead of us, and perhaps we should never reach it at all. For by all my laborious contriving and intricate manoeuvres I was hoping to win the joy of worldly happiness, the very thing which this man had already secured at the cost of the few pence which he had begged.

Of course, his was not true happiness. But the state of felicity which I aimed to reach was still more false. He, at any rate, was cheerful, while I was unhappy: he had no worries, but I was full of apprehension. And if anyone had asked me whether I would rather be happy or afraid, I should have replied that I preferred to be happy. But if I had then been asked to choose between the life which that beggar led and my own, I should have chosen my own life, full of fears and worries though it was. This would have been an illogical choice and how could I have pretended that it was the right one? For I ought not to have preferred myself to the beggar simply because I was the more learned, since my learning was no source of happiness to me. I only made use of it to try to please others, and I only tried to please them, not to teach them. This was why you broke my bones with the rod of your discipline.

My soul, then, must beware of those who say that what matters is the reason why a man is happy. They will say that it was drunkenness that made the beggar happy, while my soul looked for happiness in honour. But what sort of honour did it hope to find? Not the kind which is to be found in you, O Lord. It was not true honour, any more than the beggar's joy was true joy, but it turned my head even more. That very night the beggar would sleep off his drunkenness, but mine had been with me night after night as I slept and was still with me in the morning when I woke, and would still be with me night and day after that.

Yet I know that it does matter why a man is happy. There is a world of difference between the joy of hope that comes from faith and the shallow happiness that I was looking for. There was a difference too between the beggar and myself. He was certainly the happier man, not only because he was flushed with cheerfulness while I was eaten away with anxiety, but also because he had earned his wine by wishing good day to passers-by while I was trying to feed my pride by telling lies.

*   *   *   *   *

I probed the hidden depths of my soul and wrung its pitiful secrets from it, and when I mustered them all before the eyes of my heart, a great storm broke within me, bringing with it a great deluge of tears. I stood up and left Alypius so that I might weep and cry to my heart's content, for it occurred to me that tears were best shed in solitude. I moved away far enough to avoid being embarrassed even by his presence. He must have realized what my feelings were, for I suppose I had said something and he had known from the sound of my voice that I was ready to burst into tears. So I stood up and left him where we had been sitting, utterly bewildered. Somehow I flung myself down beneath a fig tree and gave way to the tears which now streamed from my eyes, the sacrifice that is acceptable to you. I had much to say to you, my God, not in these very words but in this strain: *Lord, will you never be content? Must we always taste your vengeance? Forget the long record of our sins.* For I felt that I was still the captive of my sins, and in my misery I kept crying 'How long shall I go on saying "tomorrow, tomorrow"? Why not now? Why not make an end of my ugly sins at this moment?'

I was asking myself these questions, weeping all the while with the most bitter sorrow in my heart, when all at once I heard the sing-song voice of a child in a nearby house. Whether it was the voice of a boy or a girl I cannot say, but again and again it repeated the refrain 'Take it and read, take it and read'. At this I looked up, thinking hard whether there was any kind of game in which children used to chant words like these, but I could not remember ever hearing them before. I stemmed my flood of tears and stood up, telling myself that this could only be a divine command to open my book of Scripture and read the first passage on which my eyes should fall. For I had heard the story of Antony, and I remembered how he had happened to go into a church while the Gospel was being read and had taken it as a counsel addressed to himself when he heard the words *Go home and sell all that belongs to you. Give it to the poor, and so the treasure you have shall be in heaven; then come back and follow me.* By this divine pronouncement he had at once been converted to you.

So I hurried back to the place where Alypius was sitting, for when I stood up to move away I had put down the book containing Paul's Epistles. I seized it and opened it, and in silence I read the first passage on which my eyes fell: *Not in revelling and drunkenness, not in lust and wantonness, not in quarrels and rivalries. Rather, arm yourselves with the Lord Jesus Christ; spend no more thought on nature and nature's appetites.* I had no wish to read more and no need to do so. For in an instant, as I came to the end of the sentence, it was as though the light of confidence flooded into my heart and all the darkness of doubt was dispelled.

I marked the place with my finger or by some other sign and closed the book. My looks now were quite calm as I told Alypius what had happened to me. He too told me what he had been feeling, which of course I did not know. He asked to see what I had read. I showed it to him and he read on beyond the text which I had read. I did not know what followed, but it was this: *Find room among you for a man of over-delicate conscience.* Alypius applied this to himself and told me so. This admonition was enough to give him strength, and without suffering the distress of hesitation he made his resolution and took this good purpose to himself. And it very well suited his moral character, which had long been far, far better than my own.

Then we went in and told my mother, who was overjoyed. And when we went on to describe how it had all happened, she was jubilant with triumph and glorified you, *who are powerful enough, and more than powerful enough, to carry out your purpose beyond all our hopes and dreams.* For she saw that you had granted her far more than she used to ask in her tearful prayers and plaintive lamentations. You converted me to yourself, so that I no longer desired a wife or placed any hope in this world but stood firmly upon the rule of faith, where you had shown me to her in a dream so many years before. And you *turned her sadness into rejoicing,* into joy far fuller than her dearest wish, far sweeter and more chaste than any she had hoped to find in children begotten of my flesh.

— Translated by R.S. Pine-Coffin

THE QUR'AN

The Qur'an contains the sacred writings of the Islamic faith, as revealed to Muhammad by the angel Gabriel in the last twenty-two years of his life. The Qur'an (Arabic, "the Recital") consists of 114 *suras*, or chapters, individually titled and arranged by later editors from the longest to the shortest. Like the Hebrew and Christian scriptures, the Qur'an was transmitted orally until it was first written down a generation after Muhammad's death. The Muslim scripture is unique in that, through his angel, God speaks directly to the faithful. While Muhammad clearly drew from Hebrew, Christian, and Arabic sources, his revelation is remarkable in the beauty of its language and the forcefulness of its vision of a single, all-powerful, and merciful God. Muslims believe the Qur'an is the final revelation of God, pronounced in a vivid language that can only be understood in the original Arabic.

In the selections provided here, the Qur'an addresses the problems that beset Arabic society in Muhammad's times. "Women" (Sura 4) establishes in the voice of God a code of conduct that protects the legal rights of women and assures the poor and unfortunate will be cared for. "The Merciful" (Sura 55) details the glory of God and the wrath that awaits wrongdoers.

For analysis and interpretation:

1. Define, as you understand it, the basic ethical principle that underlies the legal prescriptions of Sura 4. How might this principle be applied in contemporary circumstances?

2. What are the most important characteristics of the God as defined in these parts of the Qur'an? Compare this conception of God to Hebrew and Christian ideas.

Women

Sura 4:1–40

In the Name of God, the Compassionate, the Merciful

MEN, HAVE fear of your Lord, who created you from a single soul. From that soul He created its mate, and through them He bestrewed the earth with countless men and women.

Fear God, in whose name you plead with one another, and honour the mothers who bore you. God is ever watching you.

Give orphans the property which belongs to them. Do not exchange their valuables for worthless things or cheat them of their possessions; for this would surely be a great sin. If you fear that you cannot treat orphans with fairness, then you may marry other women who seem good to you: two, three, or four of them. But if you fear that you cannot maintain equality among them, marry one only or any slave-girls you may own. This will make it easier for you to avoid injustice.

Give women their dowry as a free gift; but if they choose to make over to you a part of it, you may regard it as lawfully yours.

Do not give the feeble-minded the property with which God has entrusted you for their support; but maintain and clothe them with its proceeds, and give them good advice.

Put orphans to the test until they reach a marriageable age. If you find them capable of sound judgement, hand over to them their property, and do not deprive them of it by squandering it before they come of age.

Let not the rich guardian touch the property of his orphan ward; and let him who is poor use no more than a fair portion of it for his own advantage.

When you hand over to them their property, call in some witnesses; sufficient is God's accounting of your actions.

Men shall have a share in what their parents and kinsmen leave; and women shall have a share in what their parents and kinsmen leave: whether it be little or much, they shall be legally entitled to their share.

If relatives, orphans, or needy men are present at the division of an inheritance, give them, too, a share of it, and speak to them kind words.

Let those who are solicitous about the welfare of their young children after their own death take care not to wrong orphans. Let them fear God and speak for justice.

Those that devour the property of orphans unjustly, swallow fire into their bellies; they shall burn in a mighty conflagration.

God has thus enjoined you concerning your children:

A male shall inherit twice as much as a female. If there be more than two girls, they shall have two-thirds of the inheritance; but if there be one only, she shall inherit the half. Parents shall inherit a sixth each, if the deceased have a child; but if he leave no child and his parents be his heirs, his mother shall have a third. If he have brothers, his mother shall have a sixth after payment of any legacy he may have bequeathed or any debt he may have owed.

You may wonder whether your parents or your children are more beneficial to you. But this is the law of God; God is all-knowing and wise.

You shall inherit the half of your wives' estate if they die childless. If they leave children, a quarter of their estate shall be yours after payment of any legacy they may have bequeathed or any debt they may have owed.

Your wives shall inherit one quarter of your estate if you die childless. If you leave children, they shall inherit one-eighth, after payment of any legacy you may have bequeathed or any debt you may have owed.

If a man or a woman leave neither children nor parents and have a brother or a sister, they shall each inherit one-sixth. If there be more, they shall equally share the third of the estate, after payment of any legacy he may have bequeathed or any debt he may have owed, without prejudice to the rights of the heirs. That is a commandment from God. God is all-knowing, and gracious.

Such are the bounds set by God. He that obeys God and His apostle shall dwell for ever in gardens watered by running streams. That is the supreme triumph. But he that defies God and His apostle and transgresses His bounds, shall be cast into a Fire wherein he will abide for ever. A shameful punishment awaits him.

If any of your women commit fornication, call in four witnesses from among yourselves against them; if they testify to their guilt confine them to their houses till death overtakes them or till God finds another way for them.

If two men among you commit indecency, punish them both. If they repent and mend their ways, let them be. God is forgiving and merciful.

God forgives those who commit evil in ignorance and then quickly turn to Him in repentance. God will pardon them. God is all-knowing and wise. But He will not forgive those who do evil and, when death comes to them, say: 'Now we repent!' Nor those who die unbelievers: for them We have prepared a woeful scourge.

Believers, it is unlawful for you to inherit the women of your deceased kinsmen against their will, or to bar them from re-marrying, in order that you may force them to give up a part of what you have given them, unless they be guilty of a proven sinful act. Treat them with kindness; for even if you dislike them, it may well be that you dislike a thing which God has meant for your own abundant good.

If you wish to replace a wife with another, do not take from her the dowry you have given her even if it be a talent of gold. That would be improper and grossly unjust; for how can you take it back when you have lain with each other and entered into a firm contract?

You shall not marry the women whom your fathers married: all previous such marriages excepted. That was an evil practice, indecent and abominable.

Forbidden to you are your mothers, your daughters, your sisters, your paternal and maternal aunts, the daughters of your brothers and sisters, your foster-mothers, your foster-sisters, the mothers of your wives, your step-daughters who are in your charge, born of the wives with whom you have lain (it is no offence for you to marry your step-daughters if you have not consummated your marriage with their mothers), and the wives of your own begotten sons. You are also forbidden to take in marriage two sisters at one and the same time: all previous such marriages excepted. God is forgiving and merciful. Also married women, except those whom you own as slaves. Such is the decree of God. All women other than these are lawful to you, provided you seek them with your wealth in modest conduct, not in fornication. Give them their dowry for the enjoyment you have had of them as a duty; but it shall be no offence for you to make any other agreement among yourselves after you have fulfilled your duty. God is all-knowing and wise.

If any one of you cannot afford to marry a free believing woman, let him marry a slave-girl who is a believer (God best knows your faith: you are born one of another). Marry them with the permission of their masters and give them their dowry in all justice, provided they are honourable and chaste and have not entertained other men. If after marriage they commit adultery, they shall suffer half the penalty inflicted upon free adulteresses. Such is the law for those of you who fear to commit sin: but if you abstain, it will be better for you. God is forgiving and merciful.

God desires to make this known to you and to guide you along the paths of those who have gone before you, and to turn to you in mercy. God is all-knowing and wise.

God wishes to forgive you, but those who follow their own appetites wish to see you far astray. God wishes to lighten your burdens, for man was created weak.

Believers, do not consume your wealth among yourselves in vanity, but rather trade with it by mutual consent.

Do not destroy yourselves. God is merciful to you, but he that does that through wickedness and injustice shall be burned in fire. That is easy enough for God.

If you avoid the enormities you are forbidden, We shall pardon your misdeeds and usher you in with all honour. Do not covet the favours by which God has exalted some of you above others. Men shall be rewarded according to their deeds, and women shall be rewarded according to their deeds. Rather implore God to bestow on you His gifts. God has knowledge of all things.

To every parent and kinsman We have appointed heirs who will inherit from them. As for those with whom you have entered into agreements, let them, too, have their due. God bears witness to all things.

Men have authority over women because God has made the one superior to the other, and because they spend their wealth to maintain them. Good women are obedient. They guard their unseen parts because God has guarded them. As for those from whom you fear disobedience, admonish them and send them to beds apart and beat them. Then if they obey you, take no further action against them. God is high, supreme.

If you fear a breach between a man and his wife, appoint an arbiter from his people and another from hers. If they wish to be reconciled God will bring them together again. God is all-knowing and wise.

Serve God and associate none with Him. Show kindness to parents and kindred, to orphans and to the destitute, to near and distant neighbours, to those that keep company with you, to the traveller in need, and to the slaves you own. God does not love arrogant and boastful men, who are themselves niggardly and enjoin others to be niggardly; who conceal the riches which God of His bounty has bestowed upon them (We have prepared a shameful punishment for the unbelievers); and who spend their wealth for the sake of ostentation, believing neither in God nor in the Last Day. He that chooses Satan for his friend, an evil friend has he.

What harm could befall them if they believed in God and the Last Day and gave in alms of that which God bestowed on them? God knows them all.

God will wrong none by an atom's weight. A good deed He will repay twofold. Of His own bounty He will bestow a rich recompense. . . .

The Merciful

Sura 55

In the Name of God, the Compassionate, the Merciful

It is the Merciful who has taught the Koran.

He created man and taught him articulate speech. The sun and the moon pursue their ordered course. The plants and the trees bow down in adoration.

He raised the heaven on high and set the balance of all things, that you might not transgress that balance. Give just weight and full measure.

He laid the earth for His creatures, with all its fruits and blossom-bearing palm, chaff-covered grain and scented herbs. Which of your Lord's blessings would you deny?

He created man from potter's clay, and the jinn from smokeless fire. Which of your Lord's blessings would you deny?

The Lord of the two easts is He, and the Lord of the two wests. Which of your Lord's blessings would you deny?

He has let loose the two oceans: they meet one another. Yet between them stands a barrier which they cannot overrun. Which of your Lord's blessings would you deny?

Pearls and corals come from both. Which of your Lord's blessings would you deny?

His are the ships that sail like mountains upon the ocean. Which of your Lord's blessings would you deny?

All that lives on earth is doomed to die. But the face of your Lord will abide for ever, in all its majesty and glory. Which of your Lord's blessings would you deny?

All who dwell in heaven and earth entreat Him. Each day some mighty task engages Him. Which of your Lord's blessings would you deny?

Mankind and jinn, We shall surely find the time to judge you! Which of your Lord's blessings would you deny?

Mankind and jinn, if you have power to penetrate the confines of heaven and earth, then penetrate them! But this you shall not do except with Our own authority. Which of your Lord's blessings would you deny?

Flames of fire shall be lashed at you, and molten brass. There shall be none to help you. Which of your Lord's blessings would you deny?

When the sky splits asunder, and reddens like a rose or stainèd leather (which of your Lord's blessings would you deny?), on that day neither man nor jinnee will be asked about his sins. Which of your Lord's blessings would you deny?

The wrongdoers will be known by their looks; they shall be seized by their forelocks and their feet. Which of your Lord's blessings would you deny?

That is the Hell which the sinners deny. They shall wander between fire and water fiercely seething. Which of your Lord's blessings would you deny?

But for those that fear the majesty of their Lord there are two gardens (which of your Lord's blessings would you deny?) planted with shady trees. Which of your Lord's blessings would you deny?

Each is watered by a flowing spring. Which of your Lord's blessings would you deny?

Each bears every kind of fruit in pairs. Which of your Lord's blessings would you deny?

They shall recline on couches lined with thick brocade, and within reach will hang the fruits of both gardens. Which of your Lord's blessings would you deny?

Therein are bashful virgins whom neither man nor jinnee will have touched before. Which of your Lord's blessings would you deny?

Virgins as fair as corals and rubies. Which of your Lord's blessings would you deny?

Shall the reward of goodness be anything but good? Which of your Lord's blessings would you deny?

And beside these there shall be two other gardens (which of your Lord's blessings would you deny?) of darkest green. Which of your Lord's blessings would you deny?

A gushing fountain shall flow to each. Which of your Lord's blessings would you deny?

Each planted with fruit-trees, the palm and the pomegranate. Which of your Lord's blessings would you deny?

In each there shall be virgins chaste and fair. Which of your Lord's blessings would you deny?

Dark-eyed virgins sheltered in their tents (which of your Lord's blessings would you deny?) whom neither man nor jinnee will have touched before. Which of your Lord's blessings would you deny?

They shall recline on green cushions and fine carpets. Which of your Lord's blessings would you deny?

Blessed be the name of your Lord, the Lord of majesty and glory!

5

The Middle Ages

The literature and philosophy of the European Middle Ages (approximately A.D. 500–1500) had to be refashioned from the devastated urban civilization of the Roman empire. In this world of ruined cities and barbarian rule, two vigorous new forces shaped a distinctly medieval culture: the Western Christian church and a feudal class of warrior-rulers. The literary works that arose under the patronage of the Church and the feudal nobility were composed from many elements, including the surviving classical tradition, the lore and doctrine of Christianity, and lively popular traditions. Virtually every work of medieval civilization shows evidence of the commingling and conflict of these diverse traditions.

The *Song of Roland*, the Middle Ages' greatest war epic, is a straightforward account of knightly bravery and self-sacrifice that is also overlaid with Christian values, as can be seen in Roland's heroic death. A different tension between sacred and secular animates the medieval romance tradition, as in the medieval lyric poets who blend the sensuous imagery of romantic love with philosophical and religious idealism.

By the last centuries of the Middle Ages, this fusion of literary and intellectual traditions had created the conditions for great synthetic masterpieces. Dante Alighieri assimilated medieval scholastic thought and his supreme command of poetic traditions in the visionary *Divine Comedy*. Chaucer drew together the lively narrative traditions in his vigorous tales of Canterbury pilgrims. Christine de Pisan's eloquent *Book of the City of Ladies* was able to survey the entire classical and Christian traditions to bolster her defense of women's intellectual achievements. In these works the tension among diverse traditions is resolved in consummate literary and philosophical masterworks.

THE *SONG OF ROLAND*

The *Song of Roland*, the first great literary work in French, was first recorded sometime after 1100, though perhaps composed somewhat earlier. This *chanson de geste* (literally, "song of deeds") recounts, with considerable imaginative revision, an episode in the Frankish king Charlemagne's campaign against the Muslims in Spain. A Frankish rearguard force led by Roland foolishly but bravely engages their Muslim opponents. All the Frankish knights are killed before Charlemagne can return to rescue them.

In the selection here, Roland gathers the bodies of his fallen knights around the dying Archbishop Turpin. The Muslim army frets over the approach of Charlemagne, whom Roland has summoned with his great horn (the "olifant"). Mortally wounded himself, Roland recounts his heroic achievements and dies with the gestures appropriate to a great knight.

For analysis and interpretation:

1. What evidence can be cited from this excerpt of the compromise between military and religious beliefs?

2. Analyze the warrior ethic in this poem, that is, the code of right and wrong action that governs Roland and the other characters. Where can you identify a similar ethic at work in contemporary life?

3. Compare the *Song of Roland* to similar stories of heroic deeds and noble death from contemporary life. To what extent are such stories still the province of male characters and an ethic of manliness?

From the *Song of Roland*

156.
Roland the Count fights well and with great skill,
but he is hot, his body soaked with sweat;
has a great wound in his head, and much pain,
his temple broken because he blew the horn.
But he must know whether King Charles will come;
draws out the olifant, sounds it, so feebly.
The Emperor drew to a halt, listened.
"Seigneurs," he said, "it goes badly for us—
My nephew Roland falls from our ranks today.
I hear it in the horn's voice: he hasn't long.
Let every man who wants to be with Roland
ride fast! Sound trumpets! Every trumpet in this host!"
Sixty thousand, on these words, sound, so high
the mountains sound, and the valleys resound.
The pagans hear: it is no joke to them;
cry to each other: "We're getting Charles on us!"

157.

The pagans say: "The Emperor is coming. AOI.
listen to their trumpets—it is the French!
If Charles comes back, it's all over for us,
if Roland lives, this war begins again
and we have lost our land, we have lost Spain."
Some four hundred, helmets laced on, assemble,
some of the best, as they think, on that field.
They storm Roland, in one fierce, bitter attack.
And now Count Roland has some work on his hands. AOI.

158.

Roland the Count, when he sees them coming,
how strong and fierce and alert he becomes!
He will not yield to them, not while he lives.
He rides the horse they call Veillantif, spurs,
digs into it with his spurs of fine gold,
and rushes at them all where they are thickest,
the Archbishop—that Turpin!—at his side.
Said one man to the other: "Go at it, friend.
The horns we heard were the horns of the French,
King Charles is coming back with all his strength."

159.

Roland the Count never loved a coward,
a blusterer, an evil-natured man,
a man on horse who was not a good vassal.
And now he called to Archbishop Turpin:
"You are on foot, Lord, and here I am mounted,
and so, here I take my stand: for love of you.
We'll take whatever comes, the good and bad,
together, Lord: no one can make me leave you.
They will learn our swords' names today in battle,
the name of Almace, the name of Durendal!"
Said the Archbishop: "Let us strike or be shamed!
Charles is returning, and he brings our revenge."

160.

Say the pagans: "We were all born unlucky!
The evil day that dawned for us today!
We have lost our lords and peers, and now comes Charles—
that Charlemagne!—with his great host. Those trumpets!
that shrill sound on us—the trumpets of the French!
And the loud roar of that Munjoie! This Roland
is a wild man, he is too great a fighter—

What man of flesh and blood can ever hope
to bring him down? Let us cast at him, and leave him there."
And so they did: arrows, wigars, darts,
lances and spears, javelots dressed with feathers;
struck Roland's shield, pierced it, broke it to pieces,
ripped his hauberk, shattered its rings of mail,
but never touched his body, never his flesh.
They wounded Veillantif in thirty places,
struck him dead, from afar, under the Count.
The pagans flee, they leave the field to him.
Roland the Count stood alone, on his feet. AOI.

      161.

The pagans flee, in bitterness and rage,
strain every nerve running headlong toward Spain,
and Count Roland has no way to chase them,
he has lost Veillantif, his battle horse;
he has no choice, left alone there on foot.
He went to the aid of Archbishop Turpin,
unlaced the gold-dressed helmet, raised it from his head,
lifted away his bright, light coat of mail,
cut his under tunic into some lengths,
stilled his great wounds with thrusting on the strips;
then held him in his arms, against his chest,
and laid him down, gently, on the green grass;
and softly now Roland entreated him:
"My noble lord, I beg you, give me leave:
our companions, whom we have loved so dearly,
are all dead now, we must not abandon them.
I want to look for them, know them once more,
and set them in ranks, side by side, before you."
Said the Archbishop: "Go then, go and come back.
The field is ours, thanks be to God, yours and mine."

      162.

So Roland leaves him, walks the field all alone,
seeks in the valleys, and seeks in the mountains.
He found Gerin, and Gerer his companion,
and then he found Berenger and Otun,
Anseïs and Sansun, and on that field
he found Gerard the old of Roussillon;
and carried them, brave men, all, one by one,
came back to the Archbishop with these French dead,
and set them down in ranks before his knees.
The Archbishop cannot keep from weeping,

raises his hand and makes his benediction;
and said: "Lords, Lords, it was your terrible hour.
May the Glorious God set all your souls
among the holy flowers of Paradise!
Here is my own death, Lords, pressing on me,
I shall not see our mighty Emperor."

163.

And Roland leaves, seeks in the field again;
he has found Oliver, his companion,
held him tight in his arms against his chest;
came back to the Archbishop, laid Oliver
down on a shield among the other dead.
The Archbishop absolved him, signed with the Cross.
And pity now and rage and grief increase;
and Roland says: "Oliver, dear companion,
you were the son of the great duke Renier,
who held the march of the vale of Runers.
Lord, for shattering lances, for breaking shields,
for making men great with presumption weak with fright,
for giving life and counsel to good men,
for striking fear in that unbelieving race,
no warrior on earth surpasses you."

164.

Roland the Count, when he sees his peers dead,
and Oliver, whom he had good cause to love,
felt such grief and pity, he begins to weep;
and his face lost its color with what he felt:
a pain so great he cannot keep on standing,
he has no choice, falls fainting to the ground.
Said the Archbishop: "Baron, what grief for you."

165.

The Archbishop, when he saw Roland faint,
felt such pain then as he had never felt;
stretched out his hand and grasped the olifant.
At Rencesvals there is a running stream:
he will go there and fetch some water for Roland;
and turns that way, with small steps, staggering;
he is too weak, he cannot go ahead,
he has no strength: all the blood he has lost.
In less time than a man takes to cross a little field
that great heart fails, he falls forward, falls down;
and Turpin's death comes crushing down on him.

166.

Roland the Count recovers from his faint,
gets to his feet, but stands with pain and grief;
looks down the valley, looks up the mountain, sees:
on the green grass, beyond his companions,
that great and noble man down on the ground,
the Archbishop, whom God sent in His name;
who confesses his sins, lifts up his eyes,
holds up his hands joined together to heaven,
and prays to God: grant him that Paradise.
Turpin is dead, King Charles' good warrior.
In great battles, in beautiful sermons
he was ever a champion against the pagans.
Now God grant Turpin's soul His holy blessing. AOI.

167.

Roland the Count sees the Archbishop down,
sees the bowels fallen out of his body,
and the brain boiling down from his forehead.
Turpin has crossed his hands upon his chest
beneath the collarbone, those fine white hands.
Roland speaks the lament, after the custom
followed in his land: aloud, with all his heart:
"My noble lord, you great and well-born warrior,
I commend you today to the God of Glory,
whom none will ever serve with a sweeter will.
Since the Apostles no prophet the like of you
arose to keep the faith and draw men to it.
May your soul know no suffering or want,
and behold the gate open to Paradise."

168.

Now Roland feels that death is very near.
His brain comes spilling out through his two ears;
prays to God for his peers: let them be called;
and for himself, to the angel Gabriel;
took the oliphant: there must be no reproach!
took Durendal his sword in his other hand,
and farther than a crossbow's farthest shot
he walks toward Spain, into a fallow land,
and climbs a hill: there beneath two fine trees
stand four great blocks of stone, all are of marble;
and he fell back, to earth, on the green grass,
has fainted there, for death is very near.

169.

High are the hills, and high, high are the trees;
there stand four blocks of stone, gleaming of marble.
Count Roland falls fainting on the green grass,
and is watched, all this time, by a Saracen:
who has feigned death and lies now with the others,
has smeared blood on his face and on his body;
and quickly now gets to his feet and runs—
a handsome man, strong, brave, and so crazed with pride
that he does something mad and dies for it:
laid hands on Roland, and on the arms of Roland,
and cried: "Conquered! Charles's nephew conquered!
I'll carry this sword home to Arabia!"
As he draws it, the Count begins to come round.

170.

Now Roland feels: someone taking his sword!
opened his eyes, and had one word for him:
"I don't know you, you aren't one of ours";
grasps that olifant that he will never lose,
strikes on the helm beset with gems in gold,
shatters the steel, and the head, and the bones,
sent his two eyes flying out of his head,
dumped him over stretched out at his feet dead;
and said: "You nobody! how could you dare
lay hands on me—rightly or wrongly: how?
Who'll hear of this and not call you a fool?
Ah! the bell-mouth of the olifant is smashed,
the crystal and the gold fallen away."

171.

Now Roland the Count feels: his sight is gone;
gets on his feet, draws on his final strength,
the color on his face lost now for good.
Before him stands a rock; and on that dark rock
in rage and bitterness he strikes ten blows:
the steel blade grates, it will not break, it stands unmarked.
"Ah!" said the Count, "Blessed Mary, your help!
Ah Durendal, good sword, your unlucky day,
for I am lost and cannot keep you in my care.
The battles I have won, fighting with you,
the mighty lands that holding you I conquered,
that Charles rules now, our King, whose beard is white!
Now you fall to another: it must not be
a man who'd run before another man!

For a long while a good vassal held you:
there'll never be the like in France's holy land."

172.

Roland strikes down on that rock of Cerritania:
the steel blade grates, will not break, stands unmarked.
Now when he sees he can never break that sword,
Roland speaks the lament, in his own presence:
"Ah Durendal, how beautiful and bright!
so full of light, all on fire in the sun!
King Charles was in the vales of Moriane
when God sent his angel and commanded him,
from heaven, to give you a captain count.
That great and noble King girded it on me.
And with this sword I won Anjou and Brittany,
I won Poitou, I won Le Maine for Charles,
and Normandy, that land where men are free,
I won Provence and Aquitaine with this,
and Lombardy, and every field of Romagna,
I won Bavaria, and all of Flanders,
all of Poland, and Bulgaria, for Charles,
Constantinople, which pledged him loyalty,
and Saxony, where he does as he wills;
and with this sword I won Scotland and Ireland,
and England, his chamber, his own domain—
the lands, the nations I conquered with this sword,
for Charles, who rules them now, whose beard is white!
Now, for this sword, I am pained with grief and rage:
Let it not fall to pagans! Let me die first!
Our Father God, save France from that dishonor."

173.

Roland the Count strikes down on a dark rock,
and the rock breaks, breaks more than I can tell,
and the blade grates, but Durendal will not break,
the sword leaped up, rebounded toward the sky.
The Count, when he sees that sword will not be broken,
softly, in his own presence, speaks the lament:
"Ah Durendal, beautiful, and most sacred,
the holy relics in this golden pommel!
Saint Peter's tooth and blood of Saint Basile,
a lock of hair of my lord Saint Denis,
and a fragment of blessed Mary's robe:
your power must not fall to the pagans,
you must be served by Christian warriors.

May no coward ever come to hold you!
It was with you I conquered those great lands
that Charles has in his keeping, whose beard is white,
the Emperor's lands, that make him rich and strong."

    174.
Now Roland feels: death coming over him,
death descending from his temples to his heart.
He came running underneath a pine tree
and there stretched out, face down, on the green grass,
lays beneath him his sword and the olifant.
He turned his head toward the Saracen hosts,
and this is why: with all his heart he wants
King Charles the Great and all his men to say,
he died, that noble Count, a conqueror;
makes confession, beats his breast often, so feebly,
offers his glove, for all his sins, to God. AOI.

    175.
Now Roland feels that his time has run out;
he lies on a steep hill, his face toward Spain;
and with one of his hands he beat his breast:
"Almighty God, *mea culpa* in thy sight,
forgive my sins, both the great and the small,
sins I committed from the hour I was born
until this day, in which I lie struck down."
And then he held his right glove out to God.
Angels descend from heaven and stand by him. AOI.

—Translated by Frederick Goldin

MEDIEVAL LYRIC POETRY

Medieval authors composed lyric poetry in Latin, the learned language of the Church, and in the many vernacular languages of medieval Europe. One of the liveliest vernacular traditions arose in the Provence of southern France, with an invigorating blend of the Árabic love poetry of neighboring Muslim Spain and the troubadour poets' own concept of spiritualized courtly love. In Muslim Spain, called *al-Andalus* in Arabic, poets at the courts of Córdoba and other capitals composed in the official language of Arabic. By the generation of Ibn Hazm (died 1063), the Andalusian poets had distanced themselves from Eastern Arabic influences and composed poetry of a more personal tone, though highly philosophical in its view of romantic love.

Though less intellectualized than the Hispanic-Arabic poets, the troubadour lyric also had to compromise its frank sensuality with the strictures of social respectability. The combination of joyful love and regretful lament give the songs of Bernart de Ventadorn (active ca. 1170) their bittersweet tension.

The anonymous collection of poems entitled *Carmina Burana* (thirteenth century) exemplifies the lively secular spirit of medieval times, with its frank call for respite from study.

For analysis and interpretation:

1. What images express Ibn Hazm's spiritualized view of romantic love?

2. How does Bernart de Ventadorn make his praise of his lady's beauty also a praise of God?

3. Evaluate the effect of spirituality and religious restraints on the language and tone of these poems. How do they compare to love poetry from other times, including the contemporary age?

4. Compare the hedonism of the *Carmina Burana* to the tone of self-sacrifice in Bernart's love lyrics.

Ibn Hazm

1

I love you with a love that knows no waning, whereas some of
    men's loves are midday mirages.
I bear for you a pure, sincere love, and in [my] heart there is a clear picture and an
    inscription [declaring] my love for you.
Moreover, if my soul were filled by anything but you, I would pluck it out, while
    any membrane [covering it] would be torn away from it by [my] hands.
I desire from you nothing but love, and that is all I request from you.
If I should come to possess it, then all the earth will [seem like] a senile camel and
    mankind like motes of dust, while the land's inhabitants will [seem like] insects.

2

Are you from the world of the angels, or are you a mortal? Explain this to me, for
    inability [to reach the truth] has made a mockery of my understanding.
I see a human shape, yet if I use my mind, then the body is [in reality] a celestial one.
Blessed be He who arranged the manner of being of his creation in such a way that
    you should be the [only] beautiful, natural light [in it].
I have no doubt but that you are that spirit which a resemblance joining one soul to
    another in close relationship has directed toward us.
We lacked any proof that would bear witness to your creation, which we could use
    in comparison, save only that you are visible.
Were it not that our eye contemplates [your] essence we could only declare that you
    are the Sublime, True Reason.

Bernart de Ventadorn

I   Time comes and goes and turns,
through days, through months and through years,
but I, alas! am left speechless,
with my desire always the same.
Always the same and unchanging,
for she whom I wanted and still want,
has never brought me joy.

II   Her endless laughter
pains and wounds me.
She made me play a game
in which I got the worst twice over,
for love upheld by one side only
is surely lost
until the two somehow agree.

III   It is only right
that I should blame myself,
for no man born of woman
ever served so much in vain;
and if she does not punish me,
my folly will only grow, since
"fools are fearless until beaten."

IV   I shall never sing again
nor belong to the school of Eble,
for my singing is of no avail,
nor are my trills or melodies;
nor does anything I say or do
seem to be of any use to me,
nor do I see my state improving.

V   Though I may seem joyful,
my heart is filled with grief.
Who ever saw a man do penitence
for a sin not yet committed?
The more I beg, the crueler
she becomes, and unless she changes,
we'll be forced to part.

VI   It is best that she should
bend me to her every wish,
for then, if she does me wrong
or puts me off, she'll have compassion.

Because the Scripture says
one day of happiness
is well worth a hundred.

VII As long as I, safe and sound,
may live, I'll never leave her,
for after the grain has fallen,
the chaff swings aimlessly in the wind,
and if she takes her time,
it's not for me to blame her—
but if only she could mend her ways!

VIII O love which I so covet,
well-formed body, thin and smooth,
fresh skin and high color
which God fashioned with His hands,
I have always wanted you,
for nothing else so pleases me,
no other love so tempts me.

IX O wise, gentle lady, may He
who fashioned you so beautifully,
grant me that joy which I await.

From the *Carmina Burana*

Let's away with study,
     Folly's sweet.
Treasure all the pleasure
     Of our youth:
Time enough for age
     To think on Truth.
          So short a day,
          And life so quickly hasting
          And in study wasting
          Youth that would be gay!

'Tis our spring that's slipping.
     Winter draweth near,
Life itself we're losing.
     And this sorry cheer
Dries the blood and chills the heart,
     Shrivels all delight.
Age and all its crowd of ills
     Terrifies our sight.

> *So short a day,*
> *And life so quickly hasting,*
> *And in study wasting*
> *Youth that would be gay!*

Let us as the gods do,
  'Tis the wiser part:
Leisure and love's pleasure
  Seek the young in heart
Follow the old fashion,
  Down into the street!
Down among the maidens,
  And the dancing feet!
> *So short a day,*
> *And life so quickly hasting,*
> *And in study wasting*
> *Youth that would be gay!*

There for the seeing
  Is all loveliness,
White limbs moving
  Light in wantonness.
Gay go the dancers,
  I stand and see,
Gaze, till their glances
  Steal myself from me.
> *So short a day,*
> *And life so quickly hasting,*
> *And in study wasting*
> *Youth that would be gay!*

DANTE ALIGHIERI

The *Divine Comedy* of Dante Alighieri is a monument of medieval civilization, a Christian epic that rivals the great journeys of the Greek Odysseus and Roman Aeneas. Modern readers are most attracted to the *Inferno*, with its dramatic portrayals of the suffering souls in hell.

The *Inferno*'s opening cantos emphasize the danger to Dante's own soul, since his journey is an emblem of every human's journey through the hazards of sin and temptation. When the three beasts block his path, Dante is aided by the shade of Virgil, who explains that he has been sent to guide the pilgrim by three great ladies of heaven. In Limbo, Dante sojourns with the virtuous souls of classical learning, who accept him as their equal. Then he begins his series of encounters with the damned souls of hell, by whom Dante must be instructed if he wishes to reach heaven.

Among the most famous are two episodes presented here, Dante's encounters with the adulterous lovers Paolo and Francesca and with Ulysses, the indomitable explorer of classical literature. Paolo and Francesca suffer for failing to submit their passion to divine law; Ulysses' sin is ostensibly giving evil counsel (that is, deceiving the Trojans with his wooden horse). However, Ulysses' tale of a final voyage of exploration also illustrates the perils of pursuing knowledge without divine guidance.

For analysis and interpretation:

1. Summarize the theological reasons why the great geniuses of classical learning must dwell in hell, according to Dante.

2. Analyze the way in which Francesca deflects blame from herself in her account of her passion for Paolo. How does this attitude make Francesca more deserving of her punishment?

3. In your opinion, should Ulysses be condemned for urging his companions on toward their destruction? How might Dante have seen his own journey as a similarly perilous voyage after knowledge?

From *The Divine Comedy* *Inferno:* Cantos 1–5, 26

— CANTO I

The Dark Wood of Error

Midway in his allotted threescore years and ten, Dante comes to himself with a start and realizes that he has strayed from the True Way into the Dark Wood of Error (Worldliness). As soon as he has realized his loss, Dante lifts his eyes and sees the first light of the sunrise (the Sun is the Symbol of Divine Illumination) lighting the shoulders of a little hill (The Mount of Joy). It is the Easter Season, the time of resurrection, and the sun is in its equinoctial rebirth. This juxtaposition of joyous symbols fills Dante with hope and he sets out at once to climb directly up the Mount of Joy, but almost immediately his way is blocked by the Three Beasts of Worldliness: THE LEOPARD OF MALICE AND FRAUD, THE LION OF VIOLENCE AND AMBITION, and THE SHE-WOLF OF INCONTINENCE. These beasts, and especially the She-Wolf, drive him back despairing into the darkness of error. But just as all seems lost, a figure appears to him. It is the shade of VIRGIL, Dante's symbol of HUMAN REASON.

Virgil explains that he has been sent to lead Dante from error. There can, however, be no direct ascent past the beasts: the man who would escape them must go a longer and harder way. First he must descend through Hell (The Recognition of Sin), then he must ascend through Purgatory (The Renunciation of Sin), and only then may he reach the pinnacle of joy and come to the Light of God. Virgil offers to guide Dante, but only as far as Human Reason can go. Another guide (BEATRICE, symbol of DIVINE LOVE) must take over for the final ascent, for Human Reason is self-limited. Dante submits himself joyously to Virgil's guidance and they move off.

Midway in our life's journey, I went astray
    from the straight road and woke to find myself
    alone in a dark wood. How shall I say

what wood that was! I never saw so dreary,
    so rank, so arduous a wilderness!
    Its very memory gives a shape to fear.

Death could scarce be more bitter than that place!
    But since it came to good, I will recount
    all that I found revealed there by God's grace.

How I came to it I cannot rightly say,
    so drugged and loose with sleep had I become
    when I first wandered there from the True Way.

But at the far end of that valley of evil
    whose maze had sapped my very heart with fear!
    I found myself before a little hill   15

and lifted up my eyes. Its shoulders glowed
    already with the sweet rays of that planet
    whose virtue leads men straight on every road,

and the shining strengthened me against the fright
    whose agony had wracked the lake of my heart
    through all the terrors of that piteous night.

Just as a swimmer, who with his last breath
    flounders ashore from perilous seas, might turn
    to memorize the wide water of his death—

so did I turn, my soul still fugitive
    from death's surviving image, to stare down
    that pass that none had ever left alive.

And there I lay to rest from my heart's race
    till calm and breath returned to me. Then rose
    and pushed up that dead slope at such a pace   30

each footfall rose above the last. And lo!
    almost at the beginning of the rise
    I faced a spotted Leopard all tremor and flow

and gaudy pelt. And it would not pass, but stood
    so blocking my every turn that time and again
    I was on the verge of turning back to the wood.

This fell at the first widening of the dawn
    as the sun was climbing Aries with those stars
    that rode with him to light the new creation.

Thus the holy hour and the sweet season
    of commemoration did much to arm my fear
    of that bright murderous beast with their good omen.

Yet not so much but what I shook with dread
    at sight of a great Lion that broke upon me
    raging with hunger, its enormous head   45

held high as if to strike a mortal terror
    into the very air. And down his track,
    a She-Wolf drove upon me, a starved horror

ravening and wasted beyond all belief.
    She seemed a rack for avarice, gaunt and craving.
    Oh many the souls she has brought to endless grief!

She brought such heaviness upon my spirit
    at sight of her savagery and desperation,
    I died from every hope of that high summit.

And like a miser—eager in acquisition
    but desperate in self-reproach when Fortune's wheel
    turns to the hour of his loss—all tears and attrition

I wavered back; and still the beast pursued,
    forcing herself against me bit by bit
    till I slid back into the sunless wood.   60

And as I fell to my soul's ruin, a presence
    gathered before me on the discolored air,
    the figure of one who seemed hoarse from long silence.

At sight of him in that friendless waste I cried:
    "Have pity on me, whatever thing you are,
    whether shade or living man." And it replied:

"Not man, though man I once was, and my blood
    was Lombard, both my parents Mantuan.
    I was born, though late, *sub Julio*, and bred

Rome under Augustus in the noon
    of the false and lying gods. I was a poet
    and sang of old Anchises' noble son

who came to Rome after the burning of Troy.
>   But you—why do *you* return to these distresses
>   instead of climbing that shining Mount of Joy   75

which is the seat and first cause of man's bliss?"
>   "And are you then that Virgil and that fountain
>   of purest speech?" My voice grew tremulous:

"Glory and light of poets! now may that zeal
>   and love's apprenticeship that I poured out
>   on your heroic verses serve me well!

For you are my true master and first author,
>   the sole maker from whom I drew the breath
>   of that sweet style whose measures have brought me honor.

See there, immortal sage, the beast I flee.
>   For my soul's salvation, I beg you, guard me from her,
>   for she has struck a mortal tremor through me."

And he replied, seeing my soul in tears:
>   "He must go by another way who would escape
>   this wilderness, for that mad beast that fleers   90

before you there, suffers no man to pass.
>   She tracks down all, kills all, and knows no glut,
>   but, feeding, she grows hungrier than she was.

She mates with any beast, and will mate with more
>   before the Greyhound comes to hunt her down.
>   He will not feed on lands nor loot, but honor

and love and wisdom will make straight his way.
>   He will rise between Feltro and Feltro, and in him
>   shall be the resurrection and new day

of that sad Italy for which Nisus died,
>   and Turnus, and Euryalus, and the maid Camilla.
>   He shall hunt her through every nation of sick pride

till she is driven back forever to Hell
>   whence Envy first released her on the world.
>   Therefore, for your own good, I think it well   105

you follow me and I will be your guide
>   and lead you forth through an eternal place.
>   There you shall see the ancient spirits tried

in endless pain, and hear their lamentation
    as each bemoans the second death of souls.
    Next you shall see upon a burning mountain

souls in fire and yet content in fire,
    knowing that whensoever it may be
    they yet will mount into the blessed choir.

To which, if it is still your wish to climb,
    a worthier spirit shall be sent to guide you.
    With her shall I leave you, for the King of Time,

who reigns on high, forbids me to come there
    since, living, I rebelled against his law.
    He rules the waters and the land and air   120

and there holds court, his city and his throne.
    Oh blessed are they he chooses!" And I to him:
    "Poet, by that God to you unknown,

lead me this way. Beyond this present ill
    and worse to dread, lead me to Peter's gate
    and be my guide through the sad halls of Hell."

And he then: "Follow." And he moved ahead
    in silence, and I followed where he led.

CANTO II

The Descent

It is evening of the first day (Friday). Dante is following Virgil and finds himself tired and despairing. How can he be worthy of such a vision as Virgil has described? He hesitates and seems about to abandon his first purpose.

To comfort him Virgil explains how Beatrice descended to him in Limbo and told him of her concern for Dante. It is she, the symbol of Divine Love, who sends Virgil to lead Dante from error. She has come into Hell itself on this errand, for Dante cannot come to Divine Love unaided; Reason must lead him. Moreover Beatrice has been sent with the prayers of the Virgin Mary (COMPASSION), and of Saint Lucia (DIVINE LIGHT). Rachel (THE CONTEMPLATIVE LIFE) also figures in the heavenly scene which Virgil recounts.

Virgil explains all this and reproaches Dante: how can he hesitate longer when such heavenly powers are concerned for him, and Virgil himself has promised to lead him safely?

Dante understands at once that such forces cannot fail him, and his spirits rise in joyous anticipation.

The light was departing. The brown air drew down
    all the earth's creatures, calling them to rest
    from their day-roving, as I, one man alone,

prepared myself to face the double war
    of the journey and the pity, which memory
    shall here set down, nor hesitate, nor err.

O Muses! O High Genius! Be my aid!
    O Memory, recorder of the vision,
    here shall your true nobility be displayed!

Thus I began: "Poet, you who must guide me,
    before you trust me to that arduous passage,
    look to me and look through me—can I be worthy?

You sang how the father of Sylvius, while still
    in corruptible flesh won to that other world,
    crossing with mortal sense the immortal sill.   15

But if the Adversary of all Evil
    weighing his consequence and who and what
    should issue from him, treated him so well—

that cannot seem unfitting to thinking men,
    since he was chosen father of Mother Rome
    and of her Empire by God's will and token.

Both, to speak strictly, were founded and foreknown
    as the established Seat of Holiness
    for the successors of Great Peter's throne.

In that quest, which your verses celebrate,
    he learned those mysteries from which arose
    his victory and Rome's apostolate.

There later came the chosen vessel, Paul,
    bearing the confirmation of that Faith
    which is the one true door to life eternal.   30

But I—how should I dare? By whose permission?
    I am not Aeneas. *I* am not Paul.
    Who could believe me worthy of the vision?

How, then, may I presume to this high quest
    and not fear my own brashness? You are wise
    and will grasp what my poor words can but suggest."

As one who unwills what he wills, will stay
    strong purposes with feeble second thoughts
    until he spells all his first zeal away—

so I hung back and balked on that dim coast
    till thinking had worn out my enterprise,
    so stout at starting and so early lost.

"I understand from your words and the look in your eyes,"
    that shadow of magnificence answered me,
    "your soul is sunken in that cowardice   45

that bears down many men, turning their course
    and resolution by imagined perils,
    as his own shadow turns the frightened horse.

To free you of this dread I will tell you all
    of why I came to you and what I heard
    when first I pitied you. I was a soul

among the souls of Limbo, when a Lady
    so blessed and so beautiful, I prayed her
    to order and command my will, called to me.

Her eyes were kindled from the lamps of Heaven.
    Her voice reached through me, tender, sweet, and low.
    An angel's voice, a music of its own:

'O gracious Mantuan whose melodies
    live in earth's memory and shall live on
    till the last motion ceases in the skies,   60

my dearest friend, and fortune's foe, has strayed
    onto a friendless shore and stands beset
    by such distresses that he turns afraid

from the True Way, and news of him in Heaven
    rumors my dread he is already lost.
    I come, afraid that I am too-late risen.

Fly to him and with your high counsel, pity,
    and with whatever need be for his good
    and soul's salvation, help him, and solace me.

It is I, Beatrice, who send you to him.
    I come from the blessed height for which I yearn.
    Love called me here. When amid Seraphim

I stand again before my Lord, your praises
     shall sound in Heaven.' She paused, and I began:
     'O Lady of that only grace that raises   75

feeble mankind within its mortal cycle
     above all other works God's will has placed
     within the heaven of the smallest circle;

so welcome is your command that to my sense,
     were it already fulfilled, it would yet seem tardy.
     I understand, and am all obedience.

But tell me how you dare to venture thus
     so far from the wide heaven of your joy
     to which your thoughts yearn back from this abyss.'

'Since what you ask,' she answered me, 'probes near
     the root of all, I will say briefly only
     how I have come through Hell's pit without fear.

Know then, O waiting and compassionate soul,
     that is to fear which has the power to harm,
     and nothing else is fearful even in Hell.   90

I am so made by God's all-seeing mercy
     your anguish does not touch me, and the flame
     of this great burning has no power upon me.

There is a Lady in Heaven so concerned
     for him I send you to, that for her sake
     the strict decree is broken. She has turned

and called Lucia to her wish and mercy
     saying: 'Thy faithful one is sorely pressed;
     in his distresses I commend him to thee.'

Lucia, that soul of light and foe of all
     cruelty, rose and came to me at once
     where I was sitting with the ancient Rachel,

saying to me: 'Beatrice, true praise of God,
     why dost thou not help him who loved thee so
     that for thy sake he left the vulgar crowd?   105

Dost thou not hear his cries? Canst thou not see
     the death he wrestles with beside that river
     no ocean can surpass for rage and fury?

No soul of earth was ever as rapt to seek
    its good or flee its injury as I was—
    when I had heard my sweet Lucia speak—

to descend from Heaven and my blessed seat
    to you, laying my trust in that high speech
    that honors you and all who honor it.'

She spoke and turned away to hide a tear
    that, shining, urged me faster. So I came
    and freed you from the beast that drove you there,

blocking the near way to the Heavenly Height.
    And now what ails you? Why do you lag? Why
    this heartsick hesitation and pale fright   120

when three such blessed Ladies lean from Heaven
    in their concern for you and my own pledge
    of the great good that waits you has been given?"

As flowerlets drooped and puckered in the night
    turn up to the returning sun and spread
    their petals wide on his new warmth and light—

just so my wilted spirits rose again
    and such a heat of zeal surged through my veins
    that I was born anew. Thus I began:

"Blessèd be that Lady of infinite pity,
    and blessèd be thy taxed and courteous spirit
    that came so promptly on the word she gave thee.

Thy words have moved my heart to its first purpose.
    My Guide! My Lord! My Master! Now lead on:
    one will shall serve the two of us in this."   135

He turned when I had spoken, and at his back
    I entered on that hard and perilous track.

CANTO III

The Vestibule of Hell
The Opportunists

The Poets pass the Gate of Hell and are immediately assailed by cries of anguish. Dante sees the first of the souls in torment. They are THE OPPORTUNISTS, those souls who in life were neither for good nor evil but only for themselves. Mixed with them are those outcasts who took no sides in the Rebellion of the Angels. They are neither in Hell nor out of it. Eternally unclassified, they race round and round pursuing a wavering banner that runs forever before them through the dirty air; and as they run they are pursued by swarms of wasps and hornets, who sting them and produce a constant flow of blood and putrid matter which trickles down the bodies of the sinners and is feasted upon by loathsome worms and maggots who coat the ground.

The law of Dante's Hell is the law of symbolic retribution. As they sinned so are they punished. They took no sides, therefore they are given no place. As they pursued the ever-shifting illusion of their own advantage, changing their courses with every changing wind, so they pursue eternally an elusive, ever-shifting banner. As their sin was a darkness, so they move in darkness. As their own guilty conscience pursued them, so they are pursued by swarms of wasps and hornets. And as their actions were a moral filth, so they run eternally through the filth of worms and maggots which they themselves feed.

Dante recognizes several, among them POPE CELESTINE V, but without delaying to speak to any of these souls, the Poets move on to ACHERON, the first of the rivers of Hell. Here the newly-arrived souls of the damned gather and wait for monstrous CHARON to ferry them over to punishment. Charon recognizes Dante as a living man and angrily refuses him passage. Virgil forces Charon to serve them, but Dante swoons with terror, and does not reawaken until he is on the other side.

I AM THE WAY INTO THE CITY OF WOE.
    I AM THE WAY TO A FORSAKEN PEOPLE.
    I AM THE WAY INTO ETERNAL SORROW.

SACRED JUSTICE MOVED MY ARCHITECT.
    I WAS RAISED HERE BY DIVINE OMNIPOTENCE,
    PRIMORDIAL LOVE AND ULTIMATE INTELLECT.

ONLY THOSE ELEMENTS TIME CANNOT WEAR
    WERE MADE BEFORE ME, AND BEYOND TIME I STAND.
    ABANDON ALL HOPE YE WHO ENTER HERE.

These mysteries I read cut into stone
    above a gate. And turning I said: "Master
    what is the meaning of this harsh inscription?"

And he then as initiate to novice:
    "Here must you put by all division of spirit
    and gather your soul against all cowardice.   15

This is the place I told you to expect.
    Here you shall pass among the fallen people,
    souls who have lost the good of intellect."

So saying, he put forth his hand to me,
    and with a gentle and encouraging smile
    he led me through the gate of mystery.

Here sighs and cries and wails coiled and recoiled
    on the starless air, spilling my soul to tears.
    A confusion of tongues and monstrous accents toiled

in pain and anger. Voices hoarse and shrill
    and sounds of blows, all intermingled, raised
    tumult and pandemonium that still

whirls on the air forever dirty with it
    as if a whirlwind sucked at sand. And I,
    holding my head in horror, cried: "Sweet Spirit,   30

what souls are these who run through this black haze?"
    And he to me: "These are the nearly soulless
    whose lives concluded neither blame nor praise.

They are mixed here with that despicable corps
    of angels who were neither for God nor Satan
    but only for themselves. The High Creator

scourged them from Heaven for its perfect beauty,
    and Hell will not receive them since the wicked
    might feel some glory over them." And I:

"Master, what gnaws at them so hideously
    their lamentation stuns the very air?"
    "They have no hope of death," he answered me,

"and in their blind and unattaining state
    their miserable lives have sunk so low
    that they must envy every other fate.   45

No word of them survives their living season.
    Mercy and Justice deny them even a name.
    Let us not speak of them: look, and pass on."

I saw a banner there upon the mist.
    Circling and circling, it seemed to scorn all pause.
    So it ran on, and still behind it pressed

a never-ending rout of souls in pain.
    I had not thought death had undone so many
    as passed before me in that mournful train.

And some I knew among them; last of all
    I recognized the shadow of that soul
    who, in his cowardice, made the Great Denial.

At once I understood for certain: these
    were of that retrograde and faithless crew
    hateful to God and to His enemies.   60

These wretches never born and never dead
    ran naked in a swarm of wasps and hornets
    that goaded them the more the more they fled,

and made their faces stream with bloody gouts
    of pus and tears that dribbled to their feet
    to be swallowed there by loathsome worms and maggots.

Then looking onward I made out a throng
    assembled on the beach of a wide river,
    whereupon I turned to him: "Master, I long

to know what souls these are, and what strange usage
    makes them as eager to cross as they seem to be
    in this infected light." At which the Sage:

"All this shall be made known to you when we stand
    on the joyless beach of Acheron." And I
    cast down my eyes, sensing a reprimand   75

in what he said, and so walked at his side
    in silence and ashamed until we came
    through the dead cavern to that sunless tide.

There, steering toward us in an ancient ferry
    came an old man with a white bush of hair,
    bellowing: "Woe to you depraved souls! Bury

here and forever all hope of Paradise:
    I come to lead you to the other shore,
    into eternal dark, into fire and ice.

And you who are living yet, I say begone
    from these who are dead." But when he saw me stand
    against his violence he began again:

"By other windings and by other steerage
    shall you cross to that other shore. Not here! Not here!
    A lighter craft than mine must give you passage."   90

And my Guide to him: "Charon, bite back your spleen:
    this has been willed where what is willed must be,
    and is not yours to ask what it may mean."

The steersman of that marsh of ruined souls,
    who wore a wheel of flame around each eye,
    stifled the rage that shook his woolly jowls.

But those unmanned and naked spirits there
    turned pale with fear and their teeth began to chatter
    at sound of his crude bellow. In despair

they blasphemed God, their parents, their time on earth,
    the race of Adam, and the day and the hour
    and the place and the seed and the womb that gave them birth.

But all together they drew to that grim shore
    where all must come who lose the fear of God.
    Weeping and cursing they come for evermore,   105

and demon Charon with eyes like burning coals
    herds them in, and with a whistling oar
    flails on the stragglers to his wake of souls.

As leaves in autumn loosen and stream down
    until the branch stands bare above its tatters
    spread on the rustling ground, so one by one

the evil seed of Adam in its Fall
    cast themselves, at his signal, from the shore
    and streamed away like birds who hear their call.

So they are gone over that shadowy water,
    and always before they reach the other shore
    a new noise stirs on this, and new throngs gather.

"My son," the courteous Master said to me,
    "all who die in the shadow of God's wrath
    converge to this from every clime and country.   120

And all pass over eagerly, for here
    Divine Justice transforms and spurs them so
    their dread turns wish: they yearn for what they fear.

No soul in Grace comes ever to this crossing;
    therefore if Charon rages at your presence
    you will understand the reason for his cursing."

When he had spoken, all the twilight country
    shook so violently, the terror of it
    bathes me with sweat even in memory:

The tear-soaked ground gave out a sigh of wind
    that spewed itself in flame on a red sky,
    and all my shattered senses left me. Blind,

like one whom sleep comes over in a swoon,
    I stumbled into darkness and went down.

CANTO IV

Circle One: *Limbo*
The Virtuous Pagans

*Dante wakes to find himself across Acheron. The Poets are now on the brink of
Hell itself, which Dante conceives as a great funnel-shaped cave lying below the
northern hemisphere with its bottom point at the earth's center. Around this great
circular depression runs a series of ledges, each of which Dante calls a CIRCLE.
Each circle is assigned to the punishment of one category of sin.*

*As soon as Dante's strength returns, the Poets begin to cross the FIRST
CIRCLE. Here they find the VIRTUOUS PAGANS. They were born without the
light of Christ's revelation, and, therefore, they cannot come into the light of God,
but they are not tormented. Their only pain is that they have no hope.*

*Ahead of them Dante sights a great dome of light, and a voice trumpets
through the darkness welcoming Virgil back, for this is his eternal place in Hell.
Immediately the great Poets of all time appear—HOMER, HORACE, OVID, and
LUCAN. They greet Virgil, and they make Dante a sixth in their company.*

*With them Dante enters the Citadel of Human Reason and sees before his
eyes the Master Souls of Pagan Antiquity gathered on a green, and illuminated by
the radiance of Human Reason. This is the highest state man can achieve without
God, and the glory of it dazzles Dante, but he knows also that it is nothing compared to the glory of God.*

A monstrous clap of thunder broke apart
    the swoon that stuffed my head; like one awakened
    by violent hands, I leaped up with a start.

And having risen; rested and renewed,
    I studied out the landmarks of the gloom
    to find my bearings there as best I could.

And I found I stood on the very brink of the valley
      called the Dolorous Abyss, the desolate chasm
      where rolls the thunder of Hell's eternal cry,

so depthless-deep and nebulous and dim
      that stare as I might into its frightful pit
      it gave me back no feature and no bottom.

Death-pale, the Poet spoke: "Now let us go
      into the blind world waiting here below us.
      I will lead the way and you shall follow."   15

And I, sick with alarm at his new pallor,
      cried out, "How can I go this way when you
      who are my strength in doubt turn pale with terror?"

And he: "The pain of these below us here,
      drains the color from my face for pity,
      and leaves this pallor you mistake for fear.

Now let us go, for a long road awaits us."
      So he entered and so he led me in
      to the first circle and ledge of the abyss.

No tortured wailing rose to greet us here
      but sounds of sighing rose from every side,
      sending a tremor through the timeless air,

a grief breathed out of untormented sadness,
      the passive state of those who dwelled apart,
      men, women, children—a dim and endless congress.   30

And the Master said to me: "You do not question
      what souls these are that suffer here before you?
      I wish you to know before you travel on

that these were sinless. And still their merits fail,
      for they lacked Baptism's grace, which is the door
      of the true faith you were born to. Their birth fell

before the age of the Christian mysteries,
      and so they did not worship God's Trinity
      in fullest duty. I am one of these.

For such defects are we lost, though spared the fire
      and suffering Hell in one affliction only:
      that without hope we live on in desire."

I thought how many worthy souls there were
    suspended in that Limbo, and a weight
    closed on my heart for what the noblest suffer.   45

"Instruct me, Master and most noble Sir,"
    I prayed him then, "better to understand
    the perfect creed that conquers every error:

has any, by his own or another's merit,
    gone ever from this place to blessedness?"
    He sensed my inner question and answered it:

"I was still new to this estate of tears
    when a Mighty One descended here among us,
    crowned with the sign of His victorious years.

He took from us the shade of our first parent,
    of Abel, his pure son, of ancient Noah,
    of Moses, the bringer of law, the obedient.

Father Abraham, David the King,
    Israel with his father and his children,
    Rachel, the holy vessel of His blessing,   60

and many more He chose for elevation
    among the elect. And before these, you must know,
    no human soul had ever won salvation."

We had not paused as he spoke, but held our road
    and passed meanwhile beyond a press of souls
    crowded about like trees in a thick wood.

And we had not traveled far from where I woke
    when I made out a radiance before us
    that struck away a hemisphere of dark.

We were still some distance back in the long night,
    yet near enough that I half-saw, half-sensed,
    what quality of souls lived in that light.

"O ornament of wisdom and of art,
    what souls are these whose merit lights their way
    even in Hell. What joy sets them apart?"   75

And he to me: "The signature of honor
    they left on earth is recognized in Heaven
    and wins them ease in Hell out of God's favor."

And as he spoke a voice rang on the air:
    "Honor the Prince of Poets; the soul and glory
    that went from us returns. He is here! He is here!"

The cry ceased and the echo passed from hearing;
    I saw four mighty presences come toward us
    with neither joy nor sorrow in their bearing.

"Note well," my Master said as they came on,
    "that soul that leads the rest with sword in hand
    as if he were their captain and champion.

It is Homer, singing master of the earth.
    Next after him is Horace, the satirist,
    Ovid is third, and Lucan is the fourth.   90

Since all of these have part in the high name
    the voice proclaimed, calling me Prince of Poets,
    the honor that they do me honors them."

So I saw gathered at the edge of light
    the masters of that highest school whose song
    outsoars all others like an eagle's flight.

And after they had talked together a while,
    they turned and welcomed me most graciously,
    at which I saw my approving Master smile.

And they honored me far beyond courtesy,
    for they included me in their own number,
    making me sixth in that high company.

So we moved toward the light, and as we passed
    we spoke of things as well omitted here
    as it was sweet to touch on there. At last   105

we reached the base of a great Citadel
    circled by seven towering battlements—
    and by a sweet brook flowing round them all.

This we passed over as if it were firm ground.
    Through seven gates I entered with those sages
    and came to a green meadow blooming round.

There with a solemn and majestic poise
    stood many people gathered in the light,
    speaking infrequently and with muted voice.

Past that enameled green we six withdrew
    into a luminous and open height
    from which each soul among them stood in view.

And there directly before me on the green
    the master souls of time were shown to me.
    I glory in the glory I have seen!   120

Electra stood in a great company
    among whom I saw Hector and Aeneas
    and Caesar in armor with his falcon's eye.

I saw Camilla, and the Queen Amazon
    across the field. I saw the Latian King
    seated there with his daughter by his throne.

And the good Brutus who overthrew the Tarquin:
    Lucrezia, Julia, Marcia, and Cornelia;
    and, by himself apart, the Saladin.

And raising my eyes a little I saw on high
    Aristotle, the master of those who know,
    ringed by the great souls of philosophy.

All wait upon him for their honor and his.
    I saw Socrates and Plato at his side
    before all others there. Democritus   135

who ascribes the world to chance. Diogenes,
    and with him there Thales, Anaxagoras,
    Zeno, Heraclitus, Empedocles.

And I saw the wise collector and analyst—
    Dioscorides I mean. I saw Orpheus there,
    Tully, Linus, Seneca the moralist,

Euclid the geometer, and Ptolemy,
    Hippocrates, Galen, Avicenna,
    And Averrhoës of the Great Commentary.

I cannot count so much nobility;
    my longer theme pursues me so that often
    the word falls short of the reality.

The company of six is reduced by four.
    My Master leads me by another road
    out of that serenity to the roar   150

and trembling air of Hell. I pass from light
    into the kingdom of eternal night.

CANTO V

Circle Two:
The Carnal

The Poets leave Limbo and enter the SECOND CIRCLE. Here begin the torments of Hell proper, and here, blocking the way, sits MINOS, the dread and semi-bestial judge of the damned who assigns to each soul its eternal torment. He orders the Poets back; but Virgil silences him as he earlier silenced Charon, and the Poets move on.

They find themselves on a dark ledge swept by a great whirlwind, which spins within it the souls of the CARNAL, those who betrayed reason to their appetites. Their sin was to abandon themselves to the tempest of their passions: so they are swept forever in the tempest of Hell, forever denied the light of reason and of God. Virgil identifies many among them. SEMIRAMIS is there, and DIDO, CLEOPATRA, HELEN, ACHILLES, PARIS, and TRISTAN. Dante sees PAOLO and FRANCESCA swept together, and in the name of love he calls to them to tell their sad story. They pause from their eternal flight to come to him, and Francesca tells their history while Paolo weeps at her side. Dante is so stricken by compassion at their tragic tale that he swoons once again.

So we went down to the second ledge alone;
    a smaller circle of so much greater pain
    the voice of the damned rose in a bestial moan.

There Minos sits, grinning, grotesque, and hale.
    He examines each lost soul as it arrives
    and delivers his verdict with his coiling tail.

That is to say, when the ill-fated soul
    appears before him it confesses all,
    and that grim sorter of the dark and foul

decides which place in Hell shall be its end,
    then wraps his twitching tail about himself
    one coil for each degree it must descend.

The soul descends and others take its place:
    each crowds in its turn to judgment, each confesses,
    each hears its doom and falls away through space.   15

"O you who come into this camp of woe,"
    cried Minos when he saw me turn away
    without awaiting his judgment, "watch where you go

once you have entered here, and to whom you turn!
    Do no be misled by that wide and easy passage!"
    And my Guide to him: "That is not your concern;

it is his fate to enter every door.
    This has been willed where what is willed must be,
    and is not yours to question. Say no more."

Now the choir of anguish, like a wound,
    strikes through the tortured air. Now I have come
    to Hell's full lamentation, sound beyond sound.

I came to a place stripped bare of every light
    and roaring on the naked dark like seas
    wracked by a war of winds. Their hellish flight   30

of storm and counterstorm through time foregone,
    sweeps the souls of the damned before its charge.
    Whirling and battering it drives them on,

and when they pass the ruined gap of Hell
    through which we had come, their shrieks begin anew.
    There they blaspheme the power of God eternal.

And this, I learned, was the never ending flight
    of those who sinned in the flesh, the carnal and lusty
    who betrayed reason to their appetite.

As the wings of wintering starlings bear them on
    in their great wheeling flights, just so the blast
    wherries these evil souls through time foregone.

Here, there, up, down, they whirl and, whirling, strain
    with never a hope of hope to comfort them,
    not of release, but even of less pain.   45

As cranes go over sounding their harsh cry,
    leaving the long streak of their flight in air,
    so come these spirits, wailing as they fly.

And watching their shadows lashed by wind, I cried:
    "Master, what souls are these the very air
    lashes with its black whips from side to side?"

"The first of these whose history you would know,"
    he answered me, "was Empress of many tongues.
    Mad sensuality corrupted her so

that to hide the guilt of her debauchery
    she licensed all depravity alike,
    and lust and law were one in her decree.

She is Semiramis of whom the tale is told
    how she married Ninus and succeeded him
    to the throne of that wide land the sultans hold.   60

The other is Dido; faithless to the ashes
    of Sichaeus, she killed herself for love.
    The next whom the eternal tempest lashes

is sense-drugged Cleopatra. See Helen there,
    from whom such ill arose. And great Achilles,
    who fought at last with love in the house of prayer.

And Paris. And Tristan." As they whirled above
    he pointed more that a thousand shades
    of those torn from the mortal life by love.

I stood there while my Teacher one by one
    named the great knights and ladies of dim time;
    and I was swept by pity and confusion.

At last I spoke: "Poet, I should be glad
    to speak a word with those two swept together
    so lightly on the wind and still so sad."   75

And he to me: "Watch them. When next they pass,
    call to them in the name of love that drives
    and damns them here. In that name they will pause."

Thus, as soon as the wind in its wild course
    brought them around, I called: "O wearied souls!
    if none forbid it, pause and speak to us."

As mating doves that love calls to their nest
    glide through the air with motionless raised wings,
    borne by the sweet desire that fills each breast—

Just so those spirits turned on the torn sky
    from the band where Dido whirls across the air;
    such was the power of pity in my cry.

"O living creature, gracious, kind, and good,
    going this pilgrimage through the sick night,
    visiting us who stained the earth with blood,   90

were the King of Time our friend, we would pray His peace
    on you who have pitied us. As long as the wind
    will let us pause, ask of us what you please.

The town where I was born lies by the shore
    where the Po descends into its ocean rest
    with its attendant streams in one long murmur.

Love, which in gentlest hearts will soonest bloom
    seized my lover with passion for that sweet body
    from which I was torn unshriven to my doom.

Love, which permits no loved one not to love,
    took me so strongly with delight in him
    that we are one in Hell, as we were above.

Love led us to one death. In the depths of Hell
    Caïna awaits for him who took our lives."
    This was the piteous tale they stopped to tell.   105

And when I had heard those world-offended lovers
    I bowed my head. At last the Poet spoke:
    "What painful thoughts are these your lowered brow covers?"

When at length I answered, I began: "Alas!
    What sweetest thoughts, what green and young desire
    led these two lovers to this sorry pass."

Then turning to those spirits once again,
    I said: "Francesca, what you suffer here
    melts me to tears of pity and of pain.

But tell me: in the time of your sweet sighs
    by what appearances found love the way
    to lure you to his perilous paradise?"

And she: "The double grief of a lost bliss
    is to recall its happy hour in pain.
    Your Guide and Teacher knows the truth of this.   120

But if there is indeed a soul in Hell
    to ask of the beginning of our love
    out of his pity, I will weep and tell:

On a day for dalliance we read the rhyme
    of Lancelot, how love had mastered him.
    We were alone with innocence and dim time.

Pause after pause that high old story drew
    our eyes together while we blushed and paled;
    but it was one soft passage overthrew

our caution and our hearts. For when we read
    how her fond smile was kissed by such a lover,
    he who is one with me alive and dead

breathed on my lips the tremor of his kiss.
    That book, and he who wrote it, was a pander.
    That day we read no further." As she said this,   135

the other spirit, who stood by her, wept
    so piteously, I felt my senses reel
    and faint away with anguish. I was swept

by such a swoon as death is, and I fell,
    as a corpse might fall, to the dead floor of Hell.

CANTO XXVI

Circle Eight: *Bolgia Eight*
The Evil Counselors

Dante turns from the Thieves toward the Evil Counselors of the next Bolgia, and between the two he addresses a passionate lament to Florence prophesying the griefs that will befall her from these two sins. At the purported time of the Vision, it will be recalled, Dante was a Chief Magistrate of Florence and was forced into exile by men he had reason to consider both thieves and evil counselors. He seems prompted, in fact, to say much more on this score, but he restrains himself when he comes in sight of the sinners of the next Bolgia, for they are a moral symbolism, all men of gift who abused their genius, perverting it to wiles and stratagems. Seeing them in Hell he knows his must be another road: his way shall not be by deception.

So the Poets move on and Dante observes the EIGHTH BOLGIA in detail. Here the EVIL COUNSELORS move about endlessly, hidden from view inside great flames. Their sin was to abuse the gifts of the Almighty, to steal his virtues for low purposes. And as they stole from God in their lives and worked by hidden ways, so are they stolen from sight and hidden in the great flames which are their own guilty consciences. And as, in most instances at least, they sinned by glibness of tongue, so are the flames made into a fiery travesty of tongues.

Among the others, the Poets see a great doubleheaded flame, and discover that ULYSSES and DIOMEDE are punished together within it. Virgil addresses the flame, and through its wavering tongue Ulysses narrates an unforgettable tale of his last voyage and death.

Joy to you, Florence, that your banners swell,
      beating their proud wings over land and sea,
      and that your name expands through all of Hell!

Among the thieves I found five who had been
      your citizens, to my shame; nor yet shall you
      mount to great honor peopling such a den!

But if the truth is dreamed of toward the morning,
      you soon shall feel what Prato and the others
      wish for you. And were that day of mourning

already come it would not be too soon.
      So may it come, since it must! for it will weigh
      more heavily on me as I pass my noon.

We left that place. My Guide climbed stone by stone
      the natural stair by which we had descended
      and drew me after him. So we passed on,   15

and going our lonely way through that death land
      among the crags and crevices of the cliff,
      the foot could make no way without the hand.

I mourned among those rocks, and I mourn again
      when memory returns to what I saw:
      and more than usually I curb the strain

of my genius, lest it stray from Virtue's course;
      so if some star, or a better thing, grant me merit,
      may I not find the gift cause for remorse.

As many fireflies as the peasant sees
  . when he rests on a hill and looks into the valley
      (where he tills or gathers grapes or prunes his trees)

in that sweet season when the face of him
      who lights the world rides north, and at the hour
      when the fly yields to the gnat and the air grows dim—   30

such myriads of flames I saw shine through
      the gloom of the eighth abyss when I arrived
      at the rim from which its bed comes into view.

As he the bears avenged so fearfully
      beheld Elijah's chariot depart—
      the horses rise toward heaven—but could not see

more than the flame, a cloudlet in the sky,
    once it had risen—so within the fosse
    only those flames, forever passing by

were visible, ahead, to right, to left;
    for though each steals a sinner's soul from view
    not one among them leaves a trace of the theft.

I stood on the bridge and leaned out from the edge;
    so far, that but for a jut of rock I held to
    I should have been sent hurtling from the ledge   45

without being pushed. And seeing me so intent,
    my Guide said: "There are souls within those flames;
    each sinner swathes himself in his own torment."

"Master," I said, "your words make me more sure,
    but I had seen already that it was so
    and meant to ask what spirit must endure

the pains of that great flame which splits away
    in two great horns, as if it rose from the pyre
    where Eteocles and Polynices lay?"

He answered me: "Forever round this path
    Ulysses and Diomede move in such dress,
    united in pain as once they were in wrath;

there they lament the ambush of the Horse
    which was the door through which the noble seed
    of the Romans issued from its holy source;   60

there they mourn that for Achilles slain
    sweet Deidamia weeps even in death;
    there they recall the Palladium in their pain."

"Master," I cried, "I pray you and repray
    till my prayer becomes a thousand—if these souls
    can still speak from the fire, oh let me stay

until the flame draws near! Do not deny me:
    You see how fervently I long for it!"
    and he to me: "Since what you ask is worthy,

it shall be. But be still and let me speak;
    for I know your mind already, and they perhaps
    might scorn your manner of speaking, since they were Greek."

And when the flame had come where time and place
　　seemed fitting to my Guide, I heard him say
　　these words to it: "O you two souls who pace   75

together in one flame!—if my days above
　　won favor in your eyes, if I have earned
　　however much or little of your love

in writing my High Verses, do no pass by,
　　but let one of you be pleased to tell where he,
　　having disappeared from the known world, went to die."

As if it fought the wind, the greater prong
　　of the ancient flame began to quiver and hum;
　　then moving its tip as if it were the tongue

that spoke, gave out a voice above the roar.
　　"When I left Circe," it said, "who more than a year
　　detained me near Gaëta long before

Aeneas came and gave the place that name,
　　not fondness for my son, nor reverence
　　for my aged father, nor Penelope's claim   90

to the joys of love, could drive out of my mind
　　the lust to experience the far-flung world
　　and the failings and felicities of mankind.

I put out on the high and open sea
　　with a single ship and only those few souls
　　who stayed true when the rest deserted me.

As far as Morocco and as far as Spain
　　I saw both shores; and I saw Sardinia
　　and the other islands of the open main.

I and my men were stiff and slow with age
　　when we sailed at last into the narrow pass
　　where, warning all men back from further voyage,

Hercules' Pillars rose upon our sight.
　　Already I had left Ceuta on the left;
　　Seville now sank behind me on the right.   105

'Shipmates,' I said, 'who through a hundred thousand
　　perils have reached the West, do not deny
　　to the brief remaining watch our senses stand

experience of the world beyond the sun.
     Greeks! You were not born to live like brutes,
     but to press on toward manhood and recognition!

With this brief exhortation I made my crew
     so eager for the voyage I could hardly
     have held them back from it when I was through;

and turning our stern toward morning, our bow toward night,
     we bore southwest out of the world of man;
     we made wings of our oars for our fool's flight.

That night we raised the other pole ahead
     with all its stars, and ours had so declined
     it did not rise out of its ocean bed.   120

Five times since we had dipped our bending oars
     beyond the world, the light beneath the moon
     had waxed and waned, when dead upon our course

we sighted, dark in space, a peak so tall
     I doubted any man had seen the like.
     Our cheers were hardly sounded, when a squall

broke hard upon our bow from the new land:
     three times it sucked the ship and the sea about
     as it pleased Another to order and command.

At the fourth, the poop rose and the bow went down
     till the sea closed over us and the light was gone."

—Translated, with commentary, by John Ciardi

GEOFFREY CHAUCER

Geoffrey Chaucer (1340–1400) was the greatest English poet of the Middle Ages, a master storyteller rivaled only by Dante in his command of character and voice. Chaucer was born in medieval London and spent his life in various offices of service to the English king. As courtier, soldier, and public official, Chaucer traveled widely and acquired a broad learning in the late Middle Ages' literary and philosophical genres.

Like Dante, Chaucer was influenced by the secular literature and religious attitudes of his day; like Dante, Chaucer assimilated these influences in a literary work of grand conception and piercing insight. In his masterpiece, *The Canterbury Tales*, Chaucer recounts the stories of a group of pilgrims journeying to the shrine at Canterbury cathedral. Chaucer's pilgrims represent a vibrant cross section of English society, as each is sketched in Chaucer's General Prologue. The pilgrims reveal themselves further in the tales they recount during their journey. The tales themselves are a rich sampling of medieval storytelling, from upright tales of chivalric heroism to ribald accounts of illicit love.

One of Chaucer's most vivid characters is the Wife of Bath, a lusty woman who has outlasted five husbands, as the Prologue explains:

> There was a good wife from near Bath, but she was somewhat deaf, which was a shame. . . . Her fine scarlet hose were carefully tied, and her shoes were uncracked and new. Her face was bold and fair and red. All of her life she had been an estimable woman: she had had five husbands, not to mention other company in her youth—but of that we need not speak now.

In the prologue to her tale, the Wife of Bath defends her taste for carnal pleasure, under the sanction of marriage, of course, and explains how she has cleverly prevailed over her husbands. To refute the Middle Ages' conventional wisdom regarding women as agents of temptation and sin, the Wife of Bath tells a story of women's mercifulness and the triumph of true love.

The Wife of Bath's Tale

Here begins the tale of The Wife of Bath: In the old days of King Arthur, of whom the Britons speak with such respect, all this land was filled with the supernatural. The fairy queen with her jolly band danced often in many a green meadow. At least, I have read that this was the old belief; the time of which speak was many hundred years ago. But now one can no longer see the elves, for all kinds of holy friars, as thick as dust in a sunbeam, with their great charity and prayers seek out every land and river, blessing halls, chambers, kitchens, bedrooms, cities, towns, castles, high towers, villages, dairies, barns, stables—this is why there are no fairies. For where an elf once walked there now walks a friar, mornings and afternoons, saying his prayers as he begs through his district. Nowadays women can safely travel past every bush and tree; there is no other evil spirit abroad but the friar, and he can only do us physical dishonor.

It happened that King Arthur had in his court a lusty squire who one day rode along the river where he saw a girl walking ahead of him, alone as she was born, and, despite her resistance, he ravished her. This misdeed caused such an outcry and such protest was made to King Arthur that the knight was condemned to death by a court of law. He would have lost his head—perhaps this was the law then—had not the Queen and other ladies begged so hard for mercy that the King granted him his life and gave him to the Queen to decide as she wished whether he would live or die.

The Queen heartily thanked the King, and then one day when she found the opportunity she spoke to the knight: "Your situation is still such that your life is not safe. I will grant you your life if you can tell me what it is that women desire most. Take care, now, and save your neck from the ax! And if you cannot give the answer now, I will give you leave to travel for a year and a day to seek and learn a satisfactory answer to my question. But before you go, I must have your pledge that you will return."

The knight was sad and sighed deeply, but what could he do? He was not able to do as he liked. At last he decided to go away and to return at the end of a year with whatever answer God might provide. He took his leave and went on his way.

He sought out every house and place in which he hoped he might have the luck to learn what it is that women love most. But he could in no way manage to find two creatures who were in agreement on this subject. Some said women loved riches best; some said honor; some said gaiety; some said finery; some said lovemaking and to be frequently widows and wives. Some said that our hearts are most comforted when we are flattered and pleased. I won't deny that those folk are very near the truth. A man can best win us by flattery; we are all caught by constant attentions and consideration. Some others said that we love our freedom best, and to do just as we please, so that no man will scold us for our faults, but rather say that we are wise and in no way foolish. Actually, there is no one of us that will not kick if anybody scratches us on a sore spot. Let a man try it, and he'll find that true; for no matter how evil we are inside, we wish to be thought wise and pure. Some said that we take great delight in being considered stable and discreet, steadfast in purpose, not giving away secrets told to us. But that answer is not worth a rake-handle. By God, we women can keep no secret; witness Midas—do you want to hear the story?

Ovid, among other details, mentions that Midas had two ass's ears growing on his head under his long hair, and that he was able to hide this defect cunningly from the sight of everyone except his wife; no one else knew of it. He loved her deeply and also trusted her, and he begged her to tell no one of his disfigurement. She swore that she would not tell for all the world; she would not be so low or wicked as to bring a bad name upon her own husband, nor, by telling, to bring shame upon herself. Nevertheless, she thought that she would die from keeping a secret so long. The desire to tell pained her heart so sorely that she thought the words would burst from her. Since she dared tell no one, she ran down to a nearby marsh—her heart seemed on fire until she got there—and, like a heron sputtering in the mud, she put her mouth to the water and said, "Don't betray me, water, with your sound; I'll tell you and no other:

my husband has two long ass's ears! Now it is out, and my heart is whole. Truly, I could keep the secret no longer." You see by this that, though we women can keep a secret for a while, it must come out; we can hide nothing. If you want to know the rest of that story, read Ovid and learn it from him.

When this knight, who is the subject of my tale, saw that he could not learn what women love most, his spirit was sad within him. But home he went; he could not linger, for the day had arrived when he had to return. On his way he happened to ride, greatly troubled, by the side of a forest, where he saw more than twenty-four ladies dancing. He went eagerly toward the dancers, in the hope of learning something useful. But before he reached them the dancers vanished; he could not tell where. He saw nobody except a woman sitting on the grass—an uglier creature no one can imagine. This old woman rose to meet the knight and said: "Sir Knight, there is no path this way. Tell me truly what you seek. Perhaps I can help you; old folks know many things."

"Dear mother," he said, "I am really as good as dead, unless I can say what it is that women most desire. If you can inform me, I shall pay you well."

"Take my hand and swear," she said, "that you will do the next thing I ask of you if it is in your power, and before nightfall I will tell you the answer."

"You have my word," said the knight. "I consent."

"Then I can truly say that your life is saved," she said, "for I will stake my life that the Queen will agree with my answer. Let's see the proudest wearer of kerchief or head-dress dare to disagree with what I shall teach you. Come, let us go, without more talk." Then she whispered a message into his ear and bade him be happy and not worry.

When they arrived at the court, the knight said that he had kept to the day that he had promised, and that he was ready with the answer. Many high-born wives and maidens, and many wise widows had assembled there, and the Queen herself sat as judge to hear his answer. Then the knight was told to appear. Silence was ordered, and the knight was instructed to tell the audience what thing mortal women love best. The knight did not stand like a dumb beast, but at once answered the question in a manly voice so that all the court heard: "My liege lady," he said, "in general, women wish to have complete control over both their husbands and love affairs, and to be masters of their men. That is your greatest desire, though you kill me for saying so. Do what you will with me; I'm at your disposal."

In all the court there was not one wife or maid or widow who denied what he had said; all agreed that he deserved to live.

At that decision the old woman whom the knight had seen sitting on the grass jumped up and cried, "Mercy, my sovereign lady Queen! Before you go, do me justice. I taught this answer to the knight, and in return he swore to me that he would do the first thing I asked him if it lay in his power. Before this court, then, Sir Knight, I ask you to take me as your bride, for you know well that I've saved your life. If I lie, say no, upon your honor."

The knight answered, "Alas, woe is me! I know very well that that was my promise. For the love of God, ask something else! Take all my money, and let my body go."

"No," she replied, "in that case I'd curse us both. Not for all the metal and ore that lies on this earth or is buried under it would I give up being your beloved wife, though I'm old and ugly and poor."

"My beloved?" he exclaimed, "rather my damnation! Alas, that anyone of my birth should be so foully shamed!" But all was in vain; the conclusion was that he was forced to marry her and to take his old wife to bed with him.

Now some people will perhaps say that I did not take the trouble to tell you about all the gaiety and finery which was to be seen at the wedding feast that day. I will answer them briefly: there was no joy nor any feast at all; there was nothing but sadness and much sorrow. The knight married her secretly in the morning and then hid himself like an owl all day, so troubled was he by the ugliness of his wife.

The knight's thoughts were very miserable when he took his wife to bed; he tossed and turned back and forth. His old wife lay there with a steady smile, and said: "Bless me, dear husband; does every knight treat his wife as you do? Is this the law of King Arthur's court? Is every one of his knights so standoffish? I'm your own love and also your bride, the one who saved your life, and truly I've done you no wrong. Why do you treat me so on the first night? You act like a man who has lost his mind. What have I done? For the love of God, tell me and I will amend it if I can."

"Amend it!" replied the knight. "Alas, no, no,! It will never be amended. You are so ugly, so old, and of such low birth, it's little wonder that I toss and turn. I wish to God my heart would burst!"

"Is this the cause of your discontent?" she asked.

"Yes, of course," he answered, "and no wonder."

"Now, sir," she said, "I could change all this, if I wanted to, within three days, if you conducted yourself properly toward me. But you say that nobility of character is inherent in riches; that you wealthy folk are therefore gentlemen. Such arrogance is not worth a hen. See who is most quietly and unostentatiously virtuous and most diligent in doing whatever kind deeds he can; take him as the greatest gentleman. Christ wishes us to claim our nobility of character from Him and not from our forefathers because of their wealth. Though they left us all their possessions and we claim therefore to be of a noble family, they cannot bequeath to any of us any part of the virtuous way of life which made them gentlemen, and which served as an example for us to follow.

"Dante, the wise poet of Florence, could speak well about this subject. His story runs something like this: 'Man rarely rises by his own little efforts, for God in His goodness wishes us to derive our nobility of character from Him.' We can receive only temporal things from our ancestors, things which hurt and harm man."

"Everyone knows as well as I that if nobility of character were the natural, exclusive inheritance of a particular family, the members of that family could never cease to be truly noble, because it would be impossible for them to do evil and to have faults.

"Take a torch and carry it into the darkest house between here and the Caucasus; shut the door and go away. The torch will still blaze and burn as brightly as if twenty thousand men watched it. It will carry out its natural function, I'll stake my life, until it burns out. You can clearly see from this that nobility is not connected with wealth, for people do not always act from natural causes as the torch does. God knows, one finds often enough a lord's son doing wicked and shameful deeds. The man who wishes to be considered gentlemanly because he is born of virtuous ancestors, and yet will not act virtuously as did his ancestors, is not a gentleman, even though he is a duke or an earl. For wicked deeds make a scoundrel. Nobility of character is not just the reputation of your ancestors, resulting from their noble deeds, for that is no part of you. Your nobility of character comes from God alone; from Him comes all our true distinction; it was not left to us along with our position.

"Look how noble Tullus Hostilius was, who rose, as Valerius relates, from poverty to high rank. Read Seneca and also Boethius; there you'll find it plainly stated that there is no doubt that the man is noble who does noble deeds. Therefore, dear husband, I conclude as follows: though my ancestors were lowly, God can, as I hope He will, grant me the grace to live virtuously. When I begin to live in that fashion and to give up sin, then I am a gentlewoman.

"You also scorned my poverty, but God in whom we trust chose to live His whole life in poverty. And surely every man, maid, or wife knows that Jesus, the King of Heaven, would not choose an evil way of living. Contented poverty is an honest thing, certainly; Seneca and other writers say that. I consider the man who is satisfied with his poverty rich, even though he does not own so much as a shirt. The covetous man is poor, for he desires more than he can have. But he who has nothing and covets nothing is rich, although you look down on him. True poverty sings happily. Juvenal speaks gaily of poverty: 'The poor man as he goes along the road can sing and play in front of thieves.' Poverty is a harsh virtue, but I believe it makes for industry. It also adds wisdom, if it is borne patiently. These things are true of poverty, even though it seems a wretched state no one should wish to be in. When a man is depressed by poverty he often comes to know his God and also himself. It seems to me that poverty is an eyeglass through which one may see his true friends. Therefore, since I do not trouble you, don't complain any more about my poverty.

"Now, sir, you reproached me for my age. Surely, even if there were no authority for it in any book, you honorable gentlefolk agree that one must be courteous to an old man and call him father, in order to be considered well-mannered. I think, also, that I could find support for that statement among the writers. Since you find me old and ugly, don't be afraid that I'll make you a cuckold, for ugliness and age, I'll warrant, are fine guardians of chastity. Nevertheless, since I know your pleasure, I'll satisfy your physical desire.

"Choose one of these two things," she said, "to have me ugly and old until I die, but a true and humble wife who will never displease you as long as I live; or to have me young and lovely and take your chances on the traffic there will be in and out of your house, or quite possibly elsewhere, on account of me. Take your choice; whichever you want."

The knight thought hard and sighed deeply. At last he replied, "My lady, my love, my dear wife. I put myself under your wise control. You yourself choose whichever you think will be more agreeable and honorable for both of us. I don't care which; whatever you like suits me.

"Then am I now your master," she asked, "since I can decide and do as I wish?"

"Certainly, wife," he said, "I think that will be best."

"Kiss me," she commanded, "we are no longer at odds, for, by my troth, I will be both things to you; that is to say, both lovely and faithful. I pray God that I may die insane unless I am as loyal as ever any wife since the world began. And if by tomorrow morning I am not as beautiful as any lady, empress, or queen between the east and the west, you may kill me or not as you wish. Lift up the curtain and see for yourself."

When the knight saw that she was truly beautiful and young, he joyfully clasped her in his arms, his heart filled with happiness. He kissed her a thousand times over, and she obeyed him in everything which might give him happiness or pleasure.

Thus they lived all their lives in perfect joy. May Jesus Christ send us husbands meek, young, and lusty abed, and the luck to outlast them. And I also pray Jesus to hasten the death of those who will not be ruled by their wives. And may God soon send a severe pestilence to old and stingy husbands! HERE ENDS THE WIFE OF BATH'S TALE.

— Translated by R. M. Lumiansky

CHRISTINE DE PISAN

The career of Christine de Pisan (1365–1430?) is remarkable not only for the diversity and number of her writings, but also for her success as a professional writer in late medieval society. Christine was born into the educated middle class of Italy and spent her early life at the court of the French king, immersed in the intellectual culture that would soon spawn the Renaissance. Widowed at twenty-five, she established herself as a writer of many genres and a distinctive voice in the day's literary and philosophical debates.

One such debate regarded the literary merit of the *Roman de la Rose*, the popular medieval romance, which Christine criticized for its false and disparaging depictions of women. Christine was moved to respond with the *Book of the City of Ladies* (1405), which mixes biographies of famous women, both historical and fictional, with philosophical reflections on such questions as whether women should be educated.

In the opening chapters, Christine's despair over the imperfection of women is dispelled by a visit from three ladies—Reason, Rectitude, and Justice. They direct the author to build an imaginary city, in which will dwell the upright and virtuous ladies of all history. Christine's city was inspired in part by St. Augustine's *City of God* and may also have been a reply to the less generous views of women in Giovanni Boccaccio's *On the Souls of Women* (published 1360–74). Her blending of historical and fictional characters is a medieval convention seen also in Dante's *Divine Comedy*, and her defense of women echoes Chaucer's Wife of Bath.

For analysis and interpretation:

1. Analyze the irony in Christine's opening chapters, culminating with her regretful despair over being a woman.

2. Compare the visionary concept of a "city of ladies" to Dante's vision of the afterlife. How does each provide a moral framework for storytelling?

3. How might Christine's argument regarding the education of women be applied to issues in education today?

From *The Book of the City of Ladies*

1. HERE BEGINS THE BOOK OF THE CITY OF LADIES, WHOSE FIRST CHAPTER TELLS WHY AND FOR WHAT PURPOSE THIS BOOK WAS WRITTEN.

One day as I was sitting alone in my study surrounded by books on all kinds of subjects, devoting myself to literary studies, my usual habit, my mind dwelt at length on the weighty opinions of various authors whom I had studied for a long time. I looked up from my book, having decided to leave such subtle questions in peace and to relax by reading some light poetry. With this in mind, I searched for some small book. By chance a strange volume came into my hands, not one of my own, but one which had been given to me along with some others. When I held it open and saw from its title page that it was by Mathéolus, I smiled, for though I had never seen it before, I had often heard that like other books it discussed respect for women. I thought I would browse through it to amuse myself. I had not been reading for very long when my good mother called me to refresh myself with some supper, for it was evening. Intending to look at it the next day, I put it down. The next morning, again seated in my study as was my habit, I remembered wanting to examine this book by Mathéolus. I started to read it and went on for a little while. Because the subject seemed to me not very pleasant for people who do not enjoy lies, and of no use in developing virtue or manners, given its lack of integrity in diction and theme, and after browsing here and there and reading the end, I put it down in order to turn my attention to more elevated and useful study. But just the sight of this book, even though it was of no authority, made me wonder how it happened that so many different men—and learned men among them—have been are so inclined to express both in speaking and in their treatises and writings so many wicked insults about women and the behavior. Not only one or two and not even just this Mathéolus (for this book had a bad name anyway and was intended as a satire) but, more generally, judging from the treatises of all philosophers and poets and from all the orators—it would take too long to mention their names—it seems that they all speak from one and the same mouth. They all concur in one conclusion: that the behavior of women is inclined to and full of every vice. Thinking deeply about these matters, I began to examine my character and conduct as a natural woman and, similarly, I considered other women whose company I frequently kept, princesses, great ladies, women of the middle and lower classes, who had graciously told me of their most private and intimate thoughts, hoping that I could judge impartially and in good conscience whether the testimony of so many notable men could be true. To the best of my knowledge, no matter how long I confronted or dissected the problem, I could not see or realize how their claims could be true when compared to the natural behavior and character of women. Yet I still argued vehemently against women, saying that it would be impossible that so many famous men—such solemn scholars, possessed of such deep and great understanding, so clear-sighted in all things, as it seemed—could have spoken falsely on so many occasions that I could hardly find a book on morals where, even before I had read it in its entirety, I did not find several chapters or certain sections attacking women, no matter who the author was. This reason alone, in short, made me conclude that, although my intellect did not perceive my own great faults and, likewise, those of other women because of its simpleness and ignorance, it was however truly fitting that such was the case. And so I relied more on the judgment of others than on what I myself felt and knew. I was so transfixed in this line of thinking for such a long time that it seemed as if I were in a stupor. Like a gushing fountain, a series of authorities, whom I recalled one after another, came to mind, along with their opinions on this topic. And I finally decided that God formed a vile creature when He made woman, and I wondered how such a worthy artisan could have deigned to make such an abominable work which, from what they say, is the vessel as well as the refuge and abode of every evil and vice. As I was thinking this, a great unhappiness and sadness welled up in my heart, for I detested myself and the entire feminine sex, as though we were monstrosities in nature. And in my lament I spoke these words:

"Oh, God, how can this be? For unless I stray from my faith, I must never doubt that Your infinite wisdom and most perfect goodness ever created anything which was not good. Did You yourself not create woman in a very special way and since that time did You not give her all those inclinations which it pleased You for her to have? And how could it be that You could go wrong in anything? Yet look at all these accusations which have been judged, decided, and concluded against women. I do not know how to understand this repugnance. If it is so, fair Lord God, that in fact so many abominations abound in the female sex, for You Yourself say that the testimony of two or three witnesses lends credence, why shall I not doubt that it is true? Alas, God, why did You not let me be born in the world as a man, so that all my inclinations would be to serve You better, and so that I would not stray in anything and would be as perfect as a man is said to be? But since Your kindness has not been extended to me, then forgive my negligence in Your service, most Fair Lord God, and may it not displease You, for the servant who receives fewer gifts from his lord is less obliged in his service." I spoke these words to God in my lament and a great deal more for a very long time in sad reflection, and in my folly I considered myself most unfortunate because God had made me inhabit a female body in this world.

2. HERE CHRISTINE DESCRIBES HOW THREE LADIES APPEARED TO HER AND HOW THE ONE WHO WAS IN FRONT SPOKE FIRST AND COMFORTED HER IN HER PAIN.

So occupied with these painful thoughts, my head bowed in shame, my eyes filled with tears, leaning on the pommel of my chair's armrest, I suddenly saw a ray of light fall on my lap, as though it were the sun. I shuddered then, as if wakened from sleep, for I was sitting in a shadow where the sun could not have shone at that hour. And as I lifted my head to see where this light was coming from, I saw three crowned ladies standing before me, and the splendor of their bright faces shone on me and throughout the entire room. Now no one would ask whether I was surprised, for my doors were shut and they had still entered. Fearing that some phantom had come to tempt me and filled with great fright, I made the Sign of the Cross on my forehead.

Then she who was the first of the three smiled and began to speak, "Dear daughter, do not be afraid, for we have not come here to harm or trouble you but to console you, for we have taken pity on your distress, and we have come to bring you out of the ignorance which so blinds your own intellect that you shun what you know for a certainty and believe what you do not know or see or recognize except by virtue of many strange opinions. You resemble the fool in the prank who was dressed in women's clothes while he slept; because those who were making fun of him repeatedly told him he was a woman, he believed their false testimony more readily than the certainty of his own identity. Fair daughter, have you lost all sense? Have you forgotten that when fine gold is tested in the furnace, it does not change or vary in strength but becomes purer the more it is hammered and handled in different ways? Do you not know that the best things are the most debated and the most discussed? If you wish to consider the question of the highest form of reality, which consists in ideas of celestial substances, consider whether the greatest philosophers who have lived and whom you support against your own sex have ever resolved whether ideas are false and contrary to the truth. Notice how these same philosophers contradict and criticize one another, just as you have seen in the *Metaphysics* where Aristotle takes their opinions to task and speaks similarly of Plato and other philosophers. And note, moreover, how even Saint Augustine and the Doctors of the Church have criticized Aristotle in certain passages, although he is known as the prince of philosophers in whom both natural and moral philosophy attained their highest level. It also seems that you think that all the words of the philosophers are articles of faith, that they could never be wrong. As far as the poets of whom you speak are concerned, do you not know that they spoke on many subjects in a fictional way and that often they mean the contrary of what their words openly say? One can interpret them according to the grammatical figure of *antiphrasis*, which means, as you know, that if you call something bad, in fact, it is good, and also vice versa. Thus I advise you to profit from their works and to interpret them in the manner in which they are intended in those passages where they attack women. Perhaps this man, who called himself Mathéolus in his own book, intended it in such a way, for there are many things which, if taken literally, would be pure heresy. As for the attack against the estate of marriage—which is a holy estate, worthy and ordained by God—made not only by Mathéolus but also by others and even by the *Romance of the Rose* where greater credibility is averred because of the authority of its author, it is evident and proven by experience that the contrary of the evil which they posit and claim to be found in this estate through the obligation and fault of women is true. For where has the husband ever been found who would allow his wife to have authority to abuse and insult him as a matter of course, as these authorities maintain? I believe that, regardless of what you might have read, you will never see such a husband with your own eyes, so badly colored are these lies. Thus, in conclusion, I tell you, dear friend, that simplemindedness has prompted you to hold such an opinion. Come back to yourself, recover your senses, and do not trouble yourself anymore over such absurdities. For you know that any evil spoken of women so generally only hurts those who say it, not women themselves."

3. HERE CHRISTINE TELLS HOW THE LADY WHO HAD SAID THIS SHOWED HER WHO SHE WAS AND WHAT HER CHARACTER AND FUNCTION WERE AND TOLD HER HOW SHE WOULD CONSTRUCT A CITY WITH THE HELP OF THESE SAME THREE LADIES.

The famous lady spoke these words to me, in whose presence I do not know which one of my senses was more overwhelmed: my hearing from having listened to such worthy words or my sight from having seen her radiant beauty, her attire, her reverent comportment, and her most honored countenance. The same was true of the others, so that I did not know which one to look at, for the three ladies resembled each other so much that they could be told apart only with difficulty, except for the last one, for although she was of no less authority than the others, she had so fierce a visage that whoever, no matter how daring, looked in her eyes would be afraid to commit a crime, for it seemed that she threatened criminals unceasingly. Having stood up out of respect, I looked at them without saying a word, like someone too overwhelmed to utter a syllable. Reflecting on who these beings could be, I felt much admiration in my heart and, if I could have dared, I would have immediately asked their names and identities and what was the meaning of the different scepters which each one carried in her right hand, which were of fabulous richness, and why they had come here. But since I considered myself unworthy to address these questions to such high ladies as they appeared to me, I did not dare to, but continued to keep my gaze fixed on them, half-afraid and half-reassured by the words which I had heard, which had made me reject my first impression. But the most wise lady who had spoken to me and who knew in her mind what I was thinking, as one who has insight into everything, addressed my reflections, saying:

"Dear daughter, know that God's providence, which leaves nothing void or empty, has ordained that we, though celestial beings, remain and circulate among the people of the world here below, in order to bring order and maintain in balance those institutions we created according to the will of God in the fulfillment of various offices, that God whose daughters we three all are and from whom we were born. Thus it is my duty to straighten out men and women when they go astray and to put them back on the right path. And when they stray, if they have enough understanding to see me, I come to them quietly in spirit and preach to them, showing them their error and how they have failed, I assign them the causes, and then I teach them what to do and what to avoid. Since I serve to demonstrate clearly and to show both in thought and deed to each man and woman his or her own special qualities and faults, you see me holding this shiny mirror which I carry in my right hand in place of a scepter. I would thus have you know truly that no one can look into this mirror, no matter what kind of creature, without achieving clear self-knowledge. My mirror has such great dignity that not without reason is it surrounded by rich and precious gems, so that you see, thanks to this mirror, the essences, qualities, proportions, and measures of all things are known, nor can anything be done well without it. And because, similarly, you wish to know what are the offices of my other sisters whom you see here, each will reply in her own person about her name and character, and this way our testimony will be all the more certain to you. But now I myself will declare the reason for our coming. I must assure you, as we do nothing without good cause, that our appearance here is not at all in vain. For, although we are not common to many places and our knowledge does not come to all people, nevertheless you, for your great love of investigating the truth through long and continual study, for which you come here, solitary and separated from the world, you have deserved and deserve, our devoted friend, to be visited and consoled by us in your agitation and sadness, so that you might also see clearly, in the midst of the darkness of your thoughts, those things which taint and trouble your heart.

"There is another greater and even more special reason for our coming which you will learn from our speeches: in fact we have come to vanquish from the world the same error into which you had fallen, so that from now on, ladies and all valiant women may have a refuge and defense against the various assailants, those ladies who have been abandoned for so long, exposed like a field without a surrounding hedge, without finding a champion to afford them an adequate defense, notwithstanding those noble men who are required by order of law to protect them, who by negligence and apathy have allowed them to be mistreated. It is no wonder then that their jealous enemies, those outrageous villains who have assailed them with various weapons, have been victorious in a war in which women have had no defense. Where is there a city so strong which could not be taken immediately if no resistance were forthcoming, or the law case, no matter how unjust, which was not won through the obstinance of someone pleading without opposition? And the simple, noble ladies, following the example of suffering which God commands, have cheerfully suffered the great attacks which, both in the spoken and the written word, have been wrongfully and sinfully perpetrated against women by men who all the while appealed to God for the right to do so. Now it is time for their just cause to be taken from Pharaoh's hands, and for this reason, we three ladies whom you see here, moved by pity, have come to you to announce a particular edifice built like a city wall, strongly constructed and well founded, which has been predestined and established by our aid and counsel for you to build, where no one will reside except all ladies of fame and women worthy of praise, for the walls of the city will be closed to those women who lack virtue."

[In Book II, Christine responds to Lady Rectitude with a summary of medieval arguments regarding the education of women.]

36. AGAINST THOSE MEN WHO CLAIM IT IS NOT GOOD FOR WOMEN TO BE EDUCATED.

Following these remarks, I, Christine, spoke, "My lady, I realize that women have accomplished many good things and that even if evil women have done evil, it seems to me, nevertheless, that the benefits accrued and still accruing because of good women—particularly the wise and literary ones and those educated in the natural sciences whom I mentioned above—outweigh the evil. Therefore, I am amazed by the opinion of some men who claim that they do not want their daughters, wives, or kinswomen to be educated because their mores would be ruined as a result."

She responded, "Here you can clearly see that not all opinions of men are based on reason and that these men are wrong. For it must not be presumed that mores necessarily grow worse from knowing the moral sciences, which teach the virtues, indeed, there is not the slightest doubt that moral education amends and ennobles them. How could anyone think or believe that whoever follows good teaching or doctrine is the worse for it? Such an opinion cannot be expressed or maintained. I do not mean that it would be good for a man or a woman to study the art of divination or those fields of learning which are forbidden—for the holy Church did not remove them from common use without good reason—but it should not be believed that women are the worse for knowing what is good.

"Quintus Hortensius, a great rhetorician and consumately skilled orator in Rome, did not share this opinion. He had a daughter, named Hortensia, whom he greatly loved for the subtlety of her wit. He had her learn letters and study the science of rhetoric, which she mastered so thoroughly that she resembled her father Hortensius not only in wit and lively memory but also in her excellent delivery and order of speech — in fact, he surpassed her in nothing. As for the subject discussed above, concerning the good which comes about through women, the benefits realized by this woman and her learning were, among others, exceptionally remarkable. That is, during the time when Rome was governed by three men, this Hortensia began to support the cause of women and to undertake what no man dared to undertake. There was a question whether certain taxes should be levied on women and on their jewelry during a needy period in Rome. This woman's eloquence was so compelling that she was listened to, no less readily than her father would have been, and she won her case.

"Similarly, to speak of more recent times, without searching for examples in ancient history, Giovanni Andrea, a solemn law professor in Bologna not quite sixty years ago, was not of the opinion that it was bad for women to be educated. He had a fair and good daughter, named Novella, who was educated in the law to such an advanced degree that when he was occupied by some task and not at leisure to present his lectures to his students, he would send Novella, his daughter, in his place to lecture to the students from his chair. And to prevent her beauty from distracting the concentration of her audience, she had a little curtain drawn in front of her. In this manner she could on occasion supplement and lighten her father's occupation. He loved her so much that, to commemorate her name, he wrote a book of remarkable lectures on the law which he entitled *Novella super Decretalium*, after his daughter's name.

"Thus, not all men (and especially the wisest) share the opinion that it is bad for women to be educated. But it is very true that many foolish men have claimed this because it displeased them that women knew more than they did. Your father, who was a great scientist and philosopher, did not believe that women were worth less by knowing science; rather, as you know, he took great pleasure from seeing your inclination to learning. The feminine opinion of your mother, however, who wished to keep you busy with spinning and silly girlishness, following the common custom of women, was the major obstacle to your being more involved in the sciences. But just as the proverb already mentioned above says, 'No one can take away what Nature has given,' your mother could not hinder in you the feeling for the sciences which you, through natural inclination, had nevertheless gathered together in little droplets. I am sure that, on account of these things, you do not think you are worth less but rather that you consider it a great treasure for yourself; and you doubtless have reason to."

And I, Christine, replied to all of this, "Indeed, my lady, what you say is as true as the Lord's Prayer."

— Translated by Earl Jeffrey Richards